Gordon Graham, the 'fighter pilot's fighter pilot' provides an inside story of the evolution of tactical air power into the awesome force it represents today.

Robert F. Titus, Brigadier General, USAF (Ret.)

This is no run-of-the-mill story of the daredevil fighter pilot filled with accounts of aerial dog fights and air victories, although the book contains sufficient of that fare to satisfy one's appetite for such.

His World War II experience shows him as a first class combat fighter pilot as well as a skillful leader and commander at various levels. Based on his experience in World War II, the Korean War, and our involvement in Viet Nam, he was able to effect many improvements in both tactical operations techniques and in technical development of equipment.

Numerous tours as a general officer in staff and command assignments in many parts of the world on four continents demonstrate his ability as a statesman and a diplomat. His post-military jobs as a civilian working in industry proved him to be a top-notch businessman and a wily negotiator.

Throughout all phases of the book are anecdotes which are innovative, surprising and amusing. This book is a must reading for one not only interested in military aviation but also for those who wish to learn of some of the behind-the-scenes activities in war, peace and business which we don't learn from the media.

Robert M. Lee, General, USAF (Ret.)

If you are going to understand the victory of Desert Storm you must know about the struggles of airmen in World War II, Korea, and Vietnam. Gordy Graham fought the battles that led to our being an air power nation. He is also a hero, in battle and to those of us who were the next generation of fighter pilots. Crusty but kind, he kept the faith when the Air Force was run by Generals who confused ego for brains and rudeness for leadership. This book is required reading for all who seek to understand why the United States looks to the air for her first line of defense.

Charles A. Horner, General, USAF (Ret.)

DOWN FOR DOUBLE:
Anecdotes of a Fighter Pilot

White Stone, Va.

For Paul Lippincot —

    Warmest Personal Regards,
       — Gordon

       Gordon M. Graham
       Lieut. General, USAF, Ret.

DOWN FOR DOUBLE:

Anecdotes of a Fighter Pilot

Gordon M. Graham
Lieutenant General, USAF (Retired)

BRANDYLANE PUBLISHERS
White Stone, Virginia

Brandylane Publishers, White Stone, Virginia 22578

Copyright 1996 by Gordon M. Graham
All rights reserved. Published 1996.
Printed in the United States of America

Library of Congress Cataloging-in-Publication Data

Graham, Gordon M. (Gordon Marion), 1918-
    Down for double: anecdotes of a fighter pilot / Gordon M. Graham.
       p.   cm.
    Includes bibliographical references and index.
    ISBN 1-883911-06-0
    1. Graham, Gordon M. (Gordon Marion), 1918- . 2. United States.
Air Force—Officers—Biography. 3. Fighter pilots—United States—
Biography. I. Title.
   UG626.3.G7A3 1996
   358.4'3'092—dc20   95-49836
   [B]   CIP

To all the pursuit and fighter pilots who have gone before and
to those who man the cockpits today -
And to my patient wife, Vivian, and my children and grandchildren,
this book is humbly dedicated.

CONTENTS

Acknowledgments		page *viii*
Introduction		page *ix*
Chapter 1	Busted	page 1
Chapter 2	Openers	page 5
Chapter 3	Hit Me	page 13
Chapter 4	Play These	page 23
Chapter 5	Down for Double	page 31
Chapter 6	I'm Not in This One	page 55
Chapter 7	I'm Throwing In	page 65
Chapter 8	Open a New Deck	page 73
Chapter 9	Luck of the Draw	page 91
Chapter 10	Play These	page 101
Chapter 11	I'll Take One	page 125
Chapter 12	I'll Up the Ante	page 151
A Photograph Album		page 185
Chapter 13	I'll Take Two	page 215
Chapter 14	Hit Me Again	page 221
Chapter 15	Hold These	page 251
Chapter 16	I'll Take Three	page 255
Chapter 17	A Big Raise	page 261
Chapter 18	Know When to Fold Them	page 271
Chapter 19	The Dealing's Done	page 283
Epilogue	Know When to Walk Away	page 295
Appendix	Descriptions of Aircraft	page 299
Glossary	Pilotspeak	page 306
Index		page 309

ACKNOWLEDGMENTS

The forty-one hour-long tapes of the interviews for this book were transcribed by my daughter Eloise Graham Brooks and the text was edited by my grandson James Danforth Brooks.

INTRODUCTION

Records of historic events and decisions are typically written by non-participants who place them in a context, integrate a number of corroborating sources, and interpret their significance from a broad perspective.

By contrast, oral history is an organized effort to preserve the intimate knowledge, experiences, and perspectives of a person on a theme or topic. Oral history relies on stories and anecdotes as a means for understanding the perceptions of the actors and illuminating their actions. It is important to recognize, of course, that stories are as reliable as an individual's memory and motives. Nevertheless, the stories add a depth of understanding that can not be gained any other way.

The Air Force Chief Historian determined that oral history was needed from people who participated in the creation and evolution of the Air Force to explain their reasons and logic for key decisions and events. This book is based on interviews conducted by Dr. Hugh Ahmann in the spring of 1991. Dr. Ahmann is head of the Air Force's Oral History Project in the Research Division, Office of Historical Research at Maxwell AFB, Montgomery, Alabama. The Oral History Project originated under the larger Project CORONA HARVEST, which was conducted during and following the Vietnam War. The tapes and official transcripts are maintained by the Oral History Project.

The name of the book is derived from two sources. First, like most fighter pilots, I did my share of gambling — blackjack, poker, craps. Second, I had two aircraft victories early on and decided doubles was the way to go. So my P-51 Mustang was christened "Down for Double" and it seemed a natural theme for my book.

CHAPTER 1

BUSTED

Crash! My P-51 Mustang, "Down for Double," hit the ground and the canopy slammed shut. I was riding the world's largest plowshare down a muddy brussels sprouts field about a quarter of a mile long. At the end of the field was a thick hedgerow of trees and dense cover. Mud and debris were flying over the airplane like a bow wave.

My airplane hit the hedgerow and came to a shuddering stop. Fuel splashed all over and my head slammed into the gunsight, which peeled my scalp back.

I was only half-conscious. I yanked my mask off, smelled the gas, and could think only of fire. I couldn't roll back the canopy. I stood in the seat and broke that canopy lock with my back, somehow. If I had had to do it the next day, I couldn't have done it with a jack. I climbed out and started to run in those big old fleece-lined boots, through knee-deep mud. Unbeknownst to me, my dinghy and parachute were still hooked up. Enough of my chute deployed that I felt as if I were running in place. I had barely covered thirty yards when the last frag went off and I instinctively fell forward. I thought the airplane had blown up.

On my knees in the mud, I looked back to see that the airplane had not caught fire. I struggled to my feet, disengaged the dinghy and chute and walked to the edge of the field.

Busted

A British farmer had been watching the whole time. He came up to me with a kind offer: "I say, Yank. You look a bit beat up. Would you care for a spot of tea?"

I said, "No, but I'll sure take a shot of whiskey if you have any."

"Well, I think me Missus has some whiskey," he replied. We walked about a quarter of a mile to an old British thatched-roof farmhouse with a dirt floor. His wife dug out a bottle of Scotch, with about one-third remaining, that must have been seventy-five years old. I had a couple of shots. He told me I was the thirteenth airman to hit in the area. Three others were Americans. Only one Royal Air Force (RAF) pilot and I had bellied in; the rest had bailed out.

♠ ♥ ♦ ♣

The mission had begun as a bomber-escort, but the bombers had been stood down because of weather over the target.

Our Mustangs had been rapidly reconfigured with a can of napalm on the left pylon and a cluster of frag bombs on the right. We didn't need external fuel because the target was an airfield in Holland and our internal fuel was sufficient for that mission.

We took off, climbed through the overcast and proceeded on course. The weather over the target was so bad we couldn't penetrate and expend our ordnance, so we aborted the mission.

Halfway back over the channel, Lieutenant Oran Stalcup radioed that his engine had quit. Oran, barely nineteen, was from my hometown of Taft, California. He was an artist on the side. He did all the nose paint jobs on the airplanes. I still have my leather jacket with the P-51 he painted on it.

He rode his P-51 down to about 12,000 feet, saw he wouldn't make the English coast and bailed out. I sent a flight down to CAP (Combat Air Patrol) him and radioed for air-sea rescue. We didn't have exposure suits in the fall of 1944. A downed pilot could not survive more than three minutes in that water.

I could hear the radio calls, which dragged out over three or four minutes: "The Mae West's inflated. He's pulling the dinghy in. It's inflated. He's trying to get in it. He's slowing down. I don't know whether he's going to make it. No, he's just hanging on. Nope, he didn't make it."

Just then, my engine quit. I jettisoned the napalm and attempted to jettison the cluster of frags. It had a flat plate area, like a barn door.

Simultaneously, I tried and tried to restart the engine.

About 12,000 feet, I broke out of the overcast. I could see the white cliffs of Dover. Projecting my flight path, I guessed I'd hit smack dab in the middle. I didn't want to auger in, but I didn't want to step out into that cold water, either.

I gritted my teeth and told myself I could make it. I came over the cliffs and brushed the trees, going about 150 mph in order to force the airplane onto the ground. I couldn't decrease the airspeed to a desired glide for a forced landing.

The frag cluster hit the trees. One of the frags raked off, armed and detonated. One of them hung on the wing and exploded. Fragments went all over: one creased my head; one cut my oxygen hose; one or two went through my chute; and one scarred my leg. The third frag stayed on the airplane.

After the farmer's whiskey, I felt strong enough to walk a half mile or so down the road to a phone. The base sent transportation for me.

CHAPTER 2

OPENERS
Ouray, CO

I was born in Ouray (pronounced "Yuray" by the locals), Colorado, on February 16, 1918. The town was named after Chief Ouray of the Ouray tribe. It was a county seat and a mining town. Elevation is close to 9,000 feet. It is gorgeous country, 110 air miles west of Colorado Springs, on the west side of the Continental Divide.

My father was James R. Warner, born in Wisconsin in 1882. He was a miner. He was killed in a mine accident when I was two. My mother told me Warner's parents were first-generation Scottish.

My mother, Margaret Wilson, was born in Union County, Georgia, on April 12, 1896. My mother's parents were Enos W. Wilson and Louisa Lance. Enos was a first-generation Scot who settled in Georgia. Louisa was born in Blairsville, Georgia. She came from a very large family—seven boys and three girls. The boys were Gordon, Verd, Herd, Ferd, Buford, Wilford, and Enos. The Wilson family moved to Colorado, where my parents met.

Before I was five, my mother remarried, to Alexander Graham. Alex was born in Sydney, Australia, on August 16, 1884. His father, also Alexander Graham, and his mother, Mary Bruce, were born in Maine. My stepfather was a shipfitter in the shipbuilding industry and a veteran of World War I. He died in the National Military Home for

Veterans in Los Angeles on December 19, 1946.

I had one older brother, June Claire, nicknamed "Jay," who was born July 23, 1916. My stepfather adopted my brother and me, but we did not get along well. I also had a younger half-sister, who died when she was three months old. I was about eight years old then.

After my mother remarried, we went to Denver, then to Salt Lake City. I can remember climbing pear trees when we lived there. When I was about five, we moved to southern California, where my stepfather went to work in the oil fields near El Segundo. I believe we went to Taft in 1924, where I entered first grade.

In 1926 or 1927, we drove from California back to Colorado to visit my mother's relatives. I can remember being in a bad accident in New Mexico, when our big Dodge touring car was run off the road into a ravine. We were stranded for about a week while someone fixed the car.

I went back to Colorado once in the 1950s and made an attempt to trace my grandparents. I started at the county courthouse and found a lead at the post office to one of my uncles, my mother's youngest brother as I remember, who lived in a little village in the area, near Nucla. He told me the names of many of my cousins, whom I did not know, of course. But I didn't follow up on any of them.

Taft was a booming oil town when I was growing up in the 1920s. Schools were fairly casual in towns with that kind of environment; I skipped part of the second and fourth grades because they had half grades then, with low and high halves. I finished the eighth grade in 1930 at the age of twelve and began high school.

The Depression years were pretty severe. In 1932, my stepfather lost his job and went looking for work back in the mining business. We tagged along. We lived in Nevada, Idaho (Coeur d'Alène), Montana, British Columbia, and ended up in Seattle. After six months, we came back to Taft, where I completed high school.

My mother slipped on some steps at our house at 302 Crystal St. on February 20, 1934, and fractured her spine. She underwent an operation on April 5, but died April 16, at the age of thirty-eight, of general septicemia and streptococcic infection. She is buried in the West Side Cemetery in Taft.

I graduated from high school at the age of sixteen in June 1934. My brother and I did not want to stay with our stepfather.

My brother worked for a year or so for various contractors in the oil business before he joined the Army in 1935 or 1936. During World

Openers

War II, he was captured on Corregidor, badly wounded, but survived the Bataan Death March. I received two messages from him through the Red Cross. When the war ended, the prisoners were brought home and I made a trip to Letterman General Hospital in San Francisco to see him. Jay was six feet tall and had been a very athletic, strong, friendly, outgoing fellow, who liked the outdoors—hunting and fishing. He was not fond of books and had not liked school particularly. When I saw him, he was in a wheelchair and weighed less than a hundred pounds. His teeth and hair were gone, and you could see his breastbone and cheekbones.

After the war, Jay was unable to work. He was in and out of veterans' hospitals for ten or twelve years and lost his leg because of his wound. But his health gradually improved. He married and lived with his wife, Jacquie, in Oregon on a small farm.

He never lost his bitterness toward the Japanese. Jacquie had to monitor the TV very carefully because, if he saw scenes of Japanese soldiers, he would have a flashback and go berserk. He would have to be sedated and put into the hospital for a week or two until he calmed down. The flashbacks occurred less and less frequently. Jacquie always called to let me know when Jay was back in the hospital again.

During my career, I spent a lot of time in the Orient, particularly in Japan, and this was very uncomfortable for me to explain to Jay. He used to say to me, "I don't know how you can talk to those damn Japs!"

Jay never came back to the East Coast. I went to Oregon about every year to see him. He died of a heart attack on January 21, 1991.

In September 1934 I entered junior college, a two-year equivalent of today's community college, which is now Taft College. I had been interested from a very young age in engineering. I had had a Meccano or erector set and used to make everything you could make or improvise. So engineering and construction appealed to me. I studied it in high school in preparatory work oriented toward college. Being in the oil fields, that translated into petroleum engineering; I graduated from Junior college after three years, in 1937, with an AA in petroleum engineering.

I worked part-time after classes, on Saturdays and odd hours, on whatever I could find to do. I went there three years because I was working and couldn't carry a full academic load. Besides, I liked college.

Openers

And I started flying while in Junior college.

There was a dirt strip outside of Taft and there were three or four old puddle-jumpers there. Everyone who was interested gathered around on Saturdays and Sundays and paid a dollar for a ride.

One of my jobs during Christmas season 1935 was delivering parcel post packages for the post office. It was a semi-rural community. Oil leases were five to ten miles outside the periphery of the little town, so the population was pretty spread out. The pay was great for a kid like me: fifty cents per hour.

The postmistress's son was a man by the name of Raymond Strand. I remember him well—a tall, rangy fellow. He worked for his mother as the head mail-sorter. The Strands were a big Catholic family and they all worked in the post office. As far as I know, one of their descendants is still running it. But they had some steady money during those poor economic times.

Raymond was the local aeronaut and had three airplanes. One was an Aeronca C-3, which had a 37-hp engine and looked like a pregnant duck. He also had a Taylorcraft and a Luscombe, which was all metal.

Strand took a liking to me. The rest of that winter, I spent every spare minute on Saturdays or Sundays at the airport washing his airplanes and listening to the flying talk.

As a rule, he paid me a dollar for whatever I did all day long. One day, he didn't take in any money. Raymond decided that he couldn't give me a dollar. Instead, he took me along to test fly one of his airplanes for about fifteen minutes. Man, I said, this is the way to go. So that was how I started in the flying business.

I picked up what time I could and earned my private pilot license. I accumulated enough flying time to qualify for a commercial license. Later, in the Air Force, I secured a commercial pilot license.

During the summer of 1936, I worked for the U.S. Coast and Geodetic Survey as a surveyor's helper. The head of the survey party was a Naval Reserve captain by the name of Nickerson. On the side, he was the recruiter for the U.S. Naval Reserve for that district. He took a liking to me and found out about my flying ambitions, so he asked me, "How about joining the Naval Aviation Reserve?" That sounded great to me—Pensacola and all that. In the movies, naval aviators saw a lot of flying action and I was more than willing to try it out.

Nickerson recruited five of us: two brothers, Gilbert and Walter Halliday; a fellow by the name of Higgins, who was the son of the local police chief; and a wonderful chap named Innes MacKenzie, who later was my college roommate. We were all in the same category, with two years of college, except they were all twenty and I was only eighteen.

The program was to begin in 1937. We were to go to Long Beach for ten hours of aviation instruction and associated ground training, an assessment of our capability, and then to Pensacola for the full course, culminating in commissioning as naval aviators.

Nickerson told me not to worry, even though the minimum age was twenty and I would only be nineteen and a half. He would obtain a waiver, based on my having completed more than the two-year college requirement. We went to Long Beach, completed the ten hours and soloed, except for MacKenzie. MacKenzie decided to go to work full-time.

My waiver was not approved. I was crushed and decided I'd better try to go back to school. By this time, late August or early September, college had already begun. My grades had always been good, so I was accepted at the University of California ("Cal"), Berkeley, even though I was at least three weeks late and had missed the deadline for late registration.

While in college, I continued to fly at Oakland-Alameda Airport. I flew Fleets, Travelair 2000, and Piper Cubs at Harry Sham's Flying Service. He had a Fairchild 24, a high-wing monoplane, that was the jewel in his crown. He didn't trust very many pilots in it, including me. I never did fly it.

In 1938, I went to Santa Maria and took the Air Corps physical and exam. I passed but there were no vacancies so I went back to college at Cal. While there, I worked practically full-time and finally received my degree in June.

I received an excellent offer, for a new graduate, of $300 per month from Honolulu Oil Corporation, where I had worked twice before, part-time summer and winter. The company was a very wealthy producer but not a refiner or distributor. The company had evolved from the Dollar Steamship Line, which had had coal-burning ships. When its ships were converted from coal to oil, the company needed a source of oil and established the Honolulu Oil Corporation.

My job was extremely interesting and enjoyable. I was an assistant petroleum engineer on a project to drill what turned out to be the deepest electrically-drilled oil well in the world. The well had passed two pay zones, which could have been brought in as very productive wells, but

Openers

the company wanted to continue drilling it as an exploratory well.

The draft was passed in September 1940 by one vote in congress. I was single, the right age, and nervous about having to go into the infantry. Again, I went to Santa Maria and took the Air Corps exam and physical. I passed but, again, there were no vacancies, so I kept on working.

It was with great joy that I received a telegram in December 1940 ordering me to report to Fort MacArthur in San Pedro, California, to become a flying cadet. I reported, along with several other aspiring cadets, and found my way to the appropriate building on the post.

It was a typical Army enlistment office, with a typical old grizzled Army sergeant behind the table. I said that I'd applied for the Air Corps and showed him the telegram. He gave me a form to complete. I read both sides and found it was the form for a standard three-year enlistment in the U.S. Army. I asked about this. He said, "Don't worry about it, sonny, just fill it out and sign it!"

I told him I was going outside to think this over.

I was sitting on the steps when up came a fellow, Willie B. Compton, whom I didn't know very well. I'd worked for his father once. I asked him what he was doing there. He said, "I'm going to join the Air Corps!"

I said, "Go in there. The sergeant will take care of you." He went in and, a few minutes later, emerged with the same form I had been given. "That sergeant doesn't know anything about the Air Corps," he said. "I don't know about this." So we sat there and talked for five or ten minutes.

Along came the typical Sergeant Bilko. He saw two pigeons sitting there in civilian clothes and asked, "What are you fellows doing here?"

We told him.

He said, "Well, come on down to the post exchange and we'll have a cup of coffee and I'll explain it to you." He sounded like an information source, so we followed him down a block or so.

It was only about 11:00 in the morning but he decided he wanted a beer. So we ordered three Budweisers, ten cents a bottle. He said, "Now, that recruiting sergeant up there, he'll tell you anything he thinks you'll believe. But it's a pretty good deal. Don't worry if it doesn't turn out right, if you don't fly those airplanes. Look here, you can buy a beer for ten cents!"

Willie and I paid for a second round of beers with this chap and decided we'd go back and talk to the recruiting sergeant again. As we

Openers

walked back, we decided we'd sign up. So we did. The old sergeant said, "Report to the Ryan School of Aeronautics at Hemet, California, the day after New Year's for training as flying cadets."

CHAPTER 3

HIT ME

HEMET, CA: AVIATION CADET

We went to the Rose Bowl Parade and game. I had an old beat-up Plymouth for which I was paying $30 a month. The price had been $300 and I'd had it some months. I still owed about $150 on it.

We drove out to Hemet, which is east of Los Angeles not far from March Field. We were issued gray uniforms, for which we paid out of our $75 per month flying cadet salary. In addition, our rations and laundry were deducted, so that, of our $75, we were left with $7 or $8. Cadets weren't allowed to be married or have an automobile. In sum, the cadet life was pretty well-controlled. But a cadet could fly!

I didn't tolerate the disciplinary aspects well at all. A lot of practices had been copied from the military academy. For example, we had to brace when we ate and the upperclassmen hazed us unmercifully. This really bothered me.

The flying instructors were civilians. The school, one of the first in the expanded build-up in the Air Corps, was run by the Ryan School of Aeronautics out of San Diego. There were three flying officers: Captain Lloyd P. Hopwood, who retired as a two-star from Commander, Air University; Lieutenant Ford and Lieutenant Perry Hoisington, both of whom retired as colonels. The senior instructor was in charge of all the civilian instructors. If you were in trouble with your civilian

Hit Me

instructor, you eventually were given a check ride by the senior instructor. If you didn't pass his check ride, the last chance was the lieutenant's airplane, called the "Maytag" (for the washing machine). If you had to have a check ride in his airplane, you were probably going to wash out. He was the final authority.

We flew PT-13s, Stearman biplanes with 225-hp radial engines, in primary training. Great airplane, especially for aerobatics. You still see many of them around.

Each instructor had five students. The instructor's goal in life, it seemed to us, was to reduce that student load as soon as possible. The washout rate was well over sixty percent.

My instructor was a fellow by the name of Horton. It turned out, although I didn't know it at the time, that I had as much flying time as he did. He was just pulled in off the street and given the job because this was the build-up. Horton eliminated everyone but Bud Wilson and me almost right away. Bud and I had private pilot licenses and I had enough flying time for a commercial license but hadn't taken the exam.

Horton didn't show up for two or three days at a time to give Bud and me instruction, so Bud and I would draw solo airplanes and go up and have a ball. I passed the forty-hour check ride fairly easily and so did Bud. That was pretty elementary: stalls, landings, turns, and so forth. Then we should have received some more advanced work in Army-style flying, pattern flying, that sort of thing, to prepare for a final sixty-five- or seventy-hour check-ride. But old Horton wasn't around very much.

One day, Bud and I decided we would go up and have a private little dog fight. Bud and I took off, climbed to 6,000 feet and were having a picnic. There was a broken cloud deck moving in below us, but it didn't bother me particularly.

There was a special procedure for marginal weather. We were restricted to a certain area and, at the first sign of deteriorating weather, we were supposed to come back in right away. To make sure everybody came down, all the instructors who weren't flying dual and the supervisor would jump in airplanes and herd everybody out of the sky.

Suddenly, there was an airplane right on my tail, unannounced. Man, I thought, that Bud's really gotten sharp! So I went through a couple of loops and rolls and tight turns, and this chap was just hanging right on top of me. I slowed up, leveled off, and up pulled Lieutenant Hoisington, pointing for me to go down. I gave him a signal of acknowledgment and peeled off.

The overcast had become solid. I flew around for an hour trying to find a hole in it. The endurance of that Stearman was about three-and-a-half hours, as I remember. Finally, I thought I had found a hole, but it was not really a hole. It was raining and visibility was down; the ceiling was about 500 feet. I don't know why I didn't auger in, but I managed to come down underneath it safely. I didn't recognize where I was. Finally, I saw a sign identifying Redlands.

I knew there was a municipal airport there but I couldn't find the bloody place. I guess I spent about thirty minutes milling around under that overcast. The gas gauge on the Stearman was a glass tube that allowed you to see the level going down in the fuel tank. I estimated I had about thirty minutes of fuel and said to myself, "I'd better put this turkey on the ground somewhere." So I did.

The best place I could find was right in the middle of the campus at Redlands University. They had a big quadrangle, like a park, with a statue in the middle, but there was plenty of room. I came slithering over the trees, landed, and rolled about 1,000 feet, almost the full distance to the street. I taxied the remainder, shut the engine down and climbed out. Within seconds, there were people all over.

I walked across the street, which was Corona Avenue, knocked on the door, and asked the nice lady who answered if I could use her telephone. She said yes, so I called the base. Panic had ensued because I was the only cadet who hadn't shown up. Hoisington came to the phone and roared, "You stay right there. I'll come over and pick you up."

I said, "Yes, sir," and went back out. I'd given him the instructions for Corona Avenue in Redlands. Somehow or other, it was garbled in transmission and he went to Corona, California, which was a far piece from Redlands. No one came. Time passed. This nice lady made a sandwich for me while I waited out there, guarding the airplane.

We wore heavy, fleece-lined jackets and helmets, so I really looked like a pilot. I was busy lining up dates with these queenies from Redlands University and I was really going over big. All of a sudden, while I was leaning against the wing, I heard this voice. Hoisington strolled up and he was fit to be tied. He straightened me up in a hurry and he ruined some good contacts. I was led away in disgrace.

He had brought the chief civilian pilot with him in his maroon Buick convertible. The three of us squeezed in the front seat of that convertible, with me in the middle, and they just hammered me during the two-hour drive back to Hemet.

Hit Me

They thought I'd landed there deliberately. I tried to explain to them what had happened and told them the whole story about Horton's lack of instruction, Bud and myself, and what Bud and I had been doing. I don't think they really believed me. By the time we reached Hemet, I was in terrible trouble: grounded, confined and subjected to an investigation. They grilled old Bud until they had him scared to death. I guess they dug up enough on Horton to confirm my stories. I never was allowed off base after that, but I wasn't washed out.

Graduation came and we were ordered to Randolph Field, San Antonio, Texas, for basic training. We could either ride the train or make our way there any way we could. We were given a travel voucher or could turn one in when we arrived. Six of us piled into my Plymouth. It had a soft top because they didn't have solid steel tops yet. We bought two used tires and tied them on top. We drove nonstop to San Antonio, alternating drivers.

I don't remember how long it took, but we used the two spare tires en route. The roads were two-lane, hard-surfaced, all the way through Arizona and New Mexico.

At Randolph, the "West Point of Air," we moved up to BT-9s and BT-14s. The BT-9 was made by Vultee and the BT-14, by North American. I didn't fly the BT-9 very much before I was put in the BT-14, so I don't remember much about it except it was not as good an airplane and had a very bad reputation for accidents. The BT-14 also had a little larger engine, 450 hp, so everyone wanted to get into it.

The commandant of cadets was Captain "Rosie" Grubbs. The tactical officer in my company was 1st Lieutenant Henry J. Amen, famous as "Holy Jesus Amen." He was fierce and domineering, a real tyrant. We were organized into companies and battalions. While we were there, the regiment was established because of the continuing expansion.

I had a series of instructors and all kinds of trouble. I hadn't really been trained the way I should have been in primary and wasn't flying the way I was supposed to. The fault was partly mine, in that I hadn't applied myself as hard as I should have. I had limped through the forty-hour and final check rides in primary and was far from the star of the class. I was a good pilot but I couldn't make precision turns and my altitude would vary more than Air Corps tolerance. I realized it, but I was passed.

Hit Me

Basic training at Randolph was conducted by the Air Corps with Air Corps officers as instructors. Later, after I was commissioned, I was retained as an instructor at Craig Field. At Craig, all the instructors were commissioned officers and everyone did everything by the book. That was when I developed a pretty good feel for the Air Corps way of doing business. There was no other way.

I think I had a flippant attitude, too. I wasn't the only one, though. We came close to being booted out. The elimination rate at Randolph was considerably lower than at Hemet. Only about ten percent were eliminated.

Generally, the military schools were much stricter than the private schools. That changed abruptly when the war broke out. The standards were lowered and the idea was to pass everybody.

We had a very intensive course in ground school, flying and drill at Randolph. There was a lot of pure Army drill. We drilled with Springfield rifles and had parades every Saturday morning, with white glove inspections, very much like the academy. The tactical officers were all academy graduates.

Four cadets shared a room, upper and lower bunks, with a wash basin. Latrines were at the end of the corridor. The rooms had to be spotless and the beds could never be touched except at night. The system of discipline was called "gigs." You were given a gig if anything was wrong, such as a hair on the floor or a blanket you couldn't bounce a quarter on. The name of the cadet who was room orderly was posted above the wash basin in a little slip holder.

We flipped to determine who went first as room orderly when we arrived at Randolph, and I lost. Not being thoroughly cognizant of all the rules and then, too, being prone to ignore those I didn't believe were necessary, I was caught every day that week. I accumulated so many gigs that I didn't get off the post that first weekend.

That Saturday morning, General Pershing came for the preview of a film. A big review and spit and polish parade were held in his honor. The film—*Wings,* I believe it was titled—was famous, made in the late 1930s about Randolph Field and the people of the Army Air Corps.

On Saturday afternoon, all the cadets were turned loose for the weekend except me and some other no-good ones. We were out there marching up and down the ramp with rifles on our shoulders, white gloves and white gun slings. I didn't think that was a very good idea. I thought I'd been treated very unfairly when my buddies and roommates took off for "open post."

Hit Me

The second thing that a cadet was not supposed to do after reporting in to Randolph was succumb to the wiles of a car salesman. The deal was that a cadet passed his forty-hour check ride, signed a paper, took possession of the car, and didn't pay anything until he finished at Randolph. It was virtually a guarantee that, after passing the forty-hour check ride, one would be commissioned. After a cadet was commissioned, the Bank of Fort Sam Houston took over his check and took out the payments. If a cadet washed out, the car dealer retrieved the car and the cadet paid nothing for using it. Nobody became angry.

The five cats who had come with me from Hemet promised that they would reimburse me after they received their travel pay so I could make up the back payments on the beat-up old Plymouth that I had been unable to make while I was in primary.

Well, when we arrived at Randolph, the five of them drew travel pay, bought a Ford or Chevy convertible immediately, and said, "Gee, you know, we need this money to live it up!" I never received a dime from those deadbeats. My Plymouth sat in a parking lot while I walked tours on post. I'd see the other cadets come in on Sunday nights telling stories about all the great things they'd done.

About four weeks went by. I was called to report to Lieutenant Amen. I wondered what new trouble I was in. He stood me in a brace for a while and lectured me about responsibilities and said that he'd had a telephone call from a representative of the National Automobile Theft Recovery Association. He said, "It seems you took an automobile from California to Randolph and you owed money. You haven't made payments on it since the first of the year."

I said, "Yes, sir, that's right. I didn't have any money."

"Well," he said, "this is very serious. It is cause for you to be washed out. I expect you to settle this immediately and report back to me."

He gave me a telephone number. I called the fellow and arranged to meet him at the main gate. He couldn't come on base. I met him, climbed in his car and we drove to the parking lot.

Two weeks earlier, we had had one of the most hellacious thunderstorms I'd ever seen. The hailstones were the size of baseballs. They broke windows in the barracks and in cars. You can imagine what they did to that poor old Plymouth sitting out there. The top was absolutely shredded. The windshield and back window were broken. Moreover, two of the tires were flat and the battery was dead.

As we drove to the parking lot, I told the representative that I had not intended to steal the car or default on the payments. I explained my situation, why I had no money and wouldn't have until I was commissioned. I said, "I guess you'll just have to take the car."

He said, "Well, that's all right. Just give me the keys."

When we reached the car, I gave him the keys. He asked, "How am I going to move this thing out of here?"

I said, "Mister, I don't know. That's your problem. It's your car." He managed to pump up the tires and tow the car off the lot. That was the last I heard of it. However, I did write the bank a letter to tell them how sorry I was and that I would make restitution as soon as I had some money. I paid the amount owed with interest after I was commissioned.

♠ ♥ ♦ ♣

I had several instructors at Randolph because I was in trouble. Finally, I was assigned to one by the name of Brown, a young man from Alabama. I don't think he was more than six months ahead of me in flying school. He was about my size. He took me up for about thirty minutes and put me through my paces and said, "I don't see anything wrong with your flying. Why are you in trouble?"

"Sir," I said, "I don't know. I just can't seem to pass these check rides or satisfy my instructors."

"Don't worry," he said. He worked with me and straightened me out so that I passed the check and finished the course. I'll be forever grateful to him. I was doing a lot of things I knew instinctively that I shouldn't be doing but I thought I could get away with them. For example, I'd lose 100 or 200 feet in a turn, or I'd let my air speed bleed off too much on final approach. It was still safe, but it wasn't the way it was supposed to be done.

♠ ♥ ♦ ♣

From Randolph, we went to advanced training at Craig Field, in Selma, Alabama, which was still under construction. My class, 41-F, was the first full class at Craig and the first pursuit class.

The schools all specialized in bombardment (or observation, in the case of Brooks) except Craig, which was pursuit. Prior to that, a cadet finished advanced training in AT-6s or BC-1As (an overgrown AT-6, with the same engine but more gadgets). Then he went to the

Hit Me

bomber, observation or pursuit unit, where one checked out and learned tactics. Our class was the first to have aerial and ground gunnery as cadets. That had always been unit training.

We had P-35s, P-36s, AT-6s, BC-1As, and a PB-2 (for Pursuit-Biplace, because it had a gunner in the back), which had a Curtiss-Conqueror glycol liquid-cooled, in-line engine. It had the first turbo-charger I had ever seen, which gave it better altitude performance. This ragtag Air Corps collection had been concentrated at Craig to do the pursuit training job.

Advanced training consisted of night formation, gunnery, cross country navigation, skeet and .45 pistol training, and so on, all taught by one instructor in advanced training. In basic, by contrast, we had a flying instructor, but had different instructors for ground school, where we had a code or communications class; customs of the service class, and others.

Five of us were assigned to an instructor named Nielsen, who was a Stanford graduate. To him, my being a Cal graduate called for competition like Harvard v. Yale. He developed an immediate dislike for me.

Our first week there, Nielsen led the five of us to the skeet range. I should mention that I started pulling traps and shooting skeet at a very tender age. I was a good shot and I became better. None of the others had shot skeet before.

Nielsen demonstrated the safety features and how to take the shotgun down. Then he started the introduction to skeet. He went to the Number 1 station and called, "Pull," and shot. Then he went to the Number 2 station and repeated the demonstration. He shot the whole round and broke eighteen birds of the twenty-five. Then he started with the cadets.

"Abrams," he said, "you do this." Old Abe had come from somewhere in the New York City jungle and had never seen a shotgun. Abe went around and shot fewer than five birds, as I remember. The others followed, one breaking as many as ten, and I went last. We were using old, beat-up Model 12 Winchesters, pump guns. I broke all twenty-five birds, including the optional bird, for which I used a hip shot to really show off.

Nielsen was furious. I'd humiliated him in front of the cadets. He took me aside, cursed and asked, "Why didn't you tell me you were a professional skeet shot?"

I said, "Sir, you didn't ask me. I could have told you but you didn't let me even explain."

He said, "It's just some more of that damn California arrogance." We went on through advanced training with no further incident but never exactly became buddies.

The last phase of advanced was air and ground gunnery down at Fort Walton Beach Army Air Field (now Eglin Air Force Base), Florida. Initially, AT-6s and BC-1As were used for training students in firing air-to-air and air-to-ground. Then, students were finally checked out in a P-36. Three A-12s were used for towing targets.

The A-12 was a single-engine, fixed-pitch propeller, two-seat, open-cockpit attack airplane which took off, flew, cruised, AND approached at 110 mph. A handle was used to retract the gear by collapsing the struts. The wheels would go a little way up into the wheel pants, thereby decreasing the drag by all of about three mph. If you didn't put the gear down when you landed, it was just a little harder landing but didn't hurt anything.

A towed target called a "drogue," in the shape of a cone or sleeve, was deployed manually, out a hatch in the floor, by an enlisted man in the rear (normally, gunner's) seat of the A-12. The target was about three feet in diameter and thirty feet long.

The P-36 had two .30-caliber machine guns, cowl-mounted, which fired through the prop. Virtually no one ever hit the target.

I shot the highest air-to-air and air-to-ground scores in the class. That was understandable because I was among a few there who were experienced with a gun. And I didn't hit that sleeve very many times to do that! I remember the highest score I had was hitting the sleeve or drogue three times in a mission.

The air-to-ground was a different story. The targets were ten-foot-square panels, much like the ones we use today at Nellis except smaller, because the speed and rate of fire were far less. The gunnery range was mounted on a dock that ran out from shore. We used to stand on the dock to watch each other practice—it was very close.

Upon completing training in August 1941, I received my pilot wings and a commission as a second lieutenant, U.S. Army Air Corps Reserve. My first assignment was Gunnery Instructor, Fort Walton Beach Army Air Field.

CHAPTER 4

PLAY THESE
EGLIN AFB, FL: INSTRUCTOR

The first class to show up for gunnery instruction was our lower class, 41-G. One day I was a student flying in the front seat of an AT-6 and the next, I was in the rear seat as an instructor. The transition was that swift.

♠ ♥ ♦ ♣

As an engineer, I was always curious about the technical aspect of things. My introduction to the Research and Development (R&D) community occurred at Fort Walton Beach Army Air Field. We in the gunnery detachment were tasked to test the ability of a carrier pigeon to transmit air-to-ground communications.

For the experiments, there was a tube, about five or six inches in diameter and twelve to fourteen inches long, near the throttle quadrant, with an opening that projected to the rear exterior and ended flush with the fuselage of the P-36. A pilot was given a small cage containing two pigeons, which was placed on the floor of the cockpit on the opposite side from the throttle because that was the only place it could be squeezed in. Simulating an air observation mission, the pilot would manufacture a message, such as "There are five airplanes," or "There is a gun emplacement on the northeast corner of the strip," or whatever. The pilot would slow the airplane practically to a stall and retrieve a pigeon from the cage; then, while trying to fly the airplane, put the message in a small capsule; fasten the capsule on the leg of the bird; stuff the uncooperative bird into the tube on the other side; and, while holding the stick in one hand, use the other hand to push the bird out with a small, cushioned ramrod.

The theory was that the bird went off with his head downwind into the slipstream, which was supposed to improve his chance of survival. However, the airplane simply would not fly slowly enough to allow us to force the pigeon out without killing it. Feathers would fly all over. I shoved about six or seven out. I never heard of any surviving. Some ground-pounder from World War I must have dreamed that up. I always wondered what would have happened if a bird had escaped while in the cockpit. That was my initial exposure to the R&D field. Over the years, I had reason many times to believe that our R&D efforts had not risen much above the investigative thinking of the pigeon caper.

♠ ♥ ♦ ♣

About November 1941, before Pearl Harbor, orders were published for the 41-G class. I was pretty unhappy the day the orders came out. I had been under the mistaken impression that I was only going to have to teach one class. I don't recall whether that was because I'd been told that or was just wishful thinking.

The day after the orders were published, I took four cadets from the 41-G class up on an air-to-air mission. The technique was for the instructor to perch, with the four students in echelon, then peel off and make a high side pass or a low quarter pass, or whatever tactic was to be demonstrated, at the gunnery target, fire, pull away, zoom back up, and go to the end of the string. Each student followed individually. I had instructed them about the tactic before taking off, so there wasn't anything for me to do after I made the demonstration except to sit up there and watch them to make sure they didn't do anything wrong.

These students were pretty good. They were virtually at the end of their training and about to be commissioned. So I sat there for one or two passes. By then, we'd worked our way up over the mouth of Appalachicola Bay.

Seven to ten enormous manta rays, some of them with a wing

span of fifteen feet or more, frequently would lie in the water there, with part showing above the surface. I was just drooling to take a shot at one.

That day, I looked down and saw some rays. So I said, man, I'm going after one of those hummers. I called the flight and said, "I'll be back in a couple of minutes," and peeled off. I went roaring down there as fast as that old AT-6 prop airplane would go and lined up on those rays and cut loose. The AT-6 had two .30 caliber guns mounted in the wings. All I did was scare heck out of the rays and they took off. I pulled up, making an awful lot of noise.

It was about four o'clock in the afternoon. Our camp tents were near Fort Walton Beach and we used to go swimming there after work. By four, almost everyone was through working, had changed and gone down to the beach. About twenty people were swimming and playing in the water, including Lieutenant Ed Herbes (pronounced "Her-bees"), who was the operations officer of the detachment. When I pulled up from that pass on the rays, I decided to go buzz the beach. This had been done by others on more than one occasion.

On the way to the beach was a small sailboat with a man and a woman. I decided to give this sailboat a little buzz job. I flew right at them and then pulled up at the last instant, belly to the sail, blasted the throttle, and blew it right over in the water. I pulled up and looked back. The two of them were hanging on and shaking their fists at me. I thought that was really funny. Then I went smoking across that beach and, believe me, everyone dove in the water.

I went back up to my cadets and we finished and landed. Afterwards, three or four others and I were in the common latrine cleaning up. I was washing and shaving. One of them asked, "Man, were you at the beach a while ago? Did you see that buzz job? Wonder who the devil did that? That was the best job I've ever seen!"

I was just grinning and said, "You want to know who did that? I'm the one."

Old Ed stepped out of one of the stalls about that time and said, "Thanks, Graham. I had the investigation started but you just saved me a lot of trouble."

I was fined $75, given an Article 104 (now an Article 15), set back a year on the promotion list, and transferred back to Craig in disgrace.

Six months later, I was restored to the promotion list. For the first two weeks at Craig, however, I was emptying wastebaskets while

Play These

they figured out what to do with me. Then I was shipped off to a basic flying school at Cochran Field, Macon, Georgia, to train British Royal Air Force (RAF) cadets in BT-13As, which we called "Vultee Vibrators."

♠ ♥ ♦ ♣

The RAF Liaison Officer at Cochran, a wing commander, briefed us right away that we were not allowed to eliminate any RAF cadets. All they wanted us to do was train the cadets well enough to take a bomber off from England and drop their bombs on Germany. If they couldn't make it to a safe landing, they could bail out. The RAF could get more airplanes.

The cadets came from a variety of backgrounds. The first class of cadets was the best. By the time I left, we were scraping the bottom of the barrel.

In one of my last classes, one of my cadets, named Heard, was a concert pianist for the London Philharmonic. He was thirty-four and had never even driven an automobile. He felt strongly about being a pilot to help his country.

Heard and I had two accidents. The first time on a landing, he stalled about thirty or forty feet in the air when he sunk the stick. I was in the back seat trying to shove it loose with my foot, rammed the throttle open and we just went kersplat. He was unable to fly for a couple of days due to cuts and bruises. I had a pretty good cut across the top of my head, but I was flying the next day.

The second time, he cartwheeled us. That was potentially a lot more dangerous. He fractured a collarbone and I dislocated a shoulder. But he healed and passed on to the next phase.

♠ ♥ ♦ ♣

When World War II started, I was at Cochran. On Sunday I was at a popular swimming place, having a picnic with a couple of instructors and our girlfriends. The radio was on in my swell new Plymouth. The music program was interrupted by an announcement that Pearl Harbor had been bombed.

We listened some more but couldn't believe it. As second lieutenants in an Air Corps flying school, we had no exposure to the situation. We realized that there was a terrific build-up in military forces in the U.S. and that defense was the watchword. But we weren't

Play These

briefed by an intelligence officer. What we learned, we learned on our own from open source periodicals. All I really knew was that I wanted to quit that training business and be sent to a fighter unit.

We rushed back to the base. Pandemonium reigned. The base commander, a regular Army Colonel Fitzgerald, was overwhelmed by phone calls with orders. First, we were ordered to disperse the airplanes. I think we creamed about four or five attempting to distribute them around the airfield and to outlying training fields. We all started wearing sidearms. We were warned about sabotage and that submarines were going to shell Cochran Field. At the time, we thought those things would happen. There was a herd mentality. Looking back now, it is hard to believe.

♠ ♥ ♦ ♣

Major Cy Wilson arranged for my transfer to Maxwell AFB, Alabama, in September or October of '42. He ran the advanced phase of the Maxwell Instructor School. He knew my proficiency from having been at Craig when I was there. I liked him and had a lot of respect for him.

After a stint at Maxwell, I was assigned to Tuskegee Army Air Field, Alabama, which had a pilot training school. It was almost impossible to wash out or eliminate a student there. They finally turned out about eight or ten pilots, not enough to man a squadron. So they kept these pilots, who continued to fly and gain proficiency, as second lieutenants instead of as students. When they finally had enough pilots, they activated the 99th Pursuit Squadron, under Ben Davis as commander. This squadron did a very respectable job later in Italy.

Tuskegee County was ninety-two percent black, eight percent white. Everything was controlled by the white minority. Tuskegee Institute and Tuskegee Negro Veterans Home were located there. The town was barely more than a crossroads, with a filling station, post office, bank, a diner and a garage, thirty miles from Maxwell. If you wanted anything, you drove to Montgomery.

Of the 3,500 personnel assigned to Tuskegee AAF, there were fifty-five white officers and ten white enlisted men, all of whom lived off-base. Almost all of them were married. (Very few of the black enlisted were married.) The white enlisted men all worked in the finance office and in the hospital.

One other non-volunteer, Captain Richard E. Conner, a lower

classmate of mine, arrived at the same time I did. Everybody acquired a nickname in flying school. His was "Crash." Mine was "Ace." We made quite a pair.

Colonel Parrish informed us that our job was to activate and operate a school for black instructors. Our first question was, "Where are the students?"

Answer: "Out of the graduating classes."

The second question was: "Where are the instructors?"

Answer: "You're going to recruit them."

We located only one black instructor, a pilot in Chicago. He was a nice person, but no longer an instructor. The school had folded because of the war and he was out of a job. He had taught black and white aviators and was willing to come on as an instructor, until he found out it was in Tuskegee, Alabama. He didn't like that idea.

I was a little senior to Conner, by maybe a month or two, and served as "spokesman." "Sir," I said, "we've done everything we can. There just isn't any fodder for this machine. Now may we go?"

"I'll have to think about this." Parrish told Conner, "You go down to the advanced section and start teaching down there. Graham, we need a base air inspector. This is a new function that is just being organized and you have all the qualifications."

It was a new development about which I had heard nothing. It was a combination of a Standardization & Evaluation Chief who gave all the check rides; a technical inspector who functioned like a Base Inspector General on maintenance compliance; and administrative inspector who checks files and accounts. It took me about three months to form an organization. My staff consisted of a non-rated white lieutenant; a rated white lieutenant, by the name of Lee Graham; four black officers; and about twenty black enlisted. The Air Inspector's Office handled all the complaints, like a regular Inspector General's office.

♠ ♥ ♦ ♣

Conner and I flew everything we could find. And we kept requesting a transfer. Conner finally convinced Parrish to let him go.

I was at my wit's end, until it dawned on me like turning on a light bulb—the increasing riots in the major metropolitan areas. We hadn't been disturbed in Tuskegee, but there were murmurs and concern about the areas where rioting was occurring. One black officer told me

Play These

that they felt the repercussions of it at Tuskegee occasionally.

I manufactured a story and requested an audience with Parrish. I went to his office and closed the door. "Sir," I began, "I have some really disturbing information to tell you. I came into the office this morning and my people were over in the corner. I detected mutterings about unrest..."

"Take some leave! Go to Maxwell!" he interjected. He couldn't have me off the base fast enough.

I drove to Maxwell that afternoon and stayed four or five days. I spent most of my time in the Southeast Training Command HQ, where my old friend, Ed Herbes, who had caught me buzzing down at Eglin, was a lieutenant colonel in charge of fighter replacement training. He bore me no grudge, and I immediately dropped any I might have had when I found out his job. He fixed me up and I drove back with a set of orders to go overseas as a replacement pilot.

♠ ♥ ♦ ♣

I went to Dale Mabry Replacement Training Unit (RTU), Tallahassee, Florida, for about a month. We were a special contingent of ex-instructors. Old Herbes had really fixed me up!

I wanted to fly P-38s so badly I could taste it. That was my idea of a good airplane! It achieved remarkable success in the Pacific.

Instead, I went to Naples, Florida, where we flew P-40Ns, speedy little jobs for P-40s—very lightweight. The P-40N had been designed as a trainer, with less fuel and more guns. It was a reasonably good dive-bombing platform, but the P-40 was never very good for ordnance. I logged about forty hours in it.

We weren't told of our destinations. Most of us assumed we were going to go somewhere and fly a P-40, which was becoming an obsolescent and undesirable plane. However, most or all of us went to fly P-47s and P-51s in Europe.

I was promoted to major on June 3, 1944, en route. The orders reached me at Tallahassee, before I went to Naples. There were no majors in the contingent, only company-grade officers. I was desperately afraid that if I turned the orders in to the finance office and drew my pay as a major, I'd be kicked off the shipment and find myself back in the training command. So I told only a couple of my close buddies.

CHAPTER 5

DOWN FOR DOUBLE
STEEPLE MORDEN, ENGLAND:
354TH FIGHTER SQUADRON

We went from Naples to a replacement training depot in Goxhill, England, where we were given about ten hours of P-51 training. Very quick and dirty. I figured I was safe there and became a major.

From Goxhill, I went to the 355th Fighter Group at Steeple Morden, where I spent four or five days before being assigned to the 354th Fighter Squadron. Shortly thereafter, in September 1944, I became the squadron commander.

This caused some uproar. First, I had come from training command. They had terrible reputations because people liked to hide out there. Second, I was a major, whereas half or more of the squadron had come over with the original group as second lieutenants and were now captains. The remainder, who had come along later, had been there quite a while and were on their second tours. Third, the fellow I replaced, Bert Marshall, was very popular. Bert was promoted to lieutenant colonel and moved up to group operations. He had been an all-American quarterback at Vanderbilt and weighed 135 pounds. His son Bill wrote a book, *Angels, Bulldogs, and Dragons,* about the 355th.

Before I actually took over leading the squadron, I served a short apprenticeship and learned the ropes. I flew wing, element, and flight

Down for Double

lead positions. I estimate that I flew from fifteen to twenty missions and shot down an airplane.

It was an aggressive squadron, the best in the group. One pilot, Henry "Baby" Brown, was the highest scorer in the theater. He became number one when Gabreski was shot down, which lasted until he himself was shot down.

Brown had absolutely unbelievable vision: someone would call in, "Bandits at 12 o'clock" while he'd say, "There are nine 109s" and already be halfway there!

Jim "Jabbie" Jabara was another person with super vision in my squadron. He came from the 354th Fighter Group in France as a replacement pilot, first lieutenant. He had three victories when he showed up. He'd already flown a tour with the 354th in "air-to-mud" (ground support) in Ninth Air Force. He was a superb pilot and a great person, always smoking a big black cigar.

We never had a stable manning situation; we were either under or overmanned. When we were undermanned, we flew more than we normally would and when we were overmanned, we were encouraging pilots to take a week's leave. Some replacements we did not think we should have received; these were bomber pilots who had finished a bomber tour and voluntarily remained in theater to fly fighters, if they could. This was Eighth Air Force policy.

Several of these bomber pilots joined our squadron, but without exception, they failed to become successful fighter pilots. Most of them were killed early.

Jabbie was assigned to take one of the ex-bomber boys up for a lesson in the fundamentals of air-to-air combat. He did, and spun him in right on the home base. I castigated him for putting the man through the wringer, knowing that the bomber pilots weren't used to being on their backs and that a thirty-degree bank was practically vertical for them. I reminded him that he had to creep up gradually on these special students, not have them rat-racing right over the base on the first or second run. I had to give Jabbie an Article 104 and to fine him $200 for causing the bomber pilot's death.

Down for Double

Our squadron was less than three miles from Bassingbourne, where the 91st Bomb Group was headquartered. They had B-17s. When they took off every morning at four or five o'clock, they flew right over our base and woke us up. It was an ungodly time of the morning, but that was what they had to do. That bothered us because we could have slept another hour or so.

A classmate of mine from grade school and high school, Charlie Hudson, was a bombardier in that group. He received the Distinguished Service Cross for bringing a B-17 home and landing it after the pilot and copilot had both been killed. He had washed out of flying school, so he knew a little bit about flying. That was quite an achievement, however. His book, *Combat, He Wrote,* was published in 1994.

Once when the bomb group took off on a mission in November or December of 1944, one of the bombers lost two engines, I think on the same side. The plane plunked right in our revetment area and exploded. Seven of my airplanes were destroyed and four or five more were damaged. My squadron was out of business for a week, until more airplanes arrived. But, had the plane crashed even minutes later, we would have been wiped out; crew chiefs, armorers, and communications men were on their way to the work area and the revetments in trucks, jeeps and tractors. None of my people was injured. A couple of my people earned medals for trying to pull the B-17 crew out of the fire, but none of the crew survived. The fuel caused the airplane to blow up and ignited their ammo load for hours afterward, cooking off .50 caliber rounds. None of the bombs exploded.

For a standard escort mission from England, we would be awakened by the bombers as they became airborne and circled interminably. There was a "buncher" beacon near us, which they used for a bomber rendezvous. Finally, they would set course for targets.

We would get up, go down to Ops, where there was a snack bar with a sergeant, who was my striker and who would cook for us. We gave him all of our spare PX rations and, while we were on our mission, he would take my jeep and drive all around the English countryside and trade those for fresh eggs. A package of cigarettes and a sixpence would be worth two eggs here and an egg there.

Hours after the bombers had been airborne, we would take off and catch up with them, usually at the French coast or a little ways

Down for Double

inland. Not very far inland; they wanted those fighters around when they penetrated. We would escort them to target, they would drop their bombs, we'd bring them back out, pick up any cripples and escort them, and search the withdrawal route. Different groups of fighters were assigned to the penetration and the withdrawal routes, over the target, and Combat Air Patrol (CAP).

After we had escorted the returning bombers to the coast, we'd go back to look for a target of opportunity. This was usually not a programmed target; we had a lot of latitude. In my case, I had always five or six targets pre-selected, usually airfields.

We were directed many times to strike airfields, not specific ones but airfields in general. These were usually heavily defended by anti-aircraft artillery and they were pretty hot. We never struck an airfield without somebody being zapped or lost. We lost eighty or ninety percent of our aircraft attacking ground targets—airfields, trains, and similar targets. We didn't necessarily always lose a pilot; some bellied in or bailed out.

We were known as the "Steeple Morden Strafers" and had the highest air-to-ground record of any fighter group. A book, *The Steeple Morden Strafers,* was published in 1994.

♠ ♥ ♦ ♣

I recall one mission I led which was highly successful: we had more than twenty-five kills on the ground and no losses. The mission began as an escort to Berlin. While herding the bombers to the coast for their return to England, I tucked the squadron in tight formation and directly below a box of bombers. We stayed that way for about one-hundred miles, then made a high speed dive for the water. This was to fool and elude the German radar. We made a 180-degree turn and headed for the target I had selected in Denmark—a Messerschmitt-262 base. The Me-262 was a twin-jet fighter. We flew nineteen minutes, as I recall, at high cruise, minimum altitude (meaning: wave tops) and radio silence.

My navigation was good and we split the target on the nose, made a hard pull-up and rolled in to strafe. I had pre-designated "D"-Flight as the first flak-suppression flight and they pulled up to 6,000 feet to orbit, spot and dive strafe any gun positions. We caught those clowns by complete surprise. It must have been their Physical Training (PT) period; several soccer games were in progress. After my second pass, I pulled up to 5,000 feet to conduct the show, to call in targets and gun positions, and to direct strafing attack headings. We fired down to our bingo ammo and smoked out of there. We really caught them with their knickers down! My logbook record for this mission is "Flown 30 March 1945: 6 h & 30 min., airfield near Flensburg. Strafing. Damaged 3 Ju-52s."

♠ ♥ ♦ ♣

The Germans were clever. They had dummy aircraft that, from an orbit at 10,000 feet, you would swear were Messerschmitt-109s.

In another case, they had a device with a cable that ran down the runway to an airplane, either a dummy or one that was not flyable. The cable was attached to a good airplane next to the runway. When we showed up, they started the good airplane's motor, which caused the cable to pull the broken airplane so as to simulate taking off. I rolled in and was down to 7,000 feet and wide open when I realized that I had been tricked. By the time I could pull out and jink, my fanny had been shot off.

Trains were a different matter. They were easy meat and the locomotive blew with huge clouds of steam—very satisfying! Our standard tactic was for the first flight to hit the locomotive, to stop the train, and then to set up a strafing pattern and try to destroy the cars.

Every once in a while, though, we'd hit a train that had a flak car or two. We'd start to make a pass and the sides and back of these cars would fall off. We would find ourselves flying right down those gun barrels. If we encountered a flak car, we pulled off. Anyone who wanted to duel with a flak position didn't read continued stories.

♠ ♥ ♦ ♣

The Germans had Buzz Bombs, the V-1s, which had pulse-jet engines and 1,500 pounds of high explosive. They would tootle across the Channel using a gyro guidance system. They were programmed by the amount of fuel on board to reach a selected target. They would fly over our base and others. As long as you could hear it going "pup-pup-pup" you were safe. When that quit, you dived for the bunker because the silence meant it was within striking range.

Down for Double

My squadron was one of the units that had the job of responding to these bombs. We kept the left internal wing tank full of 150/190-grade fuel. This simulated an octane rating of 150, a very high-powered fuel. That gave us enough boost—manifold pressure—to extract about another forty mph out of the P-51. No one told us about the effects on the engine, though. Normally, we didn't use it. If we were airborne or on the ground and available to fly, we had some special designations and routes to intercept. But when we saw one of these bombs, we cranked that fuel tank on to give us that extra power. We could just barely overtake them in a dive. In level flight, unless it was very close at the start, the closure rate wasn't good enough.

We had to burn this special fuel periodically, either on a mission or just to clean the engine, to keep the fluid viable.

There were negative aspects, however; this fuel had been the cause of Lieutenant Stalcup's and my engines' quitting over the channel, as I described in the first chapter.

On that same mission, the engine quit on a third pilot, a flight officer by the name of Falvey. He was across the English Channel and descending, at about 8,000 feet, and was able to make a dead-stick landing at an RAF base. They were able to determine from his airplane that the cause of the engine failures was the 150-grade fuel, which had eroded the sodium vapor valves and valve seats of the P-51's Merlin Rolls Royce engine and caused the engine to swallow the valves.

The high octane rating had been obtained by heavily increasing the tetraethyl lead content and, also, the quantity of diethylene bromide, a solvent that was used to keep the lead in solution. Apparently, no one had run a test to determine what destructive effects this fuel might have on an engine. They just shipped it out as fast as they produced it. We were sent the first batch.

Knowing a little about fuels and lubricants, I put an engine on the test block and ran it. The engine lasted twenty-five hours, almost to the minute, before the erosion caused the engine to suck in the valves. My airplane had about twenty-five hours and twenty minutes. We stopped flying every airplane right then and changed every engine. That downed the whole squadron for about a week, which led to complaints, of course. I passed on all the results, so no one else had a problem. Our squadron had the most time on the engines using this fuel. The squadron with the next highest usage had about nineteen hours and hadn't found the problem yet.

The typical bureaucratic Air Corps solution was, "Inspect it every five hours. At the end of twenty-five hours, change the engine promptly." We chose to pull off the heads and inspect the engine after every flight that used the fuel. No fix was found. We lived with it for as long as we used that fuel.

The day after I landed in the brussels sprouts patch, I went back with some tools and a helper to salvage the gunsight. The gunsight was new, a K-14 Gyro-Computing Gunsight invented by the Navy. I had one of only two in the squadron and had acquired mine in a most unusual way.

There was a U.S. Navy antisubmarine base on the south coast of Devonshire. They had Navy versions of B-24s. Someone had told me that the naval aviators flew fresh steaks in all the time from the Navy supply ships, but they couldn't obtain any liquor. I decided to visit the base with some Scotch and try to trade for some of these steaks. We had modified some external pylon tanks by cutting them and installing a hatch, so they would hold cargo. I put a case of Scotch in each tank and took off.

I landed, taxied up and asked to see their equivalent of the Base Ops officer. I didn't know a soul there. I was put on the right track and made a deal for a pile of good, fresh steaks for that Scotch.

During this trip, I was shown the new K-14 gunsight on a wrecked simulator or demo. This was curious, since there was no Navy fighter unit there.

Several days after this trip, I went to the depot at Wattisham. This was our supply depot for parts and new airplanes. They had just started to receive the K-14 gunsights, but hadn't distributed any yet. I talked them out of one, using my information from the Navy folks, took it up and practiced with it against another P-51. The next day, I shot down two airplanes with it!

The conditions that the sight solved were almost incredible; I was pulling "g's" in a chase almost in the vertical plane, i.e., a loop. With the old Mark IX sight, a pilot had to estimate the solution and put the pipper out in front by as many mils as he thought would hit the enemy plane. With the K-14, one simply put the pipper on the cockpit, tracked and squeezed the trigger. I hit both targets dead on into the cockpit area under almost identical conditions.

I was so overwhelmed with the capabilities of this K-14 sight that

Down for Double

I couldn't contain myself. I went and confessed to the group commander that we had a secret weapon. I commandeered every one in the depot at Wattisham to fill my squadron. By the next month, everyone in the group had one. We were the first pilots in Eighth Air Force with them.

♠ ♥ ♦ ♣

In all, I lost four airplanes during the war. I was shot down twice and bellied in one other airplane besides the one with the K-14 gunsight in the brussels sprouts.

One of the times I was shot down occurred during a ground-strafing mission. I was hit in the coolant system by 20 mm flak. It was late in the day. We had escorted a mission in, brought them out, gone back, and were strafing an airfield just east of the Rhine River. I don't recall hitting any airplanes. I made one pass and was hit. I started back with a wingman and the engine became rougher and rougher. I knew it was about through. I pulled up and it quit just about the time I decided to bail out. So I bailed out over Belgium. I didn't know it, though. I splashed in a small river, maybe seventy-five yards wide.

The Canadians and British, who came through the northern part of Europe, were on one side of the river and the Germans were on the other. The only thing that saved me was that I was closer to the Canadian side. I was disoriented and started trying to swim. This was almost impossible, with all that gear on. The Germans started shooting at me and the Canadians fired back at them. A couple of Canadians leapt into the water to haul me out.

I bellied the second airplane in because I couldn't lower the gear. I didn't want to mess up our runway, so I did it at an RAF base. I dinged it so badly it was totaled, but I wasn't hurt.

♠ ♥ ♦ ♣

On one unusual mission, I escorted a B-17 to a submarine pen at Bremerhaven. This was a highly classified mission, code-named "Aphrodite." I was allowed to take only four airplanes. We weren't told much, except that we were to maintain radio silence during the mission. We were told to rendezvous with a single B-17 and escort it to bomb the sub pen. We found the mother ship first and I formed up on that, not knowing that it was the mother ship. The mother ship controlled the unmanned B-17 laden with high explosive.

I trudged up alongside this B-17 and about that time one of my pilots called in to report that he was with the "Aphrodite" bomber. I pulled over there and looked at it. There was no one in it! I became suspicious. I went back alongside the other airplane, the mothership, and it was clear that pilot didn't want me around. We followed him. He turned away well before he reached the target. I never knew whether the B-17 was remotely-piloted from the mothership or was flown on auto pilot. The plane itself was loaded with TNT. The Germans were shooting at it but didn't hit it. We hung back, a couple of miles off the coast out of range of the German 88 mm anti-aircraft artillery. We were still able to watch that B-17 when it hit the ground, missed the target altogether and blew up half the cabbage patches in Germany!

One of my ground claims was a B-24. The Germans had an enormous R&D establishment at Rechlin Larz. We escorted a B-17 bomber mission there once. We were planning to go in and strafe after the bombers left, as we were permitted to do. One "box" of bombers didn't drop their bombs. They made a circle back to try again. I didn't know this and I had already launched a strafing pass. We came screaming across that Rechlin Larz seaplane R&D area and opened up on airplanes about the time the bombers unloaded. At first I didn't know what was happening. I thought they were detonating some land mines or something. I figured out what it was and we flew out and circled off to the side for a while, maybe five minutes, until we were sure it was clear. Then we went back in again.

The Germans had every kind of captured airplane at Rechlin Larz, including a U.S. B-24, which was on the end of the apron, ready to pull onto the taxiway. I saw it when I made the first strafing pass. There was a P-38 there, too. I decided to destroy the B-24 and blew that sucker apart. My film showed it beautifully, when I came home, and I turned in a claim for a B-24. Mike Glantz, the squadron intelligence officer (IO), didn't think that was going to sell. It did.

Master Sergeant Buck Wrightham, my line chief, fabricated a two-seat P-51. He removed the fuselage fuel cell, which held sixty gallons, and fashioned a back seat. The back seater had no controls, but Buck did install an interphone for communication with the front-seater. Word spread. A constant stream of maintenance crews from other units came through to see it and pretty soon everyone had built one.

Mike Glantz was always pressing us for very precise descriptions of mission results. For example, after an aerodrome strafing mission, old Mike would have each of us draw a picture, marking little Xs where the airplanes were, which ones were on fire, who shot what, and all the detail. We could blab it out, but he wanted it all down on a piece of paper, by everyone on the mission.

One time, I became exasperated because there was a conflict between my version of what happened and someone else's. I said, "Mike, I'm going to put your ass in the back seat of that piggyback (as we called the two-seated P-51). I'm going to fly inverted over the area afterwards and let YOU do the counting!" Of course, I never did.

Another incident occurred when we were on a strafing mission against trains in Holland. Bert Marshall was squadron commander at the time. We called him the "flak magnet" because, if anybody was hit, it was invariably Bert. I think he lost four airplanes to ground fire. He and another pilot in the squadron, Lieutenant Royce Priest, naturally nicknamed "Deacon," knew each other from Texas and were close friends. On this mission, Bert was hit and had to belly in. We could see Germans coming up the road toward him in Armored Personnel Carriers (APCs) and on motorcycles. We were strafing the whole area to prevent them from reaching Bert. Bert threw off his chute and dinghy. Priest landed and tossed his chute and dinghy out, too. Bert then climbed onto Priest's lap and they flew out of there! Deacon received the Distinguished Service Cross (DSC).

When the Luftwaffe executed a maximum-effort mission, they were good. They knocked a bunch of bombers down. I can remember vividly seeing parachutes and pieces of B-17s and/or B-24s floating all over the sky.

The Germans' primary tactic was to go for the bomber. That was the threat and they wanted to shoot them down. Consequently, German armament and tactics were designed for that. Conversely, our job was to protect the bombers, which showed in our strategy and tactics.

Clay Kinnard, our group commander, evolved a tactic of designating half the fighter group ("A Group") to stay very close—close enough to fly between the bombers and attacking aircraft—while flying escort for one "box" in the formation. The bomber stream was composed of 700 to 1,000 bombers flying formation in "boxes." They paraded over there all day long! The "A Group" had to find its "box," which sometimes necessitated flying up or down the stream once or twice. The bombers had some very trigger-happy gunners who didn't want any fighter pointing a nose toward their plane. It was sporty because, in order to see a bomber's tail insignia—which was how we identified our "box"—a fighter pilot had to come within firing range of the bomber's guns. One of my squadron's pilots, named Mills, was shot down by a B-17. While he was chasing an Me-109, they went by the B-17 gunner who opened up at the Me-109 but hit the P-51 instead.

The other half, "B Group," flew a couple of thousand feet higher and more spread out to intercept an incoming group of German fighters if they saw any. They would attack as soon as they identified them as hostile, to thin them out and prevent as many as possible from coming near the bombers. We would attack from any quarter—head on, abeam, astern. Our preference was a stern attack, but that didn't present itself very often.

The Luftwaffe was always present, but the real threat was the AAA (20 mm and 40 mm) and small arms while attacking ground targets—airfields, POL dumps, trains. They were positively dead-eye Dicks with the four-barreled 20 mm, which was optically-tracked. That just put out a wall! Every time I was hit, it was with 20 mm. The shells were both armor-piercing and high explosive/incendiary. Ten gun positions near a target meant a pilot would have a hell of a time.

The Germans also used air-to-air rockets against bombers. I never saw any. They weren't all that effective. We were told that they discontinued using them because of the fighters; rockets weren't any good against fighters and the German fighters couldn't carry everything.

The German acquisition and operational employment of the Me-262 virtually assured an extremely high rate of destruction of bombers with a low loss rate. They were almost invulnerable against the bomber stream. We used to watch them come, 6,000 to 10,000 feet over the bomber stream, execute a half-roll, and, booming right through that bomber stream, pick one out, knock it down, pull up, and repeat until they ran out of gas or ammunition. Our fighters couldn't fight them at that altitude and didn't have the air-to-air capabilities to defeat them.

We were virtually helpless. Only once did I have a shot at one; he had shot down a B-17 and gone down through the formation. I saw him start, so I split-S'd while he was on his way down, came out on his tail, and started firing at him wide open when I was about 1,500 yards distant, but he was accelerating away from me and I never hit him.

Hitler, however, chose not to employ them totally in the air-to-air role. This was a grave tactical error.

I lost a wingman to a Me-262. We had good photo intelligence that this jet plane was coming; we could see the runways being lengthened for them. We tried preemptive strafing attacks and were very successful in catching several of them on the ground. They were very hard to set on fire because the JP-4, or their equivalent, didn't burn like gasoline. The Germans were stamping them out, as they were other airplanes, but they were short of pilots and fuel. As a rule, a German pilot would punch out as soon as one of us was on his stern and had hit him a couple of times. He was over Germany and he'd be back the next day.

♠ ♦ ♥ ♣

Adolph Galland, a German who authored the classic *The First and the Last*, fell out of favor with Hitler primarily because of an argument over the employment of the Me-262. He had returned to operational status, however, to lead this massive effort. He was shot down and brought to England, along with an enlisted Luftwaffe pilot who had been with him.

Mike Glantz was Duty IO again the night a call came in from "Pine Tree," the Eighth Fighter Command HQ. They had a "senior German officer," unidentified, to interrogate and we could send a representative, along with the other fighter wings, to sit in on the interrogation. Mike called and woke me up to tell me there was something I might be interested in. I said, "Yeah!" and I went down there. It was Galland.

After his briefing, we were allowed to ask questions. He spoke relatively good English. I've seen him many times since and he said he remembers my question, which dealt with their formation. The Germans flew a formation that we called a "gaggle," as in "a gaggle of bandits at two o'clock." It looked like a swarm of bees; there was someone out in front but there was no rhyme or reason to their formation in the vertical or horizontal planes.

My question was, "General, what kind of tactic is this and why do you do it? What do you achieve? Why don't you fly more conventional tactics?"

The sergeant pilot, who spoke almost no English, was sitting there by him when Galland said, "It's because of the dumkopfs like him!" The sergeant sat up. Galland went on to say, "Our pilots' training is so limited because of the fuel problem that we just launch them, bunch them up, head them in the same direction, and tell them when to shoot when we're attacking the bomber stream." He wasn't apologetic about it.

♠ ♥ ♦ ♣

My squadron didn't lose many aircraft in air-to-air combat. I shot down Me-109s and Focke-Wulfe-190s. The Focke-Wulfe-190 was a better airplane. In the hands of a good pilot, it could win.

The first twin-engine fighter was the P-38. Although the P-38 pilots would defend their plane to the death, it wasn't very successful in the air-to-air role in Europe for two reasons. First, you could identify one of them from miles away, compared to a single-engine P-51. A P-51 looked a little like a Spit and a little like an Me-109. A Jug looked a little like a Focke-Wulfe-190. The Germans would fly around a B-17 to shoot at a P-38. The second reason was that the guns were mounted right in front of the cockpit. The gun ports couldn't be sealed off properly, so the cold air would come in and freeze the pilot's tail off. At high altitudes, above 20,000 ft., where most of the air-to-air escort work was done, this was a distinct drawback. The P-38 was very successful in the Pacific where different situations prevailed.

♠ ♥ ♦ ♣

Our air-to-air losses generally occurred in pretty massive air battles. I recall once, over Berlin, the air was just full of planes. It seemed to me that every one that went ziggying by had a black cross. When I returned home, I found I had picked up a few holes, I don't know how or when. The times we could control the bounce, even though we were outnumbered, we usually killed more than we lost.

We had another advantage: we had more fuel. Even though the Germans were over their home territory, they carried small drop tanks. They would shuck off those tanks, but they didn't have enough internal fuel to outlast us. The Me-262 ran out of juice pretty doggone fast. I never shot any down, but I knew pilots who did. We had a special technique. We knew which fields they were using because of the longer runways required. We would anchor a flight over one of those airfields to just loiter. If any had taken off, we knew we could attack them because they would soon run out of fuel and have to land at those airfields.

For the last three or four weeks before Victory in Europe (VE) Day, May 7, 1945, we were running up unbelievable scores by strafing airplanes in Germany. The airplanes were not on airfields; hundreds of them were concealed along autobahns, under nets and trees. The Germans had little fuel and couldn't fly many of them, but they had improvised all sorts of arrangements to conceal and use them operationally. Also, virtually all of their aircraft factories had gone underground. I later had an opportunity to tour one of them. It was a technical marvel; they came out of the underground facility, up a ramp onto the end of the runway, and took off!

The longest mission I flew was to Prague, Czechoslovakia, and back. We orbited several airfields in Czechoslovakia, but even though the visibility was decent, we never encountered any enemy airplanes. The reason they weren't flying was almost entirely because of lack of fuel. The mission took eight-and-a-half hours. I was young enough that I didn't mind it much, except that I was a little stiff when I finally landed and climbed out. I never learned to use the relief tube in that airplane. I just couldn't make it work! I learned not to drink any coffee, water or juice for a couple of hours before I took off, so I went thirsty for up to ten hours or so at a time.

I have since talked to several German pilots, mostly the high-scoring fighter aces. They formed an organization similar to the American Fighter Aces Association after the war and have come to see us. They all confirm that they just ran out of gas. Our bombers had been particularly effective against their synthetic fuel plants, which had been at the top of the target list. The strategy paid off.

It is probable that the Allied bombers could have operated without fighter escort. We had so many bombers and such well-trained crews that, even though they would have suffered heavy losses without fighter escort, they would have prevailed in delivering the munitions.

The fighters did decrease the losses. There were fifteen fighter groups in the Eighth Air Force, each with usually forty-eight or more fighters for a mission. In our group, we had several levels of effort. "Minimum" called for twelve aircraft per squadron; "normal" was four flights of four; and "maximum" was everything we could put in the air. In addition, we usually put up two airborne spares and a communications relay aircraft. And the 500 to 600 fighter pilots up there each day were a bunch of Hun-hungry studs! By the time Germany surrendered, we were really smothering them with air power.

♠ ♥ ♦ ♣

In January 1945, my squadron Intelligence Officer (IO), Mike Glantz, who was the Duty IO for the day, said he had a request for a courier to pick up a top secret document from the base Ops Officer at Bovingdon, which was the Air Transport Command (ATC) HQ. We called it, "Allergic To Combat." The courier was to fly a P-51 to Capodichino Airport in Naples, Italy, immediately, with the document. I asked Mike to tell my crew chief to hang some tanks and I'd do it. I had never been to Italy and it sounded like a great deal.

The weather was terrible. I had full external fuel tanks because I didn't know if they had anything down there, being an ATC base. I'd never been there before. I expected to pick up the message and keep going. I arrived at Bovingdon and couldn't find the base Ops Officer. No one knew anything about the message.

I spent the night there and, next day, tracked down the officer who was supposed to give me the message. He was in the base hospital with acute appendicitis, heavily sedated and about to undergo an emergency appendectomy. I finally convinced the surgeon to let me talk to his patient and elicited where this bloody message was: it was in his desk drawer! The officer had been holding it, waiting for the courier, and was stricken so suddenly that he hadn't even managed to put it in his safe.

The message was where he said it would be, addressed to "Major General Ira C. Eaker, Commander Middle East Air Force, by hand." There was "EXPEDITE" all over it, but no classification marking.

I prepared to depart the next morning. My external tanks were seeping fuel. My group was one of a few groups using tanks made of compressed paper. They were usable for a sortie so long as the airplane became airborne quickly, burned them out, and dumped them. They would start to drip if a plane sat on the ground for a couple of hours waiting to take off. Mine had been sitting overnight and were positively sagging.

I had to drop the tanks. I couldn't fly with them. I made an awful lot of ATC people unhappy because I told them I had a priority mission, they had no tanks there, and I had to return to my own base for them. I told them, "I'm going to drop them right here on the hard stand." They finally found some dollies to place under the tanks, so I wouldn't literally plunk the tanks down; removed them; and I took off for Steeple Morden.

The weather was really lousy. I never climbed over 150 feet above the deck. I brushed the trees when I tried to make the approach but landed all right.

By now, I'd been gone from the unit for three days. I thought this was too long for me to be away and said to myself, too bad about old Graham and Naples. I assigned Captain Bud Fortier, Operations Officer and the next most responsible officer, to do this. Bud went through the entire war without being shot up— I don't think his airplane received even a scratch. He was musically-inclined and used to play a clarinet for us in the evening.

The Ops order specified "one airplane." I took a dim view of sending Fortier down there by himself. I called and obtained authorization to put a wingman on the mission. Fortier took Mendenhall, his assistant. The weather continued to be bad, so another day passed. Finally, they launched. They were flying over France, ran into bad weather, became separated, and Mendenhall bellied in. He was picked up by the Free French. Bud meandered on down to Naples, arriving after about a total elapsed time of five days since the courier was to have been there.

Bud reported to General Eaker, who unwrapped the package with "Top Secret" stamp marks spilled all over it. Fortier told me afterward that smoke started coming out his ears. General Eaker asked Bud, "Captain, do you know what this is?"

"No, sir."

"Well, it's a highly classified back-up message notifying me that the Yalta Conference is scheduled for February 4. Those people went through here yesterday! Where in the hell has this been? And where have you been?"

Old Fortier blabbed the truth: "Well, my squadron commander started with it, but he was delayed."

General Eaker said, "You go back and tell your squadron commander that I want to see him, as fast as he can fly down here."

By then, Paris had been liberated and everyone wanted to go there. Fortier was no exception. He started home from Naples, figured he was in trouble anyway for losing Mendenhall, and decided to land at Orly Airport, outside Paris, and spent a couple of days living it up in Paris. Finally, he returned home.

"Gordy," Fortier broke it to me bluntly, "there is one unhappy major general down in Italy and he wants to see you right away!"

I jumped in an airplane and went down there. General Eaker had simmered down some but he really skinned me. I explained to him that I had had no idea of the magnitude of the mission, that the dumbbell who had given it to me had been completely *hors de combat,* could hardly tell me where it was. He said, "I don't ever want to see you again!"

♠ ♥ ♦ ♣

When I first arrived, in September 1944, a tour was 200 hours. Then they increased the tour to 250 and then to 300 hours because we were short on pilots. Then, we had more pilots than we needed. At the end of a tour, there were options. First, one could quit and go home. Second, one could go home on a sixty-day R&R and return to fly another tour. Third, one could continue to fly, in place, fifty-hour extensions. At the end of each extension, a physical exam was required. I was halfway through my second fifty-hour extension when the war ended. The last possibility was "involuntary reassignments," such as to higher headquarters, Forward Air Controller (FAC) with the Army.

After I finished my first tour in February 1945, I think it was, Doc Fontenot, our squadron flight surgeon, decided I needed time off and told me to go spend a week at the "flak shack." I didn't have the clanks but he thought I was becoming edgy, because I had had a real fight with Conner and had two black eyes.

The "flak shack" was in Exeter, near the Exe River, which was a great trout stream, as I discovered to my delight. This establishment was operated by the Red Cross. There were probably thirty or forty pilots there, a mix of bomber and fighter pilots. The atmosphere was one of total relaxation. You woke up when you felt like it, ate whatever you wanted for breakfast, read, played tennis, walked, rode a bicycle, or whatever. Mainly, I went fishing.

The pilots coming into the squadron through the pipeline were good. They were aggressive and really wanted to be part of the action.

Down for Double

Of course, there were a few exceptions.

♠ ♥ ♦ ♣

Whenever replacement pilots came into the squadron, I always briefed them on several things myself. One of them was escape from the airplane. There were three standard, briefed ways to exit the airplane. The first way, a "controlled bailout," was preferred if you had the altitude and control of the airplane: you unbuckled all your leads, pulled the airplane up, rolled the canopy back, rolled over, and dropped out.

The second best way was to have air speed, or dive the airplane, roll the trim tabs full forward, which meant you had to pull the stick back as hard as you could, unbuckle everything, let go of the stick, and shoot out. This works well and was used at low altitude.

Third, if you had altitude but had a problem, you could slow the airplane, under control, and try to jump to the forward edge of the wing, and hope to miss the tail.

Jack Fletcher was a new and good pilot from Atlanta in the squadron, popular, had a great sense of humor, and was a devout Christian. On his fifth or sixth mission, he was flying my wing. We were over England, returning. We had started letting down as we left the channel, and were at about 18,000 feet. He called me to say his engine had quit. I told him to keep trying to restart it. At about 15,000 feet it was clearly not going to go. I said, "You'd better start thinking about bailing out." I was flying right beside him in formation.

We wore the first "anti-g-suits." These suits were designed to prevent pilots from blacking-out during very stressful airplane maneuvers. The first ones were full uniform flying suits. They were so bad we tossed them right away. Then we received exactly the same g-suit used by the U.S. Air Force today. It had the same quick disconnect fitting, which was designed to come apart without unplugging or unscrewing if the pilot had to bail out. Jack had one of these on for the first time. I had one on, but some pilots in the squadron didn't have them yet.

I had briefed Jack on the three ways to escape from the airplane. At around 12,000 feet, I told him he'd better disconnect everything and try to bail out the first, best way. He had the altitude and control. He disconnected his radio and oxygen mask; pulled up and rolled over. His ass came out, and parachute, and dinghy, but that quick disconnect fitting hadn't come loose. He was into a half spiral, but he managed to reach the stick and righted the airplane. He plugged the mike back in and said, "Falcon Red Leader, what did you say was the next best way?"

By this time, he was down to about 7,000 or 8,000 feet. I said, "Jack, bail out!" This time, he realized what was holding him in, reached down with both hands and pulled it loose, rolled it over, and out he went. He survived.

♠ ♥ ♦ ♣

In late March or early April 1945, we had not begun standing down officially, but the war was winding down and we were looking for things to do. A Swede, Count Bernadotte, was acting as a negotiator between the German government and the Allies for the surrender at that time. A hot mission came in to go to Paris and escort an unarmed B-17 to Stockholm. That was for me! I ignored orders to take only four airplanes and took eight. I figured we'd live it up in Paris and then go to Stockholm.

We landed at Orly in mid-afternoon. HQ U.S. Forces was at Versailles Gardens, where the Chief of Staff for U.S. Forces was entertaining a group of visiting congressmen, including a congresswoman from Maine, Margaret Chase Smith. The Chief of Staff and his crew were living in the most lavish establishment I had ever seen.

The plan was for an unarmed B-17 to ferry the general and the negotiating team to Stockholm. We were to escort the B-17 to the Swedish coast. We had a penetration line that we were not to exceed. Then we were to turn around and return to England. The staff navigator, a lieutenant colonel, was responsible for planning the mission for the next day.

At nine o'clock in the evening, the general came in and asked, "Where's the fighter commander?"

We had maps and charts spread out all over a beautiful rug on the floor. I saluted and identified myself. Then he asked, "Well, is everything set?"

I said, "Well, General, there's one problem. I understood we were to escort you to Stockholm, land and refuel."

"Oh, heck, no, you can't land," he said. "It's a neutral country. This is a special mission. I'm going in on special orders and you're to return to your base in England."

"General, we can't do that," I said. "We don't have enough fuel."

"You have drop tanks, haven't you?"

"Yes, but we don't carry more than two. Permit me to suggest an alternative: we go to England and stage out of England. It will be nip and tuck, but I think we could make it if we encounter no opposition." Their fear was that there were some holdout German fighter units in Denmark and southern Norway.

He didn't like that idea worth a damn, but the navigator convinced him.

The next day, we staged out of Leiston, on the east coast of Britain. The briefing I gave to the major who was flying the B-17 was: "Don't take off and make any funny turns. Wait until we are airborne and form up on your wing." No one said anything about my taking the extra four airplanes. Maybe the general knew and wanted them. I'll never know. The major swore he wouldn't make any turns until we were airborne and had completed formation, because there was a low overcast. I told him, "If you don't wait, we won't be with you!"

The major didn't wait. Moreover, he pulled right into the overcast and leveled off at 20,000 feet. This altitude would cut our range considerably. I didn't find out about his change in the planned altitude before we took off from England. When he leveled off there, I slid over next to his cockpit before we had crossed out and started talking to him on the radio. Once we crossed out, we had to maintain radio silence.

He said, "We're going to cruise at 20,000. We have a passenger on board who can't fly above that." The general had a civilian female secretary who had a heart problem and couldn't go to altitude, because the B-17 wasn't pressurized.

Holy smokes! We're done for, I thought to myself. We escorted them to the prescribed release point, from where we could see Stockholm about fifteen miles away. We saw a couple of flights of Me-109s, but didn't have enough fuel to engage unless we came under attack. I had tried to release the escort about one-hundred miles away from Stockholm, but the general himself came on the radio and said, "This is a direct order: you WILL continue escort!"

We would have been damn lucky if everyone had made it back. I lost two pilots on the mission. They bailed out over the water and we never saw them again. Six of us made it back, of which two bellied in. The rest of us managed to land at an airfield.

I don't know if they succeeded in accomplishing anything in Stockholm.

♠ ♥ ♦ ♣

Down for Double

We had some really famous fighter pilots in my squadron. Al White was awarded the Harmon Trophy and about every other thing there was for the B-70 work. Unfortunately, during an aerial filming with an F-104, a midair collision occurred. Al bailed out but his co-pilot was killed.

Bob White was the first astronaut, that is, he earned the first astronaut wings for flying a vehicle higher than 100,000 feet, at Mach 6, I believe it was. Like Oran Stalcup, he was about nineteen years old. He was a buddy of Falvey, whose engine quit the same day mine did because of the high octane fuel corrosion problem.

I was with Bob when he was shot down on a strafing mission. He bailed out, but he was so low no one saw his chute open. He went down behind a row of trees, but the chute did open and he was not hurt when he hit the ground. I wrote a letter to his mother and told her all the circumstances, including that the likelihood of his surviving the low-altitude bailout was pretty minimal. If he had survived, he would undoubtedly have been taken prisoner. We received no word of him. By golly, he turned up as a prisoner!

Five kills earned a pilot the "Ace." I was credited with sixteen-and-a-half kills, one probable and ten damaged.

Part of the explanation for higher numbers of kills by individual pilots was their exposure time: the longer a pilot was there, the more missions he flew and, logically, the greater were the chances of seeing Germans and claiming victories. A second factor was where a pilot was in the squadron. If a pilot was a flight leader, the chances were better. By the time a pilot became squadron leader, the chances were better still because he was out in front. Third, and very important, was the individual's aggressiveness—whether he really wanted to go in there and mix things up. Last, individual pilot shooting skill counted.

Many things could go wrong. Sometimes, a pilot would fail to turn the gun switch on. This happened to me once when I flew a plane which belonged to a chap named Duffy. His airplane was really goofed up: he had had the gun switch remounted up near the gun sight. I hadn't taken the time to familiarize myself with it. We engaged the enemy very quickly and, of course, nothing happened when I pulled the trigger. I couldn't find the gun switch.

There was an unending debate about whether the .50 caliber guns used by the Allies were better than the 20 mm used by the Germans. I preferred the .50 caliber at the time (i.e., during World War II), but if we had had today's 20 mm technology, I would have taken it in a heartbeat!

Another debate occurred over the harmonization pattern. We had six guns. I chose to harmonize my outboard guns to a point of impact at 150 yards, the second one inboard at 200 yards, and the inboard guns at 300 yards. But everyone differed. Some put them all in the same "hole." I thought it could be mathematically proven that chances of achieving hits improved greatly by a dispersion pattern, the way I did it. Consider the odds of being EXACTLY at the right range, so that you could make every shot hit the same spot. If it happened, then the pilot would certainly hit the target, no question about it! But I thought those odds were unacceptably low and that the other way was better.

I shot down a Spitfire once. We had escorted a mission in and a group of eight or ten of us were returning together. There were multi-layered clouds. We engaged about a dozen Me-109s, of which I shot down one, or thought I did. The engagement was over pretty quickly because they escaped into the clouds. Everyone checked in to say he had fuel and ammo. I decided we should turn around and go back in.

We flew for about fifteen minutes in a wispy overcast eastbound over Germany. Some shapes went right over us in formation. I thought they were Me-109s. I called a hard 180-degree turn and we took off at full throttle. We were in and out of the overcast, but overtook them in about three or four minutes. It was a flight of four Spits, but from the stern a Spit looks a lot like an Me-109. There weren't supposed to be any Spits in that part of the world. Having made the turn first, I was out in front. We were starting to run low on fuel. I said, "I'll take a shot at one. If you think you're in range, fire, then we'll dive and full throttle for home. We can't stay and fight."

I gave a squirt until I saw tracers. Like most pilots, I always put five tracers ahead of the last fifty rounds in my guns. Our guns had no ammo counters, so we had no other way of knowing how much remained. Some pilots put a single tracer in at different places. I discovered that a tracer burned the magnesium very quickly and was very erratic, so there wasn't a good deflection indication from one, by itself.

I hit the Spit, although I didn't know it. We dove away and headed for England. The wing man of the destroyed Spit reported that a P-51 had shot it down. They checked out where everyone was and narrowed

Down for Double

down the likely candidate to our squadron, and me. When we looked at the gun camera film, there was no doubt. The photo interpreters (PIs) could tell instantly.

The pilot had managed to bail out in friendly territory and so avoided being captured. I found out the number of his unit and went to see him in Northern France. I had a hell of a reception from that unit! I thought I was going to be hung by the thumbs. I apologized profusely, but they were still hot. I didn't blame them.

In the mixed-up days near the end of the war, pilots in the 339th Group engaged and shot down seven or eight Russian fighters. This should not have happened; there was a buffer zone to prevent such incidents. That day, however, the visibility was very low; the group had been engaged in a fight with Me-109s, some of which had escaped; and, when the Russians showed up, they were mistakenly identified at first as the Me-109s. After the Russians had been correctly identified, some additional pot shots had been taken. Major Rod Cox, one of my old buddies, who had gone over with the original contingent that I was in, was the commander of the squadron involved.

When they were talking on the radio on the way back, they realized what they had done. They landed in France, cleaned the guns, and destroyed the gun camera film. The Russians saw enough of their unit insignia and tail numbers to identify the unit. The Russian senior officer in London claimed that they had executed their pilots who had been involved in this and they expected the U.S. Air Force to do likewise. A showy court martial trial was held. There were Russian observers, high-ranking officers from the Russian Air Force and Army. Rod Cox was selected as the fall guy. He was sentenced to life imprisonment, without chance of parole. The Russians indicated they were satisfied. Rod was flown to the U.S. that very night and no one ever heard of Rod Cox in the Air Force again. He stayed in the Air Force, but the Russians never heard about it.

We were stood down a few days before Victory in Europe (VE) Day. No more bombing missions; only some special inspections. When VE Day was announced, everyone whooped and hollered. Men fired their .45 pistols through the barracks. That day and for three days

Down for Double

following, we were confined to base. Of course, everyone headed for the bar, where stocks were rapidly depleted. We obtained special permission to take a truck to go round up some more liquor. Finally, we were turned loose and, naturally, almost everyone, especially the enlisted men, wanted to go home. They'd had a bellyful of it because they didn't have "tours"—they were there for the duration.

CHAPTER 6

I'M NOT IN THIS ONE
LITTLE WALDEN, ENGLAND: 374TH SQUADRON

After Victory in Europe (VE) Day in May 1945, I moved from the 355th to the 361st Fighter Group, where I took command of the 374th Fighter Squadron, which was one of the five groups that would be going directly to the Pacific from England. I was a lieutenant colonel, having been promoted on my twenty-seventh birthday, February 16, 1945.

We equipped with P-47Ns, which were really spiffy. The P-47N had a compressibility flap, which we now call a speed brake. It was a slotted flap that came out of the top of the wing in a dive so as to decelerate the airplane and prevent it from going into "compressibility," which caused the controls to freeze. Although we didn't know it, we were approaching the limit Mach number for the aircraft, with the result that the airflow over the surfaces became non-laminar and the pilot lost control. The compressibility flaps came on automatically, at a designed true air speed of about 500 mph. The pilot could disable it if he wished. It was a slick invention!

Before I arrived, the 361st group commander had been Roy Caviness. He had been a few classes ahead of me in flying school and an instructor at Craig.

Jack Landers came in from the Pacific to take over the group

I'm Not in This One

immediately after Roy, but stayed only a short time. He was likable and had a great reputation. Jack had originally taken the 78th Group at Duxford, and then come over to the 361st.

Jack wasn't at the 361st long enough to reorganize and weed out poor performers. I took over in August 1945 and had an easy task; there were enough people who wanted to go home and enough who wanted to stay in the Air Corps that, by the time we were ready to go, I probably had the most highly-qualified fighter group ever put together. The pilots were eager, experienced, and I had the opportunity to fly with every one of them to check them out. Morale was terrific!

♠ ♥ ♦ ♣

Enlisted men were a problem. We had very few volunteers and had to take new arrivals who had just been shipped in. The pipeline from the U.S. was flowing unabated. Some people showed up who had been sitting around a replacement depot in the states for three or four months, had waited in the theater for a month, and had just reported to their unit when the unit was on its way to ship home. The system was approaching chaos. It worsened later.

The ground echelon of the 361st Fighter group had gone to Southampton. The airplanes had been cocooned and put on carriers for shipment to the Pacific. We never saw what happened to them. Our base was to be Okinawa.

♠ ♥ ♦ ♣

On VE Day, May 7, 1945, three disarmament wings (numbered the First, Second and Third) were activated. The very next day, these wings began to take possession of all the German aircraft, primarily fighters. A lot of German airplanes couldn't be flown, because they had no fuel. These were destroyed on the spot, wherever they were. The flyable ones were flown to the central disarmament wing locations and destroyed immediately using bulldozers. The common wisdom was that holdouts and suicide corps were being formed. I only heard of one group in Bavaria that tried to hold out, but there was no air associated with it. The disarmament wings accomplished their job practically overnight.

Several of the pilots in the 361st were temporarily assigned to these disarmament wings. I was associated temporarily with one of

I'm Not in This One

them at Fritzlar, a German air base, and flew an Me-109 and a Focke-Wulfe-190. While I was at Fritzlar, one of the Air Corps officers working on the base told me about a German salt mine located to the east. Uncounted goodies were stored there. Some were shown to me. Nothing would do, but we had to go see it. We anticipated the need for trade items and collected all the cigarettes and chewing gum we could obtain, and a case of cognac. Bob Douglas, Howard Cable, Ed Tinkham, and I borrowed a command car, hooked on an empty Jeep trailer, and followed a sketchy map. We drove around for six or so hours before we found it.

We had to cross a small bridge over a stream, which served as a dividing line between the U.S. and Russian zones. The salt mine was about four or five kilometers on the other side, inside the Russian zone, guarded by Russians. There was a U.S. sentry on our side of the bridge and a Russian sentry on the far side. The military policeman (MP) stopped us. I told him what we wanted to do. He said, "Sure, that's OK. People are going in there all the time. The Russians don't care. Just give them some cigarettes." So we gave the Russian sentry a pack of cigarettes and he waved us on.

The mine had several levels, or "drifts," and went down 1,500 feet. Lighting was very dim. It had been a storage depot. For example, one whole level held surgical equipment: microscopes, surgical instruments, bandages. One level was for flying clothing, another for plain old wool socks, trousers, stuff like that.

We were like blind dogs in a meat house. We were soon separated; one person saw a pile of leather flying suits or boots that he wanted in one tunnel; someone else was snared down another shaft by another treasure. We filled the little mine cars, which were about three by five feet, as if they were shopping carts. We went crazy in there—throwing stuff in, tossing out some items for greater finds! I acquired a German typewriter, various articles of clothing, some Storm Troopers' (SS) dress uniform daggers, and a couple of beautiful fur coats.

There were half a dozen or more men around the entrance. The senior man was a Russian major, who was about my size. Several of them went into the mine with us to show us where to go and what was there. None of them spoke English and we spoke no Russian. We communicated with my inadequate German.

They were really entertained by our behavior. I was wearing a new leather flying jacket with no insignia. The Russian major pointed to my flying jacket. I thought he just wanted to try it on; I didn't realize

I'm Not in This One

he wanted to keep it. Hell, they had good equipment and he didn't need that. So my flying jacket went down the tube. I had a camera and took some pictures of the soldiers, which I still have.

One of the soldiers had a medal for being a "Hero of Stalingrad." I will never forget him. He was a very low-ranking corporal or so, standing by a big wooden door at the entrance, which opened like a barn door. That was apparently his post.

When we were organizing to leave, we broke out the cognac. It was the foulest stuff I have ever tasted! It was raw, worse than Calvados (apple brandy). Mostly, it had a very high alcohol content. I watched "Hero" take one of the bottles, turn it up, drink it without stopping! Then he threw away the bottle. Before long, he slumped by the door and was out like a light. It didn't take long for the rest of them to become well-oiled, also.

I decided we'd better get the hell out of there. We left late and the four of us alternated driving all night long back to Fritzlar. That command car and Jeep trailer were loaded to the gills and stuff was tied on top.

When we arrived at Fritzlar, we stuffed our gear and loot into every cranny of the bomb bay of a B-26, Marauder, an auxiliary airplane for our group that we had learned to fly. We raced back to Little Walden, called all our buddies, and handed out all the stuff. Then we asked them, "Give us all your goodies. We have a good thing going and might as well milk it right now. But we need a lot of trading material. These Russians are our buddies and we'll go back this time and really clean up!"

So we did. Next morning, we raced back over there, took the command car and the Jeep trailer, loaded up, and took off. When we reached the bridge, there was a different MP, who said, "You can't go in there."

"What do you mean?" I asked.

"Some Americans came through here yesterday. I wasn't on duty, but we received a report that they killed a Russian. The Russians are mighty unhappy and they won't let anybody in there."

"We heard about that," I told him. "Don't worry. They're our buddies." I didn't tell him we were the ones. So I started to walk across the bridge to talk to the Russian, who pulled up a machine pistol and put a "root-a-ti-toot-toot" right across in front of me. I threw him a pack of cigarettes, which he kicked in the water. I threw him another, which he stepped on and ground into bits, then he fired another burst from his machine pistol into the air. That was enough to convince me that we weren't the popular kids on the block!

Evidently, old Hero had died from alcohol poisoning. I could understand that. It had even tasted like poison.

♠ ♥ ♦ ♣

Crash Conner was executive officer at the 78th. He was about to go home. Pilots were running out our ears. They couldn't shut off the flow. They kept coming! They were all second lieutenants, as a rule, and eager as all get-out to fly combat. Some of them had flown from one to three missions.

One evening, Conner and I went into the bar at the 78th. There were a half a dozen men around. We ordered drinks. There was a lieutenant standing next to Conner wearing a blouse with a Distinguished Flying Cross (DFC) ribbon. This was rare. We normally wore no decoration unless it was a formal affair of some kind, of which there were virtually none. Conner nudged me and said, "See this one here? He came in not long ago. He earned the DFC, even though he didn't shoot down an airplane." Conner told me how, but I've forgotten. "But he is insufferable! We ought to pull his leg."

Duxford is an old Royal Air Force (RAF) station. The mess and bar are all in the same building, as are the rooms in the Bachelor Officers Quarters (BOQ). We went to Conner's room and worked out a plan.

I went down to the club office and typed out some applications in French for the French Foreign Legion Air Force. The application requested information on the number of flying hours, number of claims for "chausseur pilot," and so on. I stuffed a bunch of Yank magazines in a navigator's briefcase that we found, then put six of these applications (carbon copies) in on top. This took about an hour.

Then we went back to the bar. I went in one door and Conner came in the other. We hollered at each other, "Hi, Crash!" and "Hi, Ace!" We shook hands. The lieutenant didn't recognize us as having been there earlier. He was still next to the bar. By then, there must have been twenty more men in the room. I very ostentatiously slapped that briefcase on the bar.

"What do you have in your briefcase, Ace?" Crash asked me.

I answered in a mutter, with a couple of words, like "French Foreign Legion Air Force," audible to the eavesdropping lieutenant. In no time, he was trying to crowd in between us. Conner came back

I'm Not in This One

with, "That sounds like a pretty good deal! How can I be part of it?"

I looked around secretively and fished out one of the applications. The lieutenant had obviously swallowed the story hook, line and sinker. Conner puzzled over the application and filled it out. The lieutenant grabbed me by the shoulder, then, and said, "Colonel, you have to let me in on this!"

"Lieutenant," I said, "what do you think you're doing?"

He replied, "I've tasted blood!"

I just about collapsed. Conner had to leave the room. "I guess we have room for one more," I conceded. So I pulled out another application. He filled it out. Then he started to tell everyone around, all the new heads, that he had signed up for the French Foreign Legion Air Force.

Our story was that he was to pack his footlocker and ship it to a phony address, which I gave him, at the dock at Southampton. Two weeks later, to the day, he was to report to Southampton, where he would marry up with his footlocker, board the ship, and sail for the Middle East. The story was patterned after the American Volunteer Group (AVG, better known as The Flying Tigers); French Foreign Legion Air Force pilots flew Spitfires; pilots drew $1,500 a month, plus $1,000 for every airplane killed. There were other details which made it sound very attractive. For example, they would keep their Air Corps commissions, but they were seconded to the Legion. As we went along, the details became more tantalizing. The timing was exquisite! At that time, Palestine was in a terrible uproar. The French and British were involved over there. It was a real dog's breakfast trying to figure out who was running what, and a jillion frustrated U.S. fighter pilots were at loose ends.

To say that it went over big is a gross understatement. Pilots were standing in line, pounding the bar with their fists, trying to buy us drinks by the hundred, and demanding an application. We finally left, after I'd given out the six copies, and went to Conner's room.

"Crash," I said, "this is such a good deal we have to do some more!" I volunteered to find a command car, dig up Abe Morris, another old buddy, a lieutenant in the 361st, who could become the *aide de camp*, and run off some good copies on the duplicating machine. So I went back to Little Walden, where I was then based as commanding officer of the 361st, proceeded to follow through on our plan, and returned to Duxford to pick up Crash. We went to all fifteen fighter groups in the Eighth Air Force. At some point, we started to send Abe

I'm Not in This One

Morris ahead to announce our pending arrival. Pilots would be lined up, waiting for us. We were gone two weeks. It was unbelievable. The men wouldn't let us go to bed. They were mad at us when we ran out of applications.

After two weeks, we were running out of steam. We had been drinking a lot, regularly. We'd hit a base about four o'clock in the afternoon, go into a session that lasted half the night, get up in the morning and head for the next base. The last place we went was the Fourth, the proud "Fourth But First" unit to arrive over there. The Fourth had formed from the old Eagle Squadron.

About eleven o'clock, after I had just given out the last application, someone went and woke up "Red Dog" Norley, one of the original Eagle Squadron pilots. He was quite a famous character in the Fourth. He had been in the Air Corps, my lower class, but washed out. He then went up to the Royal Canadian Air Force (RCAF) and came into the Eagle Squadron through that route.

"Red Dog" came storming into the bar in his pajamas. "Graham, where the hell are you? I understand you're recruiting for the French Foreign Legion Air Force."

I acknowledged I was. I told him quietly that my *nom de guerre* was Captain John Black, which was what I was using. "Red Dog" was the last person I would ever have let sign up, because he was a good friend. I tried to take him aside and tell him it was a joke. "What the hell! You can't do that to one of your old buddies!" he accused. He became really mad and stomped off in high dudgeon.

We fled. That was the end of it. I guess about fifty people signed up. We had a lot of laughs over it. Conner took off and went home to the U.S.

Three or four months later, I was married. Soon after, my wife and I were walking down the street in Cambridge. We had been sight-seeing and shopping. A lieutenant in uniform was passing us on a narrow sidewalk. A hand grabbed me on the shoulder and knocked me flat on my can. He told me if I stood up he was going to hit me again. I didn't recognize him, but he was one of those who had fallen for the gag and had actually gone to Southampton and waited for two weeks! He told me there was a bunch of them down there—he never told me how many. I said, "Now wait a minute. I think there's some mix-up!" I was thinking of every kind of excuse. He had really pasted me. Finally, I confessed, "Yes, I did it and I'm sorry. It was just a gag."

"It damn near cost me a month's pay," he said, "plus the fact that

that Foreign Legion Air Force never did materialize! You really faked me out!" He carried on some more. Finally, I called him off. He left, still mad.

After the war, when I had left the Air Corps and was working for Socony Oil Company of Venezuela, at their headquarters in New York City, the same thing happened. I was about to enter the building where I worked and someone hit me so hard that I was knocked right through the door. He was another person who couldn't take a joke.

The third and last time someone recognized me was in 1954. I had gone to Fifth Air Force HQ to brief them on nuclear target selection, which I was doing for the Far East Air Force HQ. A major, sitting in the front row, kept looking at me as if I were a mortal enemy. I'd glance at him every once in a while and he was just looking daggers at me. When the briefing ended, he was the first person to reach the podium. He said, "I want you to know that I know who you are! You're the son of a bitch who signed me up for the French Foreign Legion Air Force." This was seven years later! He had simmered down enough that he wasn't about to slug me, but he was very unhappy.

At the 31st Fighter Group reunion in San Antonio in April 1992, I saw John Santry. He was one of my squadron commanders in the 31st between 1955 and 1959. He had not been a victim, but a couple of people who worked for him had told him this story. When I showed up as commander of the 31st and he found out who I was, he came to the office right away and said, "I understand you have some applications for the French Foreign Legion Air Force?" I thought, Oh, God, I found another one! He still calls periodically. During DESERT STORM in January 1991, I sent him a form and he obligingly filled it out.

Part of the ground support echelon had already sailed for the Pacific when Victory in Japan (VJ) Day occurred on September 2, 1945. Thousands more, waiting to board ships for the states, were held in huge cantonment areas at the ports. In spite of the security, a lot of them spilled out into the little towns and pubs, where everyone was slapping each other on the back and hoisting drinks.

We pilots were still at the base, waiting to be flown over. The Japanese surrender was good news and bad news. Everyone wanted to keep shooting down airplanes. As we used to say, "It was a sorry war,

I'm Not in This One

but it was better than no war at all." We knew we would have to find something else exciting to do.

The 361st was inactivated.

CHAPTER 7

I'M THROWING IN

ENGLAND: VIII FIGHTER COMMAND HQ

People were chosen to go home based on a point system. Points were earned for each month of service, for decorations and other accomplishments. Fifty-five points were needed for immediate departure. I had 255 points, but in October 1945 I was reassigned as Chief of Operations (the "A3") on the General Staff, VIII Fighter Command HQ, under Brigadier General Emil Kiel. My assignment was to oversee the inactivation and removal from England of all the fighter units and their equipment. Reducing the forces and removing the equipment was quick work. There were four disposal methods for the equipment. First, some airplanes were sent to the occupation forces on the continent. For example, the 355th went from Steeple Morden to Augsburg, Germany, as an occupation unit. I went over to see my buddies several times. Second, a lot went to the British. They picked over what they needed. The RAF was extremely well-stocked when we pulled out.

Third, much equipment had to be destroyed, including a lot of airplanes. Navigators and bomber, cargo and fighter pilots would fan out to the bases to collect the airplanes and fly them in to a central point. The chief point for fighters was near Birmingham. I ferried an airplane in with a flight of four once to see what they were doing. A GI

65

I'm Throwing In

jumped up on the wing and asked me, "Do you want anything out of there, Colonel?"

"What do you mean?" I asked in return.

"Most of the pilots take a compass, clock or instrument as a souvenir."

I considered the offer and asked for a compass and a clock. He whipped out a screwdriver and had them out in no time.

It made you want to cry. Hundreds of P-51s, many of them almost new, were being destroyed. While I was talking to the GI, someone else was underneath opening the fuel cocks to drain the fuel onto the ground. Almost before I could walk off the wing, a tug had hooked a tow bar and towed it over to where one of several bulldozers was waiting. After the engine was removed, it was smashed flat, dragged over to the side and stacked on end.

On another occasion, I was at the supply depot at Wattisham. GIs were sitting on stools along a bench, taking out watches, bashing them with a ball peen hammer, and pitching them in a basket. I found a noncommissioned officer (NCO) in charge in the place and said, "That's a crime! Why don't we stuff these in the cracks and crannies of ships going home and put them in the depots back home?"

"Oh, no, we can't do that!" he exclaimed. "The contract for these states that they will never be available in the United States where they could possibly reach the civilian market."

"Why not send them to Europe?" I then asked.

"We've already sent all they can handle," he admitted.

Last, high value items went home.

I did manage to keep a little German sporty motorcycle. We rode it all over the base. Occasionally, one of the bolder pilots would ride it into Cambridge or one of the villages but no one was caught. We could send home anything that would fit in a U.S. mail bag. One of my crew chiefs cut the frame into two pieces so that, when the wheels were removed, it fit in two mail bags, which I shipped home to Taft, California. It never arrived. Somebody picked it off en route, just as they emptied my banded and padlocked footlocker with my German typewriter, the SS swords and daggers, and my Schmeiser automatic pistol. The only thing left in that footlocker was a GI blanket.

♠ ♥ ♦ ♣

I'm Throwing In

I spent one whole day observing the Nuremburg Trials. Obtaining entrance to the Nuremburg Trials took some doing. The security was extraordinary. We were checked every thirty yards or less along a labyrinthine passage. There was an armed security guard at every corner to check your identification and pass. The major observation area was a balcony, rather like a choir loft, which held about fifty people. Every seat was taken. I stayed the whole day, until they drove us out. All the big wheels were there, including Göring. The trial was conducted in English and translated into German, for the benefit of the accused, as well as French and Russian. There was amplification (by headsets). I didn't hear anything profound. It seemed like a typical trial.

♠ ♥ ♦ ♣

While I was at VIII Fighter Command, I went to Berlin to look around. A Michigan policeman named Potter, whom I never will forget, flew us in a Gooney bird. He checked me out in that C-47 before he went home. "Check-out" may be an overstatement; I had flown enough in the left seat that, if another competent C-47 pilot were with me, I felt OK.

We landed at Templehof, the site of the former Luftwaffe HQ. If Berlin had been zoned, no one knew about it. There were recurring confrontations between the Russians and the Americans. The Germans were ragged, starving and begging. You could have anything you wanted for a package of cigarettes!

I wandered through the Luftwaffe HQ. It had been damaged, but was still largely intact. I went to the Reichstag, where I took some pictures. One bomb had come right through the dome. I took a picture looking up. The explosion and fire damage are visible. I finished one roll of film and put it in my new leather jacket.

While I was milling around in there, a Russian security patrol came up to me and asked to see my papers. This was just harassment. He spotted the black top of the Argus 35mm camera showing out of my jacket pocket. He reached for it and I put my hand over it. He said something in Russian and a soldier took my arm. I understood he meant, "Hands off!" He pulled out the camera and indicated to me that he wanted to keep it. We argued about it. Finally, he indicated that I should open it and he stripped out the film, then gave me back the camera. There weren't many prints on that roll, so that was no big loss, but that was the last of my film.

I'm Throwing In

We stayed a couple of nights. A warrant officer in the BOQ who was permanently assigned to Templehof showed me a footlocker full of loot that he had amassed by trading cigarettes and candy. He told me it was the third one he had filled to ship home. I asked how he knew the other two had arrived at home. He said he didn't know, but he was sending them anyway!

♠ ♥ ♦ ♣

Another interesting experience I had at VIII Fighter Command began with a story told to me by an Air Corps navigator of Dutch descent, Captain Vroegendevey. While in London on a pass, he was in a bar frequented by Dutchmen and met a civilian named Schotte. In the course of their conversation, it developed that Schotte had been the IBM representative in Europe, headquartered in Amsterdam before the war. When Holland was invaded, he was in New York City at IBM headquarters. He couldn't return to Holland to join his family. He managed to go to Portugal, buy a small boat, and sail it by himself up the coast to Holland. After locating his family he brought them out, back to Portugal, where he left them for the duration of the war. He may have had help from IBM. He then went to London and worked between London and New York.

Eighth Air Force had leased some early IBM equipment, called a "statistical control unit." In those days, IBM didn't sell anything, only leased it. All the personnel records, bombing data, and stuff like that were being processed on the equipment. After the war, there was no further use for it. It was being crated for surface shipment back to New York. Schotte was tracking all this equipment. He asked Captain Vroegendevey if someone could stop this shipment and divert it to Holland to enable the Dutch to open their securities exchange. Because it was not government equipment, this was easy; diverting it meant that precious cargo space back to the U.S. could be reallocated and they could eliminate paperwork and handling hassles.

I responded, "Sure, we'll fly it over there! How big a shipment are we talking about?"

"Schotte tells me that there are some packages, each about the size of a steel desk, and that the whole shipment weighs about 7,000 pounds. He has identified and labeled each package at Eighth Air Force HQ."

The Michigan policeman Captain Potter, a loadmaster, a couple

I'm Throwing In

of others and I flew a 3,600-pound load to Amsterdam Schipol Airport. Vroegendevey, through some channels, passed the word that we were on our way. Schotte was waiting for us in Amsterdam. We landed, unloaded, and stayed a couple of days and nights to sightsee and be entertained. We were shown all the safe houses in the underground. It was right out of James Bond! Among other things, they wanted to know what food delicacies they could give us to show their appreciation. I was introduced to their national drink, called "genever," pure gin which they drink neat. We also flew over some of the country at low level, looking at many places that we didn't visit on the ground.

We went back to England to pick up the next load. I thought, this is too good a deal. We don't need to take all of it in one more load. We managed to carve it into four more loads and gave some more officers and enlisted men a crack at this.

On the first visit, we discovered that they lacked the bare necessities, like toilet paper, razor blades and soap, let alone candy or clothing. This was another reason I cut the loads down. We managed to take half a load of consumables and clothing to them each trip after that. I told Schotte there was only one thing he had to do; he was responsible for making certain none of it reached the black market. Sure enough, within a matter of seconds after we landed, Dutch policemen arrived, cordoned off the delivery, and set up a distribution line. They must have had lists of people already drawn up for this sort of thing. We watched them distribute the load in an afternoon. They did it that fast. It was heartwarming to see. The people would almost break into tears over a bar of soap!

The second visit culminated in an invitation to a royal audience with Queen Wilhelmina and Princess Juliana, who later became the queen. At a ceremony, I received a Dutch decoration, rather like our Legion of Merit or a service award of some kind. But the paperwork disappeared and the real award never materialized. Four or five lesser decorations were handed out to the crew. They held a dinner for us at one of their prewar posh restaurants which was being restored to former glory. The proprietor had been properly briefed and he wanted to know if there was anything special we would like. I asked what he had in mind. He named lobster, which we could occasionally find in England, and, further down the list, he mentioned oysters. We never had any oysters over there. That appealed to me! He asked whether we wanted them raw or prepared some special way. I decided on a plate of raw oysters, which I consumed. Talk about sick! I couldn't fly the next day, just rolled in the right seat. It took about six hours to recover.

By the time we delivered the final load, they had succeeded in making their securities exchange operational using what we had already delivered. Schotte had made sure that the key packages were on the first shipment.

♠ ♥ ♦ ♣

While I was at VIII Fighter Command, I also sat on a general court and a special court four hours a day every day for six weeks. We'd try as many as six or seven cases in four hours. When all the good soldiers left and all the major numbers of American faces and uniforms disappeared, the riffraff who were still around started surfacing. They were easily seen and reported. Formerly, they could walk around in a uniform and they were just another GI (acronym for "Government Issue," meaning a soldier, to whom food, clothing, etc., was given with the marking, "G.I."). But they started being picked up. They were the majority of the cases. Some of them had been living with English women for two or three years. Some of them had been living off their wits or had robbed banks or grocery stores. It was a real mess.

♠ ♥ ♦ ♣

I came back from England in March 1946. First, I went to a holding cantonment, where officers and men were processed before being put on a victory ship for home, called a redeployment depot. We weren't there for very long.

We went from that camp, located near Birmingham, by train to the port. Each time the train stopped en route for a station or a break, a couple or three of the men just bailed off and said, "I'm leaving here!" I escorted the rest of the men when they left the train to be sure they boarded the ship. I was the troop commander of that unit, responsible for the unit integrity on the ship.

Boy, was this a blow. I was a lieutenant colonel, commanding the 2240 Quartermaster Truck Company. I had maybe a half-dozen noncommissioned officers (NCOs) who were good and responsible.

After we boarded the ship, we spent three or four days before we finally sailed. It took two weeks to sail from Southampton to the Camp Kilmer, New Jersey, Debarkation port. We were processed some more

I'm Throwing In

there. I was to go to California for discharge, since I had enlisted in California. I was commander of the contingent and I had the dregs. By then, most of the good soldiers had gone home and all those remaining were deserters, soldiers who had gone "Absent Without Leave (AWOL)."

I still retained the morning report of the Quartermaster Truck Company. I turned all that over and thought, boy, I'm through. Not so. I was issued another unit to take on the troop train to California; fifteen-hundred no-goodniks on a train that wasn't big enough to take that many. Finally, they cut it down to around 800. We languished there for four or five days while it was all sorted out. Anyway, I was still the boss of this unit, which was nothing more than a paper unit and a roster to make it to the separation center.

It took two weeks to go across the country on this train. It was unbelievable. We waited in the station or yard in Chicago for three days. Any other traffic had priority over troop trains going to a separation center. There was a mess car on the train for dining, where everyone ate in shifts twice a day. I again lost about ten percent of the troops en route. Whenever we had a pause for any length of time, men would peel off. Eventually, I'm sure they all ended up back at the separation center because they couldn't obtain a discharge unless they did. But they weren't manageable. I had military police there, but what were they going to do? They couldn't shoot them.

CHAPTER 8

OPEN A NEW DECK
VENEZUELA: CIVILIAN

There had been a subdued effort to pass out regular commissions. Officers could fill out an application and wait to be called to take an examination at a central location. I took it in Paris, in February 1946. The process involved a rigorous physical examination; a two-day written examination, one day on general education and the second on technical specialty (air, in my case); an all-morning interrogation by a board of officers, who asked fairly routine questions but with some depth, such as, "Why do you want to be a regular officer? Why do you feel that you are qualified?" We left with the reassuring statement, "Don't call us, we'll call you." I returned to my job and heard nothing.

I was at a loss as to whether I should try to stay on as a reserve officer. It didn't seem to me that they would issue a regular commission to someone with my kind of record when there were hordes of worthy applicants. Plus, by then, my wife was pregnant and living at her aunt's in Rochester, New York.

So I decided to return to work in the oil business. I contacted the Honolulu Oil Corporation. The aviation-loving superintendent, Herb Stark, was still there. Herb had lost an eye in an airplane accident and couldn't fly unless another pilot went with him. He owned a light plane and liked the idea that I could fly him around when he wanted to go somewhere. He insisted that I stay at his house. Over three days, he squeezed war stories out of me. I was becoming anxious about establishing a date for starting work. About the end of the third day, I said, "I appreciate all your hospitality but I am interested in settling down."

Herb told me, "We had a pretty tough time when you walked off and left us."

"But Herb, I didn't exactly walk off and leave you. I told you that I had applied for this. War was on the horizon!"

"We had a lot of work because of the war and had to find some other engineers to drill all the wells we wouldn't have drilled otherwise. We drilled up our reserves and had to prospect for more. We'd love to have you back, but you'll have to take your place in line." At that time, there was a statute on the books that stated that those people who had gone into the service were entitled to their previous job, with the salary increases that would have accrued had they stayed, no matter what the line of work. I didn't remind him of that because he didn't bring it up and he had said I could return—I just had to "take my place in the line." Their engineering establishment was small, only eight or nine petroleum engineers in that whole southern division under him. They had been unable to keep it filled with Stanford graduates and had taken in a few other mavericks, including a couple from Cal, one of whom I knew who had been a couple of years behind me. There was also one from Texas A&M, as I remember.

I replied, "Herb, I don't like that too well. I was number two of three people in the organization when I left and I don't think I should have to go to the bottom of the totem pole."

"Well, I can't put you in over these others. They've now been here longer than you were before you ran off." He kept referring to my "running off," as if I had abandoned the company to bankruptcy, which annoyed me. I thought about this that evening. The next day, I said, "I'm going to look elsewhere, Herb."

"But you're welcome to come back!"

♠ ♥ ♦ ♣

I went down to Los Angeles and started prospecting around the headquarters of the various oil companies. I went up to San Francisco; back to Houston, Texas; to Oklahoma; and to New York City. I think the Texas Company had a big office in New York City. I went to all the name-brand places, like American Oil (Amoco, now); Standard of California; Standard of Texas; Standard of Indiana; Standard of Ohio; and Socony-Vacuum Oil Company, which was Mobil. At Socony, I found out they were embarking on a pretty big drilling and exploration operation in Venezuela. To make a long story short, I signed a two-year contract with them to drill a wildcat well in Venezuela. If I completed the two years, there was a pretty husky bonus.

Socony sent me around for a month to various places in the U.S. to observe technology that had occurred in the five years that I had been gone from the industry. Then I left for Caracas. My contract called for additional compensation for flying the company supply plane, a Gooney bird, from Caracas to San Tome, which was about 160 miles south, down in the jungle. When I arrived, the operation was reasonably well-started. I don't know what had happened to my predecessor but the well was down about 2,000 feet. There was a junior Venezuelan engineer, a trainee who had graduated from their university, on the scene. I went to work and I was happy because the work was good and interesting, even though conditions were primitive.

Socony was supposed to bring my family down and locate them in Caracas within three months after I was established. By then, the baby, my daughter Eloise, was about three months old. The three-month date came and went and nothing happened. I started to complain, but still nothing happened. The company had a personnel office in Caracas that was managed by some slobbery-drunk so-and-so who couldn't have cared less about my family situation or contract. He had no responsibility for the operations or drilling people; he only looked after the people who were in Caracas. I sent telegrams and finally called the New York Office. Telephoning New York from Venezuela took about a day! Finally, I blew up and said, to hell with it.

I put the well on standby, flew that Gooney bird to Caracas, bought a ticket on Pan Am for New York, and went into the office of C.A. Moon, the Vice President for Overseas Development. He was a nice man.

I said, "Mr. Moon, your well is on standby. I came by to collect my back pay. You owe me about $1,500 and reimbursement for my airline ticket. It's all yours."

"What do you mean?" he spluttered. "What are you doing here? What about the well?"

I told him the problem. He called in the personnel weenie and started berating him. That wimp started making excuses, like, "We didn't know about this!"

Open a New Deck

I responded, "Here are copies of the telegrams I sent to you. You didn't even acknowledge them."

"They must have been misplaced." He had all kinds of excuses.

"I've said all I have to say," and I went down to the controller to collect my money.

"We have no authorization." they said. "You'll have to wait."

I left and went up to Rochester, where my wife and baby were. Moon had the address and telephone number. I started receiving telephone calls right away: "We'll double your salary! We'll arrange for your wife to go to Venezuela immediately!" All kinds of promises.

I said, "I believe you are sincere, Mr. Moon, but I don't trust the other people. They put me in a terrible situation and I have lost confidence. I don't want to work for that kind of an outfit."

He replied, "You can't just leave! This company will never give you a recommendation if you look for a job elsewhere."

I countered with, "Did you think that hadn't occurred to me? And if you think I won't be spouting and parading to everyone I know in the industry what kind of treatment I received from Socony, then you have another thought coming, too!" This conversation did not go well.

After another week, in another conversation, I said, "I haven't received a dime that you owe me. I don't think it would be in Socony's best interests to have me put an ad in the Petroleum Journal or Oil World to the effect that I'm having to sue you to secure some back pay, because that's the kind of operation you run." I received the money by return mail. It wasn't much, but in those days it amounted to something.

I returned to Los Angeles, thinking I should stay in the California area. In the back of my mind was the hip-pocket solution to go back to Honolulu Oil Corporation, if I had to. I almost signed a contract to go to Saudi Arabia with ARAMCO. I guess I verbally committed myself. But lo and behold, after eight long months, I received a telegram offering a regular commission as a First Lieutenant, Corps of Engineers, in the regular army. It had chased me all over the world. I had to pay about $20 of forwarding charges before I could read the telegram!

What to do? I went to March Field and nosed around the personnel office. Nobody could give me any information, nor did they feel motivated to find out anything. Finally, I called the Adjutant General's Office, Washington. It seemed to me it took a whole day. I finally found someone who had some knowledge. My question was, how can someone who separated as a reserve lieutenant colonel in the Army Air Force be offered a regular commission as a First Lieutenant in the Corps of Engineers? It didn't correlate.

I finally decided I had to go to the Pentagon to straighten it out. After I trudged around Fort Fumble for a couple of days, I found the right place and the right person. He explained to me that the various arms, such as infantry, armored, engineers, and air, had been issued regular commission increments. The 10,000 air slots had been soaked up very rapidly. By the time they had reached my name, the air quota had been filled. The Corps of Engineers, however, had a huge list of vacancies because few people had wanted to be regular army engineers. So, after looking at my records and seeing that I had an engineering degree, they had offered me a slot. The major told me not to worry; another increment of 10,000 was coming for the next year for regular Army Air Force; I would be commissioned in the Corps of Engineers with detached service to the Army Air Force. I would continue as a lieutenant colonel, fly airplanes, and do everything for one year, as an engineer, and then be transferred to the Army Air Force the following year. This was all verbal and I had a little trouble swallowing it. I said, "I'll have to think about it."

He assured me that it was open and above board and that this would work. That major became a brigadier general in the Air Force. He was younger than me, but a very successful and personable fellow.

I finally said, "OK," and accepted the commission right there. I was instructed to return to Rochester, where I would receive orders in the mail to report to my duty station. I went to New York and waited. Two weeks passed and no letter arrived. I was becoming nervous and was sure things had been loused up somewhere. But orders did arrive, finally, assigning me to HQ, Tenth Air Force, at Brooks AFB, Texas. Everything he had said was absolutely true. But there were a couple of hiccups en route.

♠ ♥ ♦ ♣

The first year I was back in the Air Force, I found myself going backwards pretty fast.

First, I had separated as a lieutenant colonel. If I had stayed in the Army Air Force another seven days before separating, enough to finish five years' service, I would have had an automatic promotion to colonel. I didn't know it and nobody had told me. When I came back on active duty, the personnel officer saw my history in the record and asked why I hadn't stayed on long enough to qualify for the terminal leave promotion (as they called it).

Second, in addition to orders commissioning an officer, another very important piece of paper, called "personnel orders," was required to enable a pilot to be put on flying status and be assigned to a flying unit. These had to be presented to the finance office to draw flying pay. I learned. I had my old personnel orders, but they were no longer valid because I was no longer in the Air Corps Reserve. I flew for five months. Every month, I would go in and argue with a sergeant in the finance office because I had not received any flying pay. Finally, I talked to a finance officer who checked around and discovered that I wasn't on flying status. He was incredulous and asked me, "How the hell have you been flying?"

"Everyone else accepted the orders that I had," I replied. I was issued a new set of personnel orders immediately, but I had lost five months of flying pay.

A third terrible thing happened to me practically at the same time. A reserve officer was paid $500 per year as a bonus (the Air Corps Reserve Bonus), which he collected when he went off active duty. The year started when he went on active duty. When he went off active duty, he was paid according to the number of years or increments of service. The rationale was that the $500 was to help him to readjust to civilian life, to buy clothes and other necessities. When I went off active duty, I had almost five years—within a few days of five years—so I was paid $2,493 in a lump sum total, which I went out and spent for a used car.

When I received a regular commission, I was sent a nice polite letter inviting me to return that money. I was in a group of thirty-three who were sent such letters, which was actually the second group. The first group sailed right through and collected it all. We in the second group eventually sued to keep the bonus, but we lost. The Comptroller General, I believe it was, raised the challenge and picked us off as the guinea pigs to pay the bonus back. In fact, we were the only ones who ever had to pay it back.

So I coughed up that $2,493. It was supposed to be paid back in a lump sum, but the finance department finally agreed to take it out of my pay. It took two years, I think, to pay it back.

♠ ♥ ♦ ♣

Open a New Deck

I reported into Brooks in October 1946 as the Deputy A3, the Deputy Director of Operations for Tenth Air Force. A two-star general by the name of Slim Turner was the commander— a great big man, handsome, impressive-looking—not a fighter pilot. The vice commander was Brigadier General Johnson, a crusty old type. The Chief of Staff was Colonel Ed Backus, who was an airline pilot with a reserve commission who had been recalled during the war. He was a pretty good person and I worked pretty well with him, although he thwarted me from going to jet school, which had just opened in Williams AFB, Arizona.

I was there in HQ from August to October 1946, then was assigned as Commander of the 182nd Base Unit Reserve Training (BURT) in Ft. Worth. BURT units were activated on a crash basis by the dreamers in the Army Air Force to retain the Air Force skills and expertise in reserve units all over the U.S. You could swear in anyone off the street and man one yourself—any old way to get that unit going. They issued you a variety of airplanes. I think I had three P-51s, three or four AT-6s, a couple of Gooney birds—four and five varieties, in all, because you had different kinds of pilots, of course. We also had several C-45s.

My job was to scour an assigned geographical territory and uncover reserve officers, have them come in, give them a physical, enter them on the books, process them, check them out in whatever equipment they had been proficient in previously in the Army Air Corps, and arrange for their periodic training. My territory was north and northwest Texas, southern Oklahoma, and a portion of New Mexico.

This was a seven-day-a-week job, particularly requiring work on Saturdays and Sundays because the people were working somewhere on weekdays, as a rule. I recruited a great bunch of them. We had a list to start with, but it was terribly inaccurate and incomplete. I obtained much help from the Chambers of Commerce, the banks, and everybody who knew people in the community. Towns in west Texas, southern Oklahoma and New Mexico are far apart. Amarillo and Wichita Falls were pretty good places to find people, and Ft. Worth itself. There was another unit in Dallas for east Texas; Houston for south Texas; and Oklahoma City for that part of the world.

In the short time I was there, I activated the unit. I signaled old buddies and found an Ops officer who was a classmate, Willie B. Compton, who had been recruited with me at Fort MacArthur in San

Pedro, California. Willie was a captain who had gone into bombers, flying out of Australia. He had been shot down and badly wounded early in the war. He had spent a year or so in a hospital recovering. He had married his nurse, Doris. Doris was a classy-looking gal, but turned out to be a real tramp. She ran off with Willie's best friend when we were at Brooks.

In addition, I located three others. One was Chuck Hauver, a lieutenant in my squadron during the war, and the others were Tinkham and Cable, who had been in the German salt mine caper together in the 361st. They had all separated from the Army Air Force because they had had reserve commissions. At that time, an officer could enlist with the rank of master sergeant because the Air Force was desperate for enlisted men after the war. So these three enlisted as master sergeants and they were my office staff. Of course, they checked out the reserve officers in the airplanes and they behaved just as if they were still first lieutenants. Willie was my adjutant and had every other job except the commander's job. His jobs took a whole page of orders. Tinkham, Cable, and Hauver were recalled to active duty as first lieutenants about 1947.

♠ ♥ ♦ ♣

When I was at HQ at Brooks, in San Antonio, I rented a house. It was tough to find a place to live there immediately after the war. Housing was at a premium. My wife, baby and I lived in a motel. There were two or three motels, not very classy, and they would only let you stay about a week.

Finally, I found a house to rent, paying six months' rent in advance. The facilities were minimal. The contract contained a clause which allowed me to break the contract if I was transferred on official orders. I might lose some money, but the lease was no longer valid. After three months, I was transferred to Ft. Worth. I encountered nothing but foot-dragging when I tried to claim my deposit.

The same problem occurred in Ft. Worth. I rented a place there. I had a terrible snarl with the woman who had separated from her husband. They were fighting over who owned the house. I broke that contract pretty fast. She had to refund the three months' rent and penalties. There was a rental control office in those days, still functioning after the war.

I found another house to rent in Ft. Worth. We were desperate.

Open a New Deck

We'd stayed in a motel where we had trouble trying just to warm milk for that little baby. I ran into another jewel. The house was made out of green lumber that was warping and oozing sap. But it was a place to live, under the same kind of contract with the six-month clause. We lived there four months, from November through March. Then I was transferred—where else?—back to Brooks, as commander of the Brooks unit.

♠ ♥ ♦ ♣

While I was at Ft. Worth, which later became Carswell AFB, the B-36 was being tested. They rolled one out at the Convair plant across the airfield, where it was built, and I saw it fly several times while I was there. There may have been only one or two then.

There weren't very many Strategic Air Command (SAC) bases or SAC units. As I recall, two or three bomb groups were operational or capable of doing something. There is a book titled *The Hollow Threat,* which is a history of SAC through 1950. There really wasn't any SAC. This became evident during the Korean War when it developed that the Air Force couldn't mount much of a bomber effort against North Korea.

The air division at Ft. Worth Army Air Field [later, Carswell AFB] was commanded by Brigadier General Roger Ramey. His Wing Commander was Colonel Shorty Wheeless. I met and liked them, and we were compatible. However, Shorty had a lieutenant colonel for base supply officer who was an absolute jackass. As a tenant on this SAC base, my unit was responsible for maintenance and cutting the grass around the squadron building, the headquarters, and my offices and all that. This was Standard Operating Procedure (SOP). I sent my first sergeant down to check out a lawn mower from base supply so we could comply with a big drive to neaten the base. This supply officer jerk wouldn't allow us to have a lawn mower—just wouldn't issue one to a tenant unit.

I went down there and told him I was entitled to this and I hated to go over his head to do it. His attitude was, "Well, you just try that!" Rather than generate a lot of friction, I went out and bought a used lawn mower with my own money for about $20.

I had all kinds of trouble with this clown. I couldn't order parts for our airplanes, because he just didn't think that was important. His job was to provide for that SAC wing. There were other tenants on the base, too, who were suffering as well.

Fortunately, I haven't run into many people like that.

In September 1947, the Air Force became a separate service. The enabling legislation, as I remember, was passed in May. The planning wizards foresaw and contemplated a separate service that would be responsible for its own POL (petroleum, oil, and lubricants) procurement and distribution, instead of relying on the Army and the Navy. Eighty percent of the logistics in the Air Force has been and is POL—fuel, particularly. Some logistician must have devised the arrangement for the Air Force to be responsible for its own POL because it was so unworkable.

To staff this separate POL procurement and distribution system, the Air Force screened personnel records and dug up seven or eight of us, who were petroleum engineers, for assignment on a semi-volunteer basis. I didn't really quarrel with it because I was so unhappy with this shuffle that was going on, and I was looking right down the throat of another transfer. I was desperate. The fighter units at that time were almost nonexistent. Those that were around were totally booked up. Furthermore, in many cases, pilots had to change their own plugs and do their own maintenance on their aircraft in order to fly them. It was that bad.

So I was picked. It wasn't exactly a voluntary assignment, but it certainly wasn't involuntary. It was, "Would you consider going to graduate school and into this twenty-year program?" The length of the commitment reflected the scale of the contemplated reorganization and establishment of a very heavy, large-scale POL capability in the Air Force.

The program started with graduate school, to secure an advanced degree. Then you worked for a year with an oil company, where you served as an "industrial mobilization consultant/trainee." Following that, you went on a field assignment for three or four years as an "Area Petroleum Officer," a petroleum officer on a major staff, or other such title. Then you went to the Pentagon for a tour, then to the Industrial College, followed by a senior staff assignment. The whole program added up to twenty years.

It was a well-thought-out program, but whoever did the planning didn't appreciate the magnitude of setting it up with no more than nine engineers. More than that started out, but I think a couple of them bugged out when they saw what the commitment was. Some of them were not from the Air Force because the selection occurred before the Army Air Force became the U.S. Air Force. There were two or three Army officers, infantry or something like that, and they didn't want to be part of an Air Force program. They went to school at the same time, but there were only five of us who finished and were Air Force: Lieutenant Dickey, Lieutenant Colonel Hardman, Lieutenant Colonel Chapman, Major Marshall Roberts ("Bob") Graham, and myself.

We were given our choice of college or university that we wanted to attend. I of course elected Cal, where I'd gone as an undergraduate. That was all going to happen and then a big change occurred. Air Materiel Command executed a contract with the University of Pittsburgh, a co-contract with the Army. That's why these Army officers were there. I never saw any paperwork on it. Anyway, we all went to graduate school at the University of Pittsburgh, in Pennsylvania.

I was there from July 1947 through July 1948. I had already accomplished about half of the requirements for a Master of Science in Petroleum Engineering at Cal, so I finished the first academic semester at Pitt and had everything done for the degree except the thesis. I took some more graduate courses, including one in economics.

While at the University of Pittsburgh, I took the Air Command and Staff School course from the Air University by correspondence. In the beginning, completion of the Squadron Officers' Course and the Air Command and Staff Course was not regarded as a high achievement. Nor was it regarded as a stepping stone or square to be filled. Assignments became ways to fill quotas. "Pick ol' Joe: he's about due for replacement or retirement." This changed. We became a lot more professional and a lot more selective.

Also, while I was at the University of Pittsburgh, the Air Force Institute of Technology (AFIT) was activated, under the Air Materiel Command at Wright Patterson AFB, Ohio, and took in our program.

♠ ♥ ♦ ♣

After we finished at the University of Pittsburgh, AFIT gave us a choice of assignments as Industrial Mobilization Consultant to an oil company for a year. This sounds like a fairy tale. I selected the Union Oil Company in California. Everything came to pass.

We set course for Los Angeles. We picked out a place to live in Compton.

Open a New Deck

I reported to the Union Oil HQ in Los Angeles. A.C. Rubel was the President and Chief Executive Officer of the company. I had seen his name in the journals. He didn't know anything about this program, nor did anybody else at the Union HQ. But they thought it was a pretty good idea. It didn't take very long—maybe two or three days—for them to work out the details. As a no-cost contract, they could see only benefits to be derived from it, because I would be really working for them as much as I was for the Air Force.

Everything went along swimmingly for three months, until the Union Oil Company was hit with the first oil-field and oil company refinery strike in the history of the oil business. Their major holdings were in California, with refineries in Dominguez (near Long Beach) and the Bay Area. They were a California company, although they had some pretty good-sized holdings in Texas, too. They had no overseas holdings; they were a domestic company entirely. But they had the full spectrum— drilling, production, refining, distribution and marketing.

I went to report where I was working, at the refinery in Dominguez, the day this strike started. Pickets stood in front of the plant gates. I hung around there trying to find out what was going on. All the employees were being stopped but no one was unfriendly. However, within a week the situation degenerated: the strikers were throwing rocks through and over the fence and police were beating up a few of them.

I didn't want to be involved in that at all, so I wrote a letter to the department at Wright Patterson, Air Materiel Command HQ, that was administering the program, described the predicament I was in, and asked for guidance and instructions. No answer. I waited about a week while the family and I lolled around the beach at Laguna and really lived it up. Nothing happened, no answer. So I wrote another letter. This didn't produce anything. I sent a telegram.

Finally, I made a long distance telephone call—a collect call—and that grabbed their attention. You just didn't make collect calls in the Air Force then. Someone called me back the very next day and said, "We don't think it's a good idea for you to stay there either, so find another oil company."

Shell Union had their headquarters in New York and San Francisco. They had two regional divisions or regional organizations. So I said, "I'll tackle Shell Oil in San Francisco." Fine. And I said, "By the way, does anybody know anything about this?"

"No, but we'll call them and let them know."

Open a New Deck

A day or so went by and I saddled up and went on up to San Francisco. I found a person who remembered some conversation; some Army officer had called him. But he said, "You might as well look for another place because we're combining our HQ with the New York HQ and there won't be much of a structure here." That was a stroke of bad luck.

I called Wright Patterson again, told them what had happened and said, "I don't want to move out of California right now, but I don't know what you want to do."

"Go to New York."

So I went to New York. I left the family in Compton. I was told to report to someone in personnel administration. He had been contacted but he didn't know much about it. He said, "This sounds to me as if it's bigger than just Shell Oil, more like the corporate body with Shell Union." I didn't know then, but learned, that the actual Shell Union corporate headquarters was in Holland. The personnel weenie decided he would draw on the expertise of an Air Force officer in their organization, who was located in the Rockefeller building in New York City, 36th floor.

This officer was a lieutenant colonel reservist named David Price, non-rated, who was the executive to Jimmy Doolittle. Doolittle had gone off active duty and back to Shell soon after the war ended in the Pacific. Price, a few years older than I, is a tremendous person. He retired as a major general reservist. He kept his reserve commission and moved up slowly in the political world of Washington Reserve affairs. He listened to my story and said, "Oh, you were in Eighth Air Force!"

I said, "Yeah, I was in fighters."

He said, "General Doolittle has to talk to you. He just loves to see his old Eighth Air Force fighter commanders. I know he'll want to see you."

I said, "OK." I had met General Doolittle. He had come to our base once and passed out a bunch of decorations, of which I had received one. But he didn't remember me from Adam. So, shortly, I went to his office, we shook hands and he was reminiscing about the Eighth Air Force and fighters. He was an old fighter pilot and a highly successful speed racer and one of the most extraordinary people I've ever met in my life. He died in September 1993.

He was also peppery, intense and one of the most profane people I've ever met. Finally, he said, "Well, enough of this bullshit. I have to put you to work here. Now let's see."

He punched some buttons, yelled a few words in his squawk boxes and, the next thing I knew, I was being flogged down the corridor, sat down and an agenda was already being typed up—bing, bing, bing. His last words were, "And now you're working for me. I give you your orders. I want to hear from you pretty much on a daily basis." He had in mind that I was going to be his troubleshooter, but I didn't know that at the time. It sounded like a pretty interesting deal. And it was very educational.

I went charging off and worked wherever there was a major Shell installation that had a problem, whether it was a fuel development problem; an aviation fuel detonation problem with engines; a subsurface geology problem, as I coped with in Alaska; or a refining problem in Curaçao. I went to Houston and Wood River, Illinois. I was constantly on the go. I arranged whenever I could to pass through California, because my family was still out there.

I'd call in or write in and receive more instructions. I made a two- or three-page weekly report out and mailed that in. He was very satisfied with my work. Periodically, I'd return to New York and touch base for a few days.

Whenever I touched base with Doolittle, he seemed to have a reason to run and jump in an airplane with me and take off. He kept a converted A-26, civilianized, at Teterboro Airport in New Jersey. That airplane was supposed to be ready to go on one minute's notice, literally. Invariably, at four or five o'clock in the afternoon, he'd buzz into my office when I was there in the building and say, "Gordy, come on! We have to go to Houston. Meet you downstairs in five minutes."

We'd leap into his car and his driver would roar through town. When we arrived at Teterboro, he wouldn't kick the tires, look at the Form 1, nothing. Into the airplane we'd go and full throttle all the way. He didn't even bother to get taxi instructions from the control tower. He would be taxiing out saying "This is Doolittle. I'm taking off on Runway 18."

And we'd do whatever function he had to do. Usually it was just a visit to say, "Hey, fellas, I have my thumb on you from up there and I'm just checking to see what you're doing down here," to see the refinery superintendent or the boss. And we'd go back and jump in the airplane. Sometimes it was midnight, one o'clock in the morning, and we'd go back to New York.

I don't know how many times he did that. Seemed to me at least once every time I went back to New York City, and usually to wherever there was a major installation. I never found that there was a problem, that I understood.

I became jet-qualified in a P-80 at the Air Training Command at Williams Air Force Base in 1948 while I was working for Doolittle. Ed Herbes was the commander of the school! I just showed up on the doorstep one day, told Ed I could arrange for some time off, and that I wanted to be checked out in a P-80. He set it up and I was back at work after a week in school.

My first, overwhelming impression from flying a jet was that the controls were extremely sensitive, compared to a prop airplane. I must have looked like a porpoise going down the runway on my first takeoff! I'd been warned about it.

There was a device called "CAPTIVAIR," a precursor of the flight simulator, which consisted of a P-80 cockpit and engine, with an intact fuselage and stubby wings, embedded in concrete pillars. The feel of the controls was authentic because there were hydraulic boost pumps. The instructor pilot would stand on the steps leading up to the cockpit and tell the student what to do and what was happening. It ran and did everything, except taxi or fly, and was used to check out pilots, since the P-80 had only one seat. The only CAPTIVAIR was at Williams AFB, or "Willie Field," as we called it, in Arizona. After a couple of hours of ground instruction, a reading of the Tech Order and a couple of thirty-minute simulated flights, a pilot could fire up and go. It really simplified the checkout procedures!

There were no jets at Andrews or Bolling in Maryland. I flew out of March AFB, California. I knew a lot of people there, including Robin Olds, and they made it easy for me, whenever I came out. There were a reconnaissance and three fighter squadrons there. Ennis "The Menace" Whitehead was commander. Later, he became the first commander of Far East Air Force (FEAF), in Japan.

♠ ♥ ♦ ♣

In those days, when you were on Temporary Duty (TDY) in the Air Force, you could claim $6 per day per diem. At the end of thirty days, that dropped to $4. At the end of sixty days, it dropped to $2. A the end of ninety days, you were supposed to have finished your TDY because you could claim zilch.

I tried to make sure I returned to my point of base reference, which was New York City, once every thirty days. But I missed it a few times. Getting a hotel room and eating three times a day on $4 a day even in those days wasn't very easy. I was slowly going in the hole, out of pocket. Of course, there was no compensation from Shell.

After about a year, I went into Doolittle's office and told him what the situation was. I said, "This is great and I've been enjoying it. It has been challenging and interesting, and I think I've been doing some good for you and the Air Force" and so on. But I was beginning to feel the pangs of hunger.

He said, "Well, hell, that's easy. We'll give you some money."

I said, "Sir, you know I can't take any money from Shell. This is a 'no compensation' arrangement. I don't know what the legalities or illegalities are, but I have a gut feeling that I can't accept any compensation from the oil company because of conflict of interest."

He said, "Hell, it's time you went back to the Air Force then."

I said, "That's kind of what I had in mind."

"What do you want to do?"

I said, "We've talked about this. I want to go back and have a fighter unit. Of course."

He said, "You dumb son of a bitch. What do you think you're doing? Look at all the time and money and effort—you want to throw that away? You are out of your mind. Now you go down to the Pentagon and you stay there until you find something that resembles pretty much what you should be doing in the POL business. And you call me and tell me what it is. I'll tell you whether you should take it or not." That's the way he worked.

I went down there and couldn't find anything. I didn't really search that diligently, either. I was hoping it would go away, though, and maybe I'd wear him down. I went back and told him.

He said, "You should be getting some orders. My personnel people have been in touch with Wright Field." Sure enough, I had a set of orders right away. They were an assignment as Petroleum Officer to the 19th Bomb Wing on Guam.

I went hot-footing it up to Jimmy's office with these orders in my hand and said, "Well, I have orders to the 19th Bomb Wing on Guam, as the Petroleum Officer." I didn't even know what a Petroleum Officer was supposed to do or that they were authorized.

He said, "GUAM? Those pigs! Who's your boss again?"

I said, "The commander of Air Materiel Command is the big boss—General Ben Chidlaw."

"I'll call him. Get me Ben Chidlaw!" he said to his secretary. Pretty soon the call came through. He said, "Ben, this is Jimmy. Now I know you have to take an old bull and hook him up to a plow once in a while to make him understand that everything in life isn't roses and doing what to cows, but," he said, "a Lieutenant Colonel Gordon Graham is working for you. And you're assigning him to Guam. That's the dumbest damn thing I ever have seen. Don't you understand what he's been doing for the last year?"

I couldn't hear Chidlaw's comments. He was probably saying, "Who the hell is Graham?"

Doolittle said, "Fine, Ben, I thought you'd see it my way." To me he said, "Go over there to Wright Pat and check in with him and then go back down to the Pentagon. They're going to contact the Pentagon. And you find that job I told you to find."

I caught a transient airplane, a Gooney bird, that was going to Wright Patterson AFB, Ohio, out of Mitchell. Word had preceded me. A colonel met the airplane. This was unheard of. He was looking and I was the only lieutenant colonel who climbed off. He collared me and said, "Is your name Graham? Get in the car. We're going to General Chidlaw's office." We went.

Chidlaw was fit to be tied. This was my only contact with him. He was sort of ruddy, husky and a little overweight— looked like a case for a heart attack. He ran up and down my backbone with both feet for a while. All I was doing was saying "Yes, sir" and "No, sir" and I had the last word, "Yes, sir." So I was off to the Pentagon.

The first morning in the Pentagon, I ran into Vernon Leffingwell, nicknamed "Monk," in the corridor. I hadn't even found the personnel office. Monk and I had gone to high school and college together. He had gone into the Air Corps at the same time I did, washed out, and become a navigator bombardier.

Monk had been on active duty all this time and been promoted to lieutenant colonel. He was working for Brigadier General Brooke Allen, who at that time was head of the Air Targets Division of the Directorate of Intelligence, HQ USAF. That Division's mission was to pick the targets and weapons for the SAC war plans. Highly classified. And high on the target system's list was POL. Old Monk and I had lunch. I hadn't seen him for a few years and we exchanged lies. I told him what

I was doing and my sad story.

He said, "You don't know how lucky you are!" He had entered petroleum engineering at Cal but he had flunked out and majored in letters and science, economics or something. "My boss is super and you're the expert we've been looking for. As soon as we finish lunch, we'll go talk to him," meaning General Allen.

We went to see Allen, who described the job in the vaguest terms. Brooke Allen was one of the greatest snake oil salesmen you'd ever meet. He could charm the gold teeth out of a mummy. He must have talked for twenty minutes and I never did find out what this job consisted of. I was wary.

So I punted. I said, "General, I have to touch base with the personnel people and find out what they have in mind, but more importantly, whatever I come up with, I have to clear it with General Doolittle. He's my boss and his specific instructions were that I was not to do anything unless he was consulted."

"Oh, I know Jimmy." He'd been one of Doolittle's bomb group commanders. He telephoned Doolittle.

Doolittle and Allen talked, and Allen said, "Fine. Fine, General," and put the phone down. "You're assigned."

CHAPTER 9

LUCK OF THE DRAW
HQ USAF: Air Targets Division (DI)

I reported as a lieutenant colonel to the Petroleum Section of the Strategic Vulnerability Branch. I had no clearances besides the standard secret. It took several months for the appropriate clearances to be granted. I worked without those clearances. They were desperate.

The Petroleum Section was a great bunch of people— most of them had PhDs in economics. In fact, I think all but one of them did, and he had a master's degree. Dr. Pettee was the most senior and the branch chief. They were very good at preparing studies and analyses, but there was no engineer, no pilot, no expert in weapon delivery, and none of them had a background in petroleum. They hadn't set foot in a refinery, even. Everything they had was out of books, maps and intelligence folders.

I moved to the Target Research Branch fairly soon, then became the branch chief. The group became the Air Targets Division and finally the Directorate of Targets. I worked my fanny off in that place. I obviously did a good job because I was promoted to colonel in January 1951, just before my 33rd birthday. I thought my contract would be up the second year and I would be allowed to return to the fighter business. But even though I fought to leave, I spent almost four years there.

It was a joint service activity. We had very few officers— maybe a total of twenty officers out of 200 people when I arrived. By the time I left there four years later, there were about 800 people but the increase was chiefly in the number of civilian analysts.

The Air Targets Division consisted of five branches. The Target Research Branch selected the installations and the most vulnerable aiming points—not only oil, but electric power, transportation, and all the target systems. Second, there was a Physical Vulnerability Branch, which consisted of the weapons assignment people. These were the nuclear experts. The third major branch was the Target Materials Branch. They had the photo-mosaics and provided all the target folders and associated materials. A fourth, little Tactical Branch over in the corner, was concerned with tactical targets and tactical weapons. There were no tactical nukes yet. A fifth, Allied Vulnerability Branch, was concerned with the U.S. and its possessions.

The POL target system was not very precise. There were examples of tremendous overkill on a petroleum refinery with a 20-kiloton weapon having sufficient yield to demolish ten targets. Likewise the reverse: bombs were applied against targets that weren't warranted.

After a year of working very closely with SAC and putting in lots of twelve-hour days, we prepared a decent target list for approval by the Joint Chiefs of Staff. It seemed to me that I was in and out of Omaha every other day! Their people also came to us.

I had a lot of technical help from my old Shell connections, especially from Doolittle's Exec, David Price. He had been transferred to Washington, in the meantime, as a senior Shell lobbyist.

♠ ♥ ♦ ♣

While assigned to the Air Targets Division, I was flying P-51s out of Andrews Air Force Base, because of the longer runways, and B-25s as a shirttail B-25 co-pilot out of Bolling Air Force Base. About every other month, I flew a P-51 to the West Coast. I could make it comfortably with one stop. I would leave on a Friday after work, have a good visit with my friends out there, return on a Sunday night and log my flying hours.

One Sunday, there was a national model aircraft meet at Andrews. There was no mention in the Notice to Airmen (NOTAM) or, if there was, I overlooked it. I returned that night around midnight. I had told my wife when I would return and she was waiting for me. The weather was clear. I came smoking in there, penetrated, let down, landed, and was talking to the tower. The tower reported that there had been a model aircraft meet and that one runway and ramp had been blocked off to fly the model airplanes off. They had not been restored to use. The tower said they would give me taxi instructions and requested that I flash my landing lights. I flashed my lights.

"We have you," the tower reported. "Turn left at the next intersection." A P-51 is a tail-dragger and the nose has to be moved back and forth all the time to see where one is taxiing. I kept taxiing.

"Tower," I called in after a while, "this is [whatever my call sign was]. Do you have me?"

"Roger, turn right now at the next diagonal." This went on for about twenty minutes more, in which time I could taxi all over Andrews! I had been vectored onto a narrow, blacktopped path, totally unfamiliar, and after ten minutes of motoring I saw a boulevard stop sign about forty yards ahead.

I called the tower and said, "Tower, I don't know whether you have me or not. Whoever you think you're watching must not be me. I'm looking at a stop sign at an intersection."

"Oh, my God! Flash your landing lights." I did.

"You're not in sight!" I guess I was facing away from the tower so they couldn't see the lights.

"I'm not going any farther," I declared. "I'm shutting down right here."

"How are we going to find you?"

"That's your problem," I said. I cut the power and climbed out, with my parachute and bug-out bag, and walked up to the intersection. Along came a car with some GIs from the base. They damn near drove into the ditch when they saw the airplane. They'd been drinking. They stopped and one of them hollered at me. I asked, "How about a ride back to Base Ops?"

"Base Ops?" he exclaimed. "That's about three miles from here!" But they took me back.

I filled out the airplane Form 1, gave it to the Base Ops Dispatcher, and said, "That airplane is somewhere out there in the community. I don't know where to tell you to look for it, but you should send someone out and put a guard on it." The sergeant must have thought I was pulling his leg or drunk.

He said he would.

The next day, a telephone call came in from Andrews Ops: they had found the airplane at nine o'clock that morning. They had started

Luck of the Draw

late and didn't know where to look. Someone had found it and called them to tell them where it was. There followed a big investigation into the misuse and abandonment of government property. I obtained a statement from the control tower operator that totally absolved me from anything.

♠ ♥ ♦ ♣

As SAC had grown, the demands for better targeting material had increased. Our organization had expanded by doubling in size about every year. My job didn't become any easier. There were constant upgrades and improvements in the intelligence we received and in the process for selecting targets. The Russians were building more, so more targets had to be added.

By summer of 1951, I had a pretty good handle on the work of the whole division. General Allen had been promoted to a two-star and left. Soon after, he became the Air Force Director of Public Relations, which was his last job. Allen had a good war record. He had been at Pearl Harbor when the Japanese attacked. He flew a B-17 in there while all the shooting was going on.

I went to my boss, Brigadier General Garland, who was relatively new, and appealed for a return to a flying job. I pointed out what I had accomplished. He was very unsympathetic to my appeal to be released. At that time, the nominal tour was three years, not four. The average was probably closer to four in our department. In most of the other departments, particularly in Ops, I remember, a tour was three years. He said flatly, "No. Go back to work." I sulked a while but resumed my work.

Garland didn't stay long. He was followed by Brigadier General Fowler, a very nice, personable individual who liked a good time more than hard work. But Fowler wasn't very sympathetic to letting me go, either. It sounds immodest, but I did a good job and my bosses didn't want to let a good performer leave. I know I wouldn't have, in the same situation.

Luck of the Draw

Under Pearre (pronounced "Pree") Cabell, then the Deputy Chief of Staff, Intelligence (DCSI), there was a Targets Division, Estimates Division, Collection Division, and a sort-of-catchall division. Brigadier General Mickey Moore, an ex-fighter division commander from World War II who went on to become a two-star, headed this last. Cabell was a great man who went to the CIA before I left. He retired as a four-star. Every once in a while, Cabell would call me up to fly with him. He flew B-25s.

Ben Davis was a colonel in the Directorate for Operations (DO). I went to him in late 1951 and said, "Ben, you have to help me. These folks have me in jail and won't let me out!" The Korean War was going full-bore.

Ben went with me to talk to Cabell and plead my case. I didn't say much; I'd already said my piece. Ben made a great effort, not because he owed me anything but because he is a great person, but old Cabell insisted that I was doing a great job and he needed me there.

♠ ♥ ♦ ♣

Fowler finally let me go, after I had been there over three years. I was pretty unhappy, but my orders were for the 92nd Fighter Group, at Itazuki, Japan.

In August 1953, I reported to Far East Air Force (FEAF) Headquarters, at Tokyo, after which I was to proceed to report into Fifth Air Force, at Nagoya, to be the vice-commander of the 92nd, under Ed Backus. Ed had been Chief of Staff of Tenth Air Force, under Turner, when I was at Brooks Field. He remembered me and wanted me, which explains how I was given the job. The group had F-94s—Lockheed overstretched T-33s, to be precise—which were all-weather fighters, equipped with radar and 2.75 mm folding fin rocket tubes all around the nose and in wing tip pods.

At FEAF HQ, I received a real kick in the teeth; there was a big red flag because of all my swell clearances. A non-rated colonel in charge of the estimates division had gone to Korea on a visit shortly before I arrived, had wangled a ride on a recce aircraft, possibly a C-47, on a snooping trip over Manchuria and the plane never returned. Presumably, it was shot down. The fear was that the officer, who had all the clearances I had, had been captured. The word went out that anyone like that was absolutely forbidden to put a foot over enemy territory.

Luck of the Draw

The Director of Intelligence at FEAF, Brigadier General Don Zimmerman, knew of the disappearance of the airplane and somehow heard about my coming and that I would be halted. I had gone TDY to FEAF once, early in 1951, from Washington and knew a lot of the cats there, but Don didn't remember me from all the other pilgrims from the Pentagon. He had a bona fide vacancy for head of Targets Division for FEAF, although the person in the job, Bob Gould, thought he had arranged for an extension of a year. He didn't want to leave and was making every effort to remain.

As it happened, I did replace Gould and he did leave. In his files, I found a note he had signed to Don: "I understand Gordon Graham is coming in here. What are you going to do with him?" That made me feel really useful.

We never had any positive indication that the Chinese had captured the non-rated colonel. The possibility always existed, of course, and if they had, they would never have allowed that information to leak out.

♠ ♥ ♦ ♣

The job I held was really unnecessary. That headquarters was so overmanned it was pathetic. There were four times as many people as they needed; no one was doing anything really productive, and the attempt to manage the conflict in Korea from Japan was very ineffective.

I flew with the Fourth Group, out of Kimpo, Korea, under restrictions which kept me out of air-to-air combat. I also flew T-33s out of Johnson, which was a small strip collocated with Yokota.

When I found myself hopelessly trapped in Japan, I brought my hunting buddy, Bob Graham, over to be my deputy. The duck hunting was fabulous. The ducks would settle into the rice fields to feast and the Japanese didn't like that. There was no limit and a duck hunter needed no license. Bob and I terrorized the natives. We hired a Japanese guide who owned a little skiff with an inboard Citroën engine. When we showed up, he would take us duck hunting on Tokyo Bay. We'd bring back from twenty-five to fifty ducks every time, take them back to the hotel, where the maids would pick and clean them for nothing just to keep the feathers for their futons. You couldn't find a duck on

Luck of the Draw

Tokyo Bay now. In fact, they have filled in a lot of the area where we had built three blinds.

I ran the skeet range there, too. I always managed to wangle that. I discovered a warehouse of skeet shells left over from World War II. So we had all the skeet shooting we wanted.

One Sunday, Bob and I planned to go duck hunting. This was a pretty leisurely deal; we didn't have to be up at four o'clock in the morning and freeze our tails off. First, we went to a Sunday brunch at the University Club around ten o'clock. They served punch, which I discovered contained some alcohol. I have an inviolate rule about mixing guns and alcohol, but I drank some, anyway.

Around eleven o'clock, we returned to our quarters in the Senior Officers' Billet in Tokyo, which was the Sanno Hotel, to collect our gear. The Sanno Hotel is still the Senior Officers' Billet today! It was a famous old hotel with a lot of history because it had been the headquarters of the dissident Japanese who plotted to overthrow the military in 1936. I lived on the second floor.

Behind the hotel was an alley. The Japanese would call it a street, but it was only wide enough for one car. On the far side were telephone poles. There were crows all over Japan. They were, and probably still are, a protected bird. One damned crow used to perch on a telephone pole about twenty feet directly across from my screened window and wake me up just before daylight every single morning. I threw rocks at it; I sneaked out of the hotel on several occasions and tried to pop him with a high-powered air rifle; but he always eluded me.

This particular Sunday, Bob and I had our shotguns on the bed, as well as a .22 pistol that I carried to pick off cripples from the blind, because I didn't want to shoot into the decoys with a shotgun. The .22 and a .38 comprised a beautiful matched pair of K-22 Masterpiece pistols with ivory grips, engraving and silver inlay. It was difficult to tell the guns apart without looking down the barrels.

We were changing our clothes when this obnoxious crow chose the moment to sit down outside the window. He was a BIG crow. I said to Bob, "There's that blankety-blank crow!" I grabbed the .22 pistol without thinking and shot three times. I broke an insulator on the pole, but had the great satisfaction of knowing that I had hit the crow. I knew I'd be in hot water about the insulator, but didn't think much about it.

More seriously and unbeknownst to me, one of the bullets ricocheted off the insulator and knocked a chip, about the size of my fist, out of a tile on the famous old Sanno shrine at the top of the hill, less than fifty yards away. If I had tried to do this, it would have been impossible!

I reloaded the .22 and put it back in the holster on the bed. We had picked up our shotguns and I was on the verge of stuffing the pistol into a bag when two military policemen (MPs) with drawn .45 pistols burst through the door. I thought they were going to shoot us! Our shotguns hit the floor as our hands went skyward. They cuffed our hands behind our backs and summarily hauled us off to the pokey. There, they tested our blood alcohol, thinking we were drunk. The test revealed nothing. They impounded the .22 and also the .38, which happened to be lying on the bed at the same time, and the shotguns. They didn't check the locked gun cabinet, in which I still had three or four rifles and pistols.

In 1952, shortly before this incident, the Treaty of Peace and Mutual Cooperation between the Japanese and the U.S. had been signed, which ended the formal U.S. occupation. Consequently, U.S. forces were under the Status Of Forces Agreement (SOFA) and subject to Japanese law. Those dumb MPs turned us over to the Japanese police that Sunday night and never reported to anyone that they had arrested us. They just wrote it up in their report and took off. The MP commander, Colonel Mabardy, read their report the following day.

Bob and I were put in separate cold, damp, stone-floored Japanese cells at the Kojimachi Police Station. We could talk to each other but had no access to a lawyer or anyone from the American Embassy. After two or three hours, we were taken out and interrogated individually. For the next several hours, we were asked questions by a Japanese official who spoke very limited English. With great difficulty, he asked and obtained answers to the simplest questions and eventually succeeded in completing some typical Japanese forms on our life history. After the interrogation, they gave the results to us to check. Of course, it was all in Nihongo, which we did not understand. They also took our fingerprints. We were given some rice in a bowl that evening and a blanket for the night.

The next morning, a lieutenant from the Judge Advocate's office showed up. He finally obtained permission to see us. He had his notebook in his briefcase and was going to take a statement from us. I asked, "Lieutenant, aren't you here to take us out of this place?"

He said, "No disposition of your case has been made."

We stayed there all that day and another night before the Japanese police released us. They fined us $4.84 for the insulator and 1,000 yen or so (worth about $3.00) for the chip off the shrine. Then Bob and I each received a letter of administrative reprimand from Major General McNaughton, the deputy to Lieutenant General Partridge.

Major General McNaughton was big, gruff, and loud-talking, but a pretty good man. He was noted for his flash temper, but he always apologized later. He had spent a lot of time in training command. He loved to shoot ducks, geese, and pheasant over there.

Senior officers and their families, including McNaughton's, lived in a dependent housing area called Washington Heights. One morning after my incident, a crow landed outside his bedroom window, started making noise, and woke him up. He leaped out of bed, grabbed his shotgun from his closet, shoved it out the window, and shot the crow. Of course, it woke everybody up. The MPs were there in a hurry to investigate who was being shot and try to restore quiet.

Bob and I were notified by mail the next day that our administrative reprimands had been withdrawn and the record expunged. I finally served my sentence and was allowed to leave Japan in December 1954.

Eighteen years later, when I returned to Japan in 1970 as Commander, Fifth Air Force and Commander, U.S. Forces, Japan, I could have asked for anything and no one would have challenged me. I asked my aide to arrange for me to go look at the Kojimachi Police Station. My big Chrysler, with the flags flying, drove up. I dismounted and a respectful official gave me a tour of every corner of the police station, which hadn't changed a bit! The interrogation room was exactly the same. Only one person, Miyagi-san, a maid at the Sanno Hotel, recognized me and remembered the incident. She must not have read the papers or realized that I was coming back as the number one U.S. military commander in Japan. She came up to me and, in typical Japanese fashion, she was bowing incessantly. My wife Vivian was not certain what to think!

Chapter 10

PLAY THESE

Albany, GA: 31st Tactical Fighter Wing

My next assignment, beginning in January 1955, was Deputy Commander of 31st Strategic Fighter Wing, which was under Second Air Force (SAC), at Turner AFB, Albany, Georgia. It was my first assignment to SAC, which was then under the command of General Curtis LeMay. I was at Turner for four full years, the longest assignment of my career.

There were two SAC fighter wings at Turner, the 31st and the 508th, under the 40th Air Division. Brigadier General Thayer Olds was the division commander. Colonel Cy Wilson commanded the 508th and Colonel Dave Schilling, the 31st. When I received my orders, I was to replace Colonel Jerry Johnson as Cy's Deputy Commander.

However, things changed considerably while I was on the way back from FEAF. I hopped rides with my gear, which included a footlocker full of guns and another full of clothes. I caught a ride to Okinawa, then to Guam, and so forth for four days. I had wired my itinerary to Turner. While I was on Guam, I received a telegram: Cy Wilson had been killed.

Cy had tried to belly an F-84F in. He was on his way to Bergstrom AFB, Texas, to go hunting and had taken a very expensive shotgun with him. It was a presentation Browning over-and-under. There was speculation that he stuck with the airplane instead of bailing out because he wanted to avoid losing the gun.

Cy's airplane had what was later determined to be "engine shroud rub," which could occur in an icing condition, such as super-cooled air at altitude. Under these conditions, the ring which surrounded the compressor section would shrink, by three thousandths of an inch, and reduce the clearance between the compressor section and the shroud. This reduction in the clearance was enough to bind the compressor and kill the engine. A pilot could dead-stick a straight-wing F-84G; a flameout landing (i.e., with the engine off) was no big deal. But the F-84F was a swept-wing airplane and flew quite differently, such as significantly higher approach speeds and sink rate.

Shroud rub was a particularly acute problem that surfaced rapidly and for which there was no known fix. Several pilots died unnecessarily; the airplanes should have been grounded until the problem was corrected.

Cy bellied the airplane successfully into a field. After he was on the ground, however, the left wing slashed through a pine tree about eight inches in diameter. The pine tree came into the cockpit, hit him on the head, and broke his neck. This was the only mark on him.

Cy's death changed the picture. Jerry moved up to take the 508th. I was senior to Jerry, so I couldn't be his deputy. Thus, when I arrived at Turner, I had no job.

"Pudge" Wheeler moved up to replace "Monty" Montgomery as the Division Director for Operations (DO) because Monty was leaving for National War College. So I wound up going into the 31st as Dave Schilling's deputy.

I was in a holding basis because Monty was still there. I found things to do. I went out to Luke AFB to check out in the F-84F, then up to Nellis to get refresher gunnery in F-86s.

This didn't last long. Three or four months later, Dave received orders to England. The job was a promotion, even if there was no increase in rank. So I became the commander of the 31st Wing. For two or three months, I had no deputy. The powers that be may have allowed that to be deliberately; Colonel Hubert ("Hub") Zemke was coming down from the Pentagon. Zemke took the wing in January 1956 and I dropped back to become his deputy.

Hub Zemke was a very successful commander of the 56th and the 479th Fighter Groups in World War II, a fighter Ace. On one mission

Play These

with the 479th, he became disoriented and bailed out. He became a POW.

♠ ♥ ♦ ♣

In October 1956, Olds left and Zemke became division commander. Thus, I became commander of the 31st Tactical Fighter Wing again. Jerry Johnson stayed as Commander of the 508th all this time.

Jerry Steeves arrived and became my deputy commander. That situation prevailed until the spring of 1957, when the 508th was inactivated, converted to the 4080th Strategic Reconnaissance Wing and transferred to Laughlin AFB, in Laredo, Texas. Turner became a single wing base and, simultaneously, was transferred from SAC to TAC.

♠ ♥ ♦ ♣

The 508th and the 31st were converting from F-84Gs to Fs. By late winter 1954, we had completed the conversion. We had a stable group of operational and maintenance personnel. The force retrenchment in 1954 and 1955 after Korea had been completed. Converting to an earlier alphabetical designation for the F84-F was an anomaly, but that was how that system worked.

The F-84F had no drag chute. On a wet runway, the F-84F was like a hog on ice. One day, during a thunderstorm, I had three airplanes run into the barrier simultaneously. We complained. The manufacturer installed a metal container under the tail, put in a chute, and installed a handle in the cockpit to activate the chute. When the pilot touched down, he pulled the handle and the chute was supposed to deploy.

There was no waterproofing system. There were many leaks around the drag chute compartment. Naturally, any moisture would freeze at altitude. Thus, when the pilot pulled the handle, only a sack of wet laundry was deployed. This was finally fixed.

The airplane was terribly underpowered. In summer with a full fuel load, we used four jet-assisted takeoff (JATO) bottles to assure takeoff. Mobile control would monitor the airplanes. If there were fewer than four bottles lit, control would call to inform the pilot so he could abort immediately. There wasn't time to jettison the fuel, the bottles and bottle-rack and still become airborne. It was definitely sporty. The runway was 9,200 feet long. It ended with an overrun barrier, an extended overrun and, one-half mile past, there was a swamp. That's where we jettisoned all the iron—1,200 pounds of rack and bottles—promptly after takeoff so we could climb. The bottles would fire until the airplane reached an altitude of 200 feet and just about over the jettison area, if everything worked right. When the JATO quit, it just went "pfft."

We flew as lightly configured as we could to avoid using bottles, but if the airplane carried two full tanks and any weapons to practice, it needed the bottles in the summer.

In spite of the fixes, the F-84F was a lousy airplane. In twenty-eight months at Turner, I lost twenty-two airplanes and four pilots. I personally accounted for three of the airplanes. Of the thirteen F-84F wings around the world, however, I had the lowest accident rate. The Air Force accident rate statistic is "accidents per 100,000 flying hours." Mine was thirty-three. The worst rate was over 200, for the 81st wing in England. Because of the accident rate, the pilots lacked confidence in the airplane.

The F-84F was probably the worst disaster that was ever visited on the Air Force. It was made by Republic Aviation, which we derided as "Repulsive Aviation." They had had a great success in World War II with the "Thunderbolt" but they never had a successful fighter afterwards. They built the F-105 and the A-10, later, neither of which was a good fighter airplane. The management team had not changed.

The first airplane in the F-84 series to go into production was the B model, a straight-wing, lousy airplane. The F-84G was a fairly good model, still a subsonic, straight-wing airplane but had been significantly upgraded with a new engine and was nearly bug-free after two years of operational experience, when I came on the scene. Then we started to convert to Fs.

The F-84F engine was the British Sapphire. It started with 8,700 pounds of thrust. The engine had to be down-rated to 7,200 pounds to be put in the F-84F. This made an astronomical difference. Loss of 1,500 pounds of thrust pushed it into the dog category. The engine was built by more than one manufacturer. One plant from which we received some was in Kansas. Another "foundry," as we called it, was on Long Island.

It took almost five years to correct all the problems with that aircraft. After the airplanes were fixed, we dumped them on the National Guard.

♠ ♥ ♦ ♣

Play These

An interesting SAC fighter competition, Operation LEFT HOOK, was held at Offutt AFB, Omaha, in 1956. LEFT HOOK was structured by Captain John "J.J." Burns, who had been drafted from Bergstrom for a tour at SAC HQ to provide information about fighters. SAC HQ didn't want many fighter types and they didn't want any senior fighter officers running around up there causing trouble.

LEFT HOOK involved all seven SAC fighter wings. Half of each wing participated, with thirty-six pilots and airplanes. A series of missions was flown for trophies in three areas: navigation, bombing accuracy and maintenance. The missions were profile missions for assigned war plan targets. Penalties were incurred for being late over the target, off-course, and other mistakes.

The turning point for the run in to the Initial Point (IP) was Bemidji, Minnesota. There was a mink farm near there. Jeez, did we play hell with that. The Air Force bought that farm. This did not endear fighters to LeMay. They were always causing trouble.

Our wing won the navigation and maintenance trophies and took second in the bombing. I was the team Captain and led the lead element. Chuck Horton, now retired as a colonel, was one of the best bombers we had, so he was the bomber in my element and I did the navigating.

♠ ♥ ♦ ♣

Another exercise which we planned was a non-stop mission to Guam to illustrate our capability for deployment to augment PACAF. The plan called for us to air refuel the entire way— 18.5 hours from Albany. This was impractical; the F-84F had an oil system that vented the oil overboard from the aft main bearing. Once the bearing was lubricated, the oil did not return to the reservoir. Although the airplane used oil sparingly, it was exhausted after eight hours of flying. The plan was never seriously considered for execution.

I decided, however, to see how long we could fly in a local exercise. We christened it OIL BURNER. I put an engine on a test stand with a full seven-gallon reservoir and ran it to borderline exhaustion, since I didn't want to destroy the engine. That's why I know about the eight-hour limit.

The airplane also had a five-gallon tank for anti-icing fluid, which we never used. It was supposed to pump anti-icing fluid in through the intake to deice the compressor blades. I calculated that adding five gallons of oil to the other oil supply would have enabled us to fly the full 18.5 hours plus. We converted this tank for oil in four airplanes. I took the flight off and we flew eight and a half hours. One pilot aborted for oxygen system malfunction but we had no oil-related problems. On a second flight, we flew twelve hours. Then I modified four more airplanes for the big operational eighteen-hour test.

The mission profile was for the eight airplanes to take off from Albany, fly to Miami, New York, Minneapolis, Seattle, Los Angeles, and return to Albany. There were tankers scattered from hell to breakfast. I limited the exercise to eight airplanes because of the availability of tankers. The tankers had to land, refuel and take off again to handle everyone.

We planned to take off before daylight. The F-84F had an autopilot. A SAC directive required fighter pilots to use celestial navigation. To pass an Operational Readiness Inspection (ORI), a pilot had to achieve an accuracy of ten nautical miles in a thousand miles by celestial navigation alone. For this exercise, we used an octant, precomputed the sunshots and the starshots, which meant that we had to take off in a narrow time bracket and make good the times fairly closely. The octant was mounted on three rubber bands or bungee cords so the pilot could pull it with one hand and sight on a star while flying the airplane. It is hard to imagine anything dumber than a fighter pilot trying to do celestial navigation in a single-engine cockpit. But we did it.

I never could use a relief tube in an airplane. I just avoided fluids for twenty-four hours before I flew, so I became terribly thirsty on long sorties. For this flight, we invented a device with a thermos bottle behind the headrest. The tube came down and hooked into the oxygen mask. The pilot could pinch a little valve to get a drink of water. We fixed bite-size pieces of meat and bread and put them in a bag, which hung on the right side of the cockpit on a bracket under the canopy sill. Later, our ideas were adopted by others, upgraded to more sophisticated devices and used in the precursor to the space program. Another invention, to keep us alert during the long flight, was the forerunner of the modern "seat-shaker." This was a device, powered by an electric motor, to expand and contract the seat cushion periodically to increase blood circulation.

We took off at three o'clock, plus or minus a minute or two, one morning. Everything went fine. Then we started to lose airplanes for a variety of reasons. Finally, we dropped to two, myself and my wing man, Cy Strain. He had radio failure. That was an automatic abort, but

Play These

he wouldn't quit. He would write a grease pencil message on a page of the Form 1, the book in which we wrote up flights. A typical message was, "When is the next refueling time?" Then he would fly up next to me and hold the message up to the canopy.

The flight surgeon constructed some "go/no go" sticks, with a pill on each end, and gave four sticks to each pilot. The red "go" pills were amphetamines. When a pilot felt drowsy, he bit off one of these pills. After landing, the pilot could bite off a blue "no go" pill to counter the effects of the red ones. Most of the pilots used them but I didn't take any.

We were forced to land at Barksdale AFB, less than two hours from Turner, after twelve plus hours because the tankers had flat run out. It was a disappointment to have come so far and not finished, but we had used up a lot of the wing's assets trying.

I had a very imaginative and talented officer, Captain Bob Krone, who conjured up a public relations caper that was a real hummer. The 31st would fly non-stop air-refueled from the West Coast to Australia to symbolize carrying the Olympic Torch to open the Olympic Games. Chuck Horton computed the fuel off-load requirements, the tankers, and the rendezvous. Before landing, the pilot would roar over and the exhaust would simulate the Olympic Torch, a "Torch of Freedom." Reade Tilley, the SAC Public Information Officer (PIO), who had been a Spitfire ace with the RAF on Malta in World War II, thought this was a great idea. LeMay threw him out of the office.

In the fall of 1955, I went elk hunting as I did almost every year with my old friend, Bob Graham, who had been in Washington and FEAF with me. A KB-29 dropped me off at Peterson AFB, Colorado Springs, where Bob was Deputy of Intelligence (DI) for Air Defense Command. We drove in his car up to Lander, Wyoming, where his wife's father lived. We kept a Jeep in his father-in-law's garage on blocks. We had bought it from an old uranium prospector. It was a real bargain, but required some work. Every year when we came in, we spent a couple of days making it ready.

We each killed an elk and a deer. We had to rent a truck to get the 800 to 1,000 pounds of packaged meat back from Wyoming to Colorado Springs. We rented a frozen food locker in downtown Colorado Springs for storage. I was going to return to Turner and bring a tanker back to haul it. Things intervened so that I was delayed in returning up there. The elk and deer meat took a back seat until the following June.

I couldn't get a tanker. Walt Bruce and I flew out in F-84Fs. I thought we could fit the meat in the two nose decks if we removed the guns and ammo cans. We did.

I was violating every rule in the book. We were never supposed to take a combat unit airplane into places like Peterson. I did it more than I should have and I was in trouble more than once when I was caught.

It was hot in June. Peterson AFB had an 8,200-ft. runway. They also had a 6,700-ft. runway, which was way too short. I had no JATO and I needed two tanks to return nonstop to Turner.

I made arrangements with the locker to go by at four o'clock in the morning. The coldest part of the day was at six o'clock. If we loaded half fuel in the internal tanks, we could get airborne and, although we would be sweating fuel, we could make it to Turner.

Peterson did not have a compressor that could pump the F-84's starter bottle up to the pressure of 3,000 psi for a good start. Walt's starter worked but mine didn't, so Walt shut down. It took over an hour to pump it up again. I hit the button again. No joy. We tried that three times. The third time, it fired. By this time, it was eleven o'clock and mighty hot. We had a hand-held Batori computer, for calculating takeoff distance and roll. It was mounted in the cockpit. I figured we could make it if we took off downhill, even though it was a little downwind. We taxied out to the overrun and had our tailpipes hanging over the fence. We started our takeoff together. He was right beside me, just the way a good wing man should be, when we reached the end of the runway.

We had prearranged that if we reached the end of the runway and weren't airborne that we would jettison the tanks as we hauled back on the stick. That's what we did.

We executed a low-altitude toss bombing maneuver as we jettisoned those tanks. One of the four fired and burned the corner of a barn and destroyed about 200 feet of fence on an adjacent ranch.

We had 1,200 pounds of fuel. This was enough to make the pattern, come back in and land. My buddy Bob had sweated us out until we took off. He thought we were gone, so he had started to drive away. He saw a big column of black smoke and thought one of us had augered in. He raced back. We had taken that meat out of the airplanes and put it back a couple of times already. We loaded it all back into his car and took it to the locker.

Play These

We had to start all over, except that now we had no tanks. In the meantime, the Base Ops Officer, who was a buddy and had worked for me, took me out to meet the irate rancher. He had some blooded horses and, although none had escaped through the damaged fence, he was afraid he would not have the fence repaired in time. I ran him down, finally, in his pickup, told him who I was and apologized. I asked how much it would cost to fix.

We sat in his truck while he did some calculations on an envelope. $492.00.

I whipped out a check and Quit Claim form and handed it to him. He was all smiles. Sure enough, he never sent in a claim.

That wasn't the end of the story. The dum-dums at the base had seen the fire and the fire engines had to put in their report. I answered correspondence for a month or two and was given some hell for it, but since no one was hurt and there was no damage claim, I skinned out of that one.

The next day, I said, "Walt, you stay here. I'll take your airplane. I know it will fire. I can take one load to Oklahoma City [Tinker AFB] on internal fuel." I called Dick Hunziger, who had the 506th, and told him my plan. He said he'd have everything ready for me.

I told Walt to stay there and do nothing. I would bring a tanker, some tanks and JATO bottles for the other airplane. Then he could come on straight back.

En route to Tinker, I had to fly around a big thunderstorm and lost seven minutes. At 32,000 feet, flying on fumes, I called to tell them I had the field in sight and cancel my IFR. Walt came on the radio. He was about twenty minutes behind me. He had elected to try for a start and come on anyway. He had not had to detour and had plenty of fuel. We both landed. Instead of one set of tanks, Dick's people had to sling two sets, but they did it and fast. We took off and made it back to Albany. By then, that elk and deer meat was mighty expensive!

♠ ♥ ♦ ♣

We rotated a squadron from the 31st to the deployment base at Sturgate, England, for six months' duty at a time. We had three squadrons with twenty-five aircraft each.

We had a secondary deployment base at Eielson AFB, near Fairbanks, Alaska, with a tanker squadron at Elmendorf, to reach targets in Siberia. These targets were exclusively Russian airfields. If we deployed out of Eielson, we needed a prestrike refueling from KB-29s to reach those targets and a poststrike refueling to return to base.

In November 1956, during the Suez crisis, one of our squadrons, with twenty-five F-84F airplanes, was sent to Eielson.

We landed at Malmstrom AFB, Montana, to refuel and spent the night. We took off the next day, rendezvoused with the tanker, refueled, and were climbing to cruise altitude at about 20,000 feet when I lost one aircraft, Schafer. He flamed out, for reasons unknown, and bailed out forty miles from Ft. Nelson, British Columbia. The snow was about six feet deep and the temperature was near zero.

In those days, radio communications between the U.S. border and Alaska were limited to some low-frequency beacons and airfields at Calgary, White Horse, Big Delta, and Eielson. I managed to communicate with the tanker before he was out of range and the tanker started the rescue net, such as it was. A chopper bush pilot at Ft. Nelson happened to hear of the bailout, voluntarily went down the next day and picked up the pilot. Schafer joined us two days later at Eielson.

When we left Albany, Georgia, on November 11, 1956, the temperature was eight-four degrees. When we landed at Eielson, it was minus forty-four degrees. The weather was 2,000 ft. ceiling, visibility a half-mile, broken clouds and light snow. And it was deteriorating. Eielson has a 15,000 ft. runway, the longest in the world. Every inch is needed in winter.

I had requested an emergency tanker be stationed over Big Delta, less than one-hundred miles from Fairbanks. One lieutenant found that tanker. The rest of us started making penetrations. I had the lead flight. Usually, we landed in pairs, the flight leader and his wing man. We were so low on fuel that we tightened up formations and went in four at a time. We slid the full 15,000 ft. I flamed out taxiing in, just past the first taxi strip crossing. Everyone made it safely, however.

We immediately went on alert, with sixteen airplanes. All the airplanes, including those on alert, were kept in a hangar. A twenty-foot high thermometer was suspended at the end of the hangar. The hangar was heated to about freezing, seventy degrees warmer than the weather outside. This was adequate to do our work. The doors were rarely opened because, if the temperature descended below sixteen degrees, the mechanism that opened the doors would freeze.

We developed a system for ensuring the alert airplanes could be ready. If we had to go, everything had to work.

For practice sessions, pilots would sit in the cockpits of the alert airplanes. Eight airplanes were each tied to a tug. Then we would open the doors. The eight tugs would jerk those airplanes out as fast as they could. The pilots would promptly hit their start buttons and move to prevent the hydraulic system, the battery and the tires from freezing. The eight tugs returned for the other eight airplanes and repeated the process.

We rehearsed this exiting procedure until we had it down cold (literally). We never had a problem with the hangar doors.

After a pilot landed, he went into the hangar. From there, it took two hours to turn an airplane around.

Over time, the Suez situation became more tense. At about three o'clock one morning, the command post was given the word to go. The alert force was notified. I was in the lead airplane. I remember asking myself for the jillionth time, what in the hell am I doing here?

It was snowing as we all taxied out. There was never any wind there. A three-knot wind was a gale at Eielson.

We had twenty-two minutes of "slop time," meaning that we could lose up to twenty-two minutes from the time we fired up until the time we took off, but still meet the KB-29 tankers from Elmendorf AFB for the prestrike refueling; reach the target; and make it to a poststrike refueling. Everything had to work; the airplanes had to be refueled at precisely the right place in space with the preplanned quantity of fuel.

The engine heat melted snow as it landed on the fuselage, but not on the wings. Two people worked valiantly on each airplane with mops and glycol to prevent ice from forming on the wings.

I watched the clock as the minutes passed. Eighteen. Twenty. Twenty-two. I was constantly asking the command post whether there was a recall. At twenty-six minutes, they called me. I was thinking, oh my gosh. Here we go. Maybe we can pick up four minutes. But it was a recall. So we taxied in. We had the damnedest blast in the club that night that you ever heard of. The redecoration cost us a bundle.

♠ ♥ ♦ ♣

After the alert passed, we were stuck with training there until our normal rotation of six months. Two squadrons rotated up there for three months each. Training in that environment was a real thrill.

We used eight airplanes on a training day to fly the whole squadron. Four airplanes at a time would take off with two tanks and a rack of practice bombs. A tanker from Elmendorf AFB at Anchorage, which

Play These

was 200 miles away, would orbit Eielson at 12,000 ft. The squadron pilots would fly up to the bomb range, practice dropping bombs, return at bingo fuel, which was about 1,800 pounds, and hit the tanker. After refueling, they would land immediately, stop, but not shut down the engine. Although it was a heavy landing, it was not dangerous because the runway was so long.

We had built a shack at each end of that long runway for an armorer, a communicator and a crew chief. The replacement pilots would be waiting there. The crew would quickly check out the returned airplane, rearm it, and the replacement pilots would turn it around and, because there was never any wind, take off in the opposite direction. Thus, the airplanes never had to shut down and we saved two hours per turnaround. We did this twelve hours a day, using eight airplanes. We trained more than we would have in the U.S.

We built a bombing range because there wasn't one. Base support had two T-33s. I filled a T-bird tip-tank with sea-marker dye, an iridescent yellow-orange powder that came in life vests. I tried this on the ground first, to experiment, but then took the T-bird to a perfectly circular, glacial lake about forty miles away. About ten feet off the ground, I made a tight, perfect turn, dispensing that powder. We held a contest to guess what the diameter of the bomb circle really was. I estimated it was about 1,800 feet in diameter, so the pilot who guessed the closest to 1,800 won a case of beer, whether that was accurate or not. If it snowed hard, we had to remark it.

We had one terrible accident up there. A KB-29 from my tanker squadron took off from Elmendorf on Christmas Day 1956 on a routine training flight. Of course, it was dark all but about two hours a day and it was dim then. The pilot flew right into a 12,000 foot mountain, less than forty feet from the top. The cause was clear from the long plowed track in the snow after the plane first hit; the navigator was using true heading and the pilot was using magnetic heading. The compass declination there is twenty-eight degrees, so he just flew twenty-eight degrees off course. Twelve died.

♠ ♥ ♦ ♣

As a result of ejecting from an aircraft because of fuel starvation, Hub Zemke directed that Jerry Steeves and I personally ensure that returning pilots sat on the ramp and burned down to 930 pounds of fuel, where the "Low Fuel" red light was set to illuminate, and verify

Play These

that the light came on in every airplane.

Soon after, at Ramey AFB, Puerto Rico, with the 309th, I landed from a gunnery mission. I checked the Form 1. There was no indication that that particular airplane's fuel had been run down per Hub's directive. I had 1,100 pounds of fuel. I pulled off the taxiway, sat on the end of the ramp, unbuckled my chute, g-suit and dinghy, and ran it up to ninety-eight percent. I still had my mike hooked up. All of a sudden, that plane just blew up like a bomb! The fourth stage compressor had disintegrated and pieces had penetrated the fuselage fuel cell. The Air Force had lost two airplanes in other wings from such explosions, but hadn't pinned down the reason.

As soon as a pilot landed, he put pins in the ejection seat so he didn't inadvertently blow himself out. This had happened on earlier airplanes. I had already put in the pins, of course, but I came out of that cockpit like a Roman candle! I was pretty badly burned on the back and side. The damn mike was still connected and wouldn't let go, so it pulled me into a somersault. I did a tumble spin, hitting the wing root and ground. But I got to my feet and ran as hard as I could.

A B-47 was refueling about 200 yards from me. Under SAC rules, there had to be a fire truck at hand every time a bomber was refueled. This didn't apply to fighters. The fire truck slammed into gear and they were on that airplane before I could move away, but the fire was so intense that it melted down to a puddle of aluminum and magnesium. There was nothing left.

The base commander, Bert Harrison, later became the Inspector General (IG) and retired as a three star. He was a BG when I blew that one up on his ramp. He was a nice man and came around to see me after the accident.

He said, "Gordy, please don't blow any more up on me. My bone yard's full of F-84Fs!"

Of course, I had to report that one. Typically, the interviews with General LeMay only lasted fifteen to twenty minutes. There were pre-meetings with the DO, the IG and Chief of Safety which usually lasted two to three hours. They went over every single thing in a "cover your ass" kind of thoroughness. They were concerned about being caught short on something they should have been doing or known about.

Another airplane I accounted for occurred when I was on an ORI. I was south of Orlando and had just pulled up behind the tanker after hitting the target. We refueled between 12,000 and 15,000 feet, which was the maximum altitude for the tankers. The pilot had to slow the airplane and hit a switch, which opened a refueling door in the left wing of the F-84F. The tanker then stuck the boom in the door. The switch ran off the main hydraulic system. I had just started to take fuel when I saw the utility hydraulic gauge start to bobble, then slump and go down. I called the boomer and told him that I was going to disconnect because I had a hydraulic malfunction. I backed off. In ten seconds or less, I had lost all hydraulic pressure. Fortunately, I could see McCoy AFB, a big SAC bomber base, and headed for it.

The F-84F had an emergency hydraulic system which ran off a battery with a fifteen-minute life. This was enough juice to power the system, providing there was fluid in the system. If everything else failed, an "electric-electric" switch enabled the pilot to fly the airplane on the emergency battery using the trim tab. The ailerons and rudder were manual, but the slab was electric. The "electric-electric" capability was not meant to be used for landing, only to take the airplane to a bailout area over friendly territory.

There was a specific directive that we were not to try to land that airplane "electric-electric" because some pilots had died trying. After the air speed bled off, it was virtually impossible to control the descent rate on the approach for a successful landing.

The system came back on and the pressure rose. I told myself I could make it. I should not have tried, but that is hindsight. I was down to about 500 feet or less when I lost all hydraulics again. Then the "electric-electric" cut in and I was committed. I splashed it hard and "class 26ed" the airplane; I drove the struts clear into the wing. But I had no choice: I was too low to bail out. Back then, we had no zero/zero bailout capability. The minimum bailout altitude was 1,000 feet.

Twelve days before we converted from SAC F-84s to TAC F-100s, the last accident in my wing occurred when Lieutenant Del Corum, who retired as a colonel and whom I saw at the 31st Reunion in San Antonio in April 1992, punched out of an F-84 over the bombing range south of Savannah, Georgia. I flew an F-84 up to Omaha to report it, since we were still under SAC. I was on downwind, had already pitched out, on a beautiful, clear day. I dropped the gear and flaps and turned on final—and flamed out.

This was just one more evidence of the design deficiencies in that airplane. After I had put the gear down, I retarded the throttle and the throttle linkage broke. In any other airplane, if the throttle quadrant linkage failed, it automatically went to eighty-seven percent, which

Play These

was about standard cruise. But not in the F-84; it went to zero.

I was executing an approach to Offutt that comes over a very high bank. The runway is 10,000 feet and slopes down. I don't know how many times I have flown in there. I knew I had to come in over that bank. I barely made it, touched down in the overrun just short of the runway. I don't think you could have slipped a cigarette paper between the wheels and that bank! I coasted ignominiously to the end of the runway and climbed out. A vehicle showed up. Of course, I'd called and told them. Talk about stacking one up right on the Old Man's doorstep! I never climbed in another F-84. I had a T-33 come up to take me home.

♠ ♥ ♦ ♣

A SAC Commanders' Conference was scheduled at Carswell AFB, Ft. Worth, Texas, for three days in January 1957. The division commander was Brigadier General Jack Ryan, who was commanding one of the first SAC B-47 wings there. Ryan later became CINCSAC, CINCPACAF and Chief of Staff.

I had met Ryan in 1951 when we were both colonels and he was a bomber wing commander at Roswell, New Mexico. We had become acquainted through Peter Hurd, a very well-known painter, who owned a ranch near Albuquerque. Peter had gone to West Point with Ryan, but Peter had dropped out. One of my good friends, Major Will Ray, knew Peter from World War II, when Peter was executing paintings for the AAF in England at Will's bomber base. Will was a bombardier-navigator. Will and I flew to Albuquerque and spent a delightful weekend at Peter's ranch as his guests. Ryan was the senior Air Force officer at the barbecue and party while we were there. I remember that Ryan came from Cherokee, Iowa, and had lost a couple of fingers in World War II. I believe he told me that he caught them between the flap handle and the gear handle, or some damn thing.

Hub had put out a directive that no F-84F flights would be made by the colonels on official business. Jerry and I ignored this and both of us took F-84Fs to Carswell, arriving the day before the conference began.

The morning before I left, however, I had gone hunting with a Major "Mac" McClure. Mac was very big and strong. I shot a deer about seven-thirty in the morning and Mac came to the shot to help dress the deer out. He shoved back two big limbs on a pine tree. I was going to hoist the hind legs of the deer up one at a time and tie each one to a limb so the deer would be spread for dressing. I bent down to tie a line on one deer leg and then raised up to tell Mac I was lifting the deer leg.

Mac misunderstood and let the limb go. The limb hit me across the forehead and left eye and knocked me off my feet. I was dazed for a couple of minutes and couldn't see anything out of my left eye. We dressed and skinned the deer and took it to a local butcher and freezer locker. I went home and dressed and went to the base to go to Carswell.

I still couldn't see out of my left eye so en route to Base Ops I went by the hospital. The medical officer on duty was a baby doctor. I didn't tell him I couldn't see. He put a patch on my eye and told me to come back if I had any trouble.

Weather en route to Carswell was "Ceiling & Visibility Unlimited (CAVU)," but Carswell was reporting one mile visibility in blowing dust and strong surface winds. I filed an Instrument Flight Rules (IFR) flight plan and took off. I was going to be a little tight on fuel because of very strong head winds, but I was not really concerned about it.

As I neared Dallas, I could see the base at Ft. Worth. I had been stationed there in 1947 and knew the runway layout and approach. I canceled my IFR and rolled into a hi-speed letdown to save fuel, rolled out at 1,700 feet on a heading to line up with the landing runway and told the tower I was on a long final. I saw a runway coming up, dropped the gear and flaps, and landed.

I immediately realized I had landed at Meacham Field, the commercial airport northeast of Carswell. A strong crosswind, the reduced visibility, only one eye and my complacency and stupidity made for a bad situation; instead of a 12,000 ft. runway, I had only 6,500 ft. I jumped on the binders [pilot talk for, "I applied full brakes"]. I knew the runway had a short overrun and then a twenty-five-foot embankment to railroad tracks. I didn't want to go off and into a real crash.

When I reached the overrun, I was still going too fast, so I hit full left brake, ground looped and slid sideways a good bit, hit full throttle, and pulled back 180 degrees to landing heading. I taxied slowly up to the taxiway, raised the canopy and slowly taxied in. The tires were shredded but not blown.

I was still on the Carswell tower frequency. I called and told them that I had mistakenly landed at Meacham. I requested a local area clearance to Carswell and was cleared. As I taxied by the Meacham

Play These

tower en route to take off position, someone in the tower stepped out onto the railing and gave me the hands overhead shaking congratulations. I taxied and took off very carefully, didn't retract the gear, and went on into Carswell.

Ryan was meeting each wing commander for the conference as he landed and welcoming him to the base. He had monitored the radio and knew what had happened. When I climbed out, he made some very uncharitable remarks about fighter pilots flying around with an eye covered and unable to find the base.

There were no replacement tires available at Carswell. By the time the conference ended on the third day, I had had some tires flown in from Bergstrom.

I had removed the eye patch, but couldn't see and was in some pain. Zemke did not know anything had happened. He had flown in in a C-45.

General LeMay was scheduled to go from Carswell direct to Turner to hunt birds for five days. Zemke was having a cocktail party for LeMay at his quarters that evening, which Jerry Johnson and I were to attend. So Jerry and I had an incentive to return as soon as possible.

We arrived at the flight line together and Jerry had a hydraulic leak. Transient alert people were still mounting my tires, so I helped Jerry fix the leak in his airplane and he took off.

I left soon after with plenty of time to arrive at Turner, change and report to the party. Then the next blow fell.

One of my external tanks wouldn't feed. I had to land at Barksdale to refuel. It was still daylight and I landed OK. But it was dark by the time I had turned the aircraft around. It was about eight o'clock when I reached Turner. I made eight or nine passes and go-arounds. Weather was fine; I just had no depth perception. Finally, I bit the bullet, made a hard landing, and taxied in. The cocktail party was over and Zemke was in a screaming fit of anger. I had ignored his edict, taken an F-84F and, worst of all, failed to return in time for the party for LeMay. He had every right to be angry. I wasn't proud of that caper.

In the fall of 1956, we were informed that the 31st was going to transfer out of SAC to TAC. We were to activate a fourth squadron, the 306th. The Table of Equipment (T/E) for each squadron was reduced from twenty-five to eighteen, a wing total reduction of three aircraft.

Play These

The wing would become the 31st Tactical Fighter Wing.

The base turnover negotiations began in January 1957. Bruce Holloway was the Vice Commander of Ninth Air Force, to which command the 31st was to be transferred. Zemke had pneumonia, so I was the chief negotiator.

This is a very involved procedure. Each command representative is trying to earn a Legion of Merit for screwing the other one. The SAC representatives were trying to take everything off the base to Laredo and I was trying to hold it down there at Turner.

♠ ♥ ♦ ♣

The conversion from SAC to TAC occurred in the spring of 1957.

We were given the F-100D, a brand new atomic delivery platform. It had a Swedish toss-bombing computer which was a Rube Goldberg contraption. It seemed ironic that the pacifist Swedes would build this.

It had a good air-to-air capability but the system was not all-weather. There were four 20 mm guns with 200 rounds apiece. There was a good gunsight system with radar ranging, but it had no ground-map mode or navigation radar. It had no computer, Doppler, inertial, or otherwise. It was like an overgrown F-86, except that it had a great engine, the J-57 with afterburner. This engine had plenty of thrust and never a problem with the thrust-to-weight ratio. The airplane was fairly maneuverable, although not so good as the F-86. The F-100 was the first airplane in production that would go supersonic in level flight.

Conversion went rapidly. We dumped the F-84Fs as fast as we could. Check-out was minimal. I took a dozen senior pilots to George AFB, California, where they had "Cs." George Laven was the division commander there. Then we came home and checked out the rest of the pilots.

The first F-100Ds were single-seaters. I named one of the F-100Ds we received "Miss Albany." We found the prettiest gal downtown to have her picture taken with it.

♠ ♥ ♦ ♣

The first nonstop air-refueled squadron deployment was FOX ABLE-73. I led the 307th in F-100s to Hahn, Germany, via Nouasseur, Morocco, and Chaumont, France. We couldn't go into Europe without first going through Africa because of political aspects. Chaumont was the home of our parent 48th Fighter Bomber Wing that the squadron at Hahn would be assigned to for operational purposes in USAFE. Colonel Stanton T. Smith was the commander of the 48th.

Hahn has the worst weather of all air bases operated by the U.S. Air Force. It sits at a bend of the Moselle River and has constant rain and fog. The Germans probably flew out of there during World War II. We were there for six months. In November and December of 1957, we didn't take off for twenty-two straight days. We'd crank up, taxi but not take off. We had no suitable alternate. Bitburg and Spangdahlem were our two alternates and they were below minimums most of that time, although not sustained for so long.

After six months, I brought the 308th Squadron over and brought the 307th home the next day. It was about a six-hour flight each way. Back then, I was young enough to do that sort of thing.

♠ ♥ ♦ ♣

One other interesting feature of this period was my relationship with Charlie Blair. Charlie was a captain for Pan Am and a captain in the Naval Reserve. He was a real aviator and a navigation expert. He'd grown up flying amphibs and flying boats in Pan Am. Before the war, he laid out some of the routes that Transport Command used and trained Army pilots. Pan Am ran one of the first navigation schools for Army pilots in the early 1940s.

Charlie was a real educator. I learned an enormous amount from him. He is responsible for my personal as well as professional interest in improving the navigational capabilities of fighters.

While I was in the Pentagon in May 1951, he flew a P-51 over the North Pole from Oslo, Norway, to the U.S. and achieved a lot of notoriety. His book, *Red Ball in the Sky,* describes this. He was an extraordinary man. Soon after I met him, Charlie transferred from the Naval Reserve to the Air Force Reserve as a colonel. He could pursue his hobby with the Air Force's blessing. He worked with Dave Schilling at Fighter Ops, there also in the Pentagon at the time, which is how I met Charlie. He affiliated with Schilling when Schilling commanded the 31st at Turner.

Charlie embraced the Air Force as being a lot more responsive, aggressive, forward-thinking, and taking greater initiative than the Navy. He became very valuable as a consultant and as an Air Force Reserve Officer because he could be yanked in on four days' active duty to perform a test flight. Unbelievable as it sounds, the Air Force bailed an F-84G to him, his own personal airplane! When the 31st converted to F-84Fs, Charlie's G was replaced with an F. He kept it in Connecticut because he flew for Pan Am out of New York. Charlie even serviced the airplane. One day, one of my people reported that he had seen Charlie walking down the road to the gas station with the 3,000 psi glass starter bottle to have it pumped up so that he could put it on the airplane and take off for Turner. This was believable, for Charlie.

When I came to Turner, strategic fighter pilots used octants to perform celestial navigation. Blair and Schilling decided that celestial navigation was primitive compared to Doppler.

Charlie and some of his protégés, including Cy Strain, had test flown a Doppler installation in an F-84G. When we converted to the F-84F at Turner, he wanted to put it on an F. The magnetron was about thirty inches in diameter and ten inches deep. We installed it in the belly of the F-84F. I worked with Charlie on it and learned an awful lot.

The early Doppler would have been more suitable for a cargo aircraft. In a fighter, a turn at a twenty degree bank or more would disable it because the magnetron was not gimbaled. It would be looking at space and stop working until the plane rolled back. Of course, by then an error would have been introduced.

Charlie kept at it. Minneapolis Honeywell, which we called "Honeybucket," who made the Doppler, shrunk the magnetron so we could put it in an F-100. We could not persuade Systems Command to do this sort of thing because they were so bomber and missile-oriented.

However, the Doppler still would not fit in the F-100 without major modifications. I took my airplane to North American, where John Casey, the Chief of Technical Design, removed the two 20 mm guns in the right gun bay. He made a bolt-on, Plexiglas bulge to accommodate everything.

I flew the first non-stop air-refueled squadron deployment across the Atlantic with that in 1957. I had some fun with it when I flew over the Air Defense Identification Zone (ADIZ) from North Africa into Spanish territory. I was giving them my ground speed and correcting their bearings! They thought I had something magic. Eventually, the Air Force took this system and developed it into the Doppler system that was installed in the F-105.

Then we became interested in follow-on technical advances, such as whether we could put an inertial system in a fighter, which we did in

Play These

the 1960s. The first one was about the size of a five-gallon jerry can and was installed in an F-104G. I flew the first sortie in the F-104G in Palmdale, California. I succeeded in having one made by Litton installed in the F-4 as a modification. The Navy version had only a dead-reckoning computer. Inertial systems are much smaller and more capable today. In a fighter, it is tied to the bombing system and, in the commercial airlines, it is coupled to the Doppler for a computerized selection of the best reading. The DC-10 has three, non-redundant Doppler-inertial navigators. A pilot can't stray off course unless he enters the wrong coordinates at takeoff.

♠ ♥ ♦ ♣

Our team won second overall flying F-100s at the World Wide Fighter Weapons Meet at Nellis in early November 1958. I was the team captain. The team had four members and a spare. Walt Bruce, of the elk and moose meat return caper, was my nuclear weapons officer. He won overall first in nuclear delivery.

The Nellis team, from the Fighter Weapons School which was still in the training command, came in first by exploiting the rules. Bruce Hinton, one of my best friends, was very crafty!

We should have won had all the units been operational units. Bruce's unit, however, was not. He did not have to think about deploying, night operations or refueling. Their work was primarily weapons delivery and fighter tactics. That was and still is regarded as one of the plush assignments for a fighter pilot. The flying weather is great, the equipment is always the latest and there is a lot of ordnance delivery, not to mention the glitzy end of the town.

For that meet, we used the old target banner that pilots had probably trained on since World War I. The banner was eight by thirty feet, towed on a harness on the end of 1,000 feet of cable. One pilot in a flight of four might have three hits. That was a pretty good score. However, you couldn't know if you had hit it until you looked at the banner on the ground afterwards and counted the color smears from each pilot's different ammo nose paint. Then came the problem of jettisoning the banner. We liked the mission because we could shoot the guns, but it was pretty depressing to have so few hits.

Bruce had nothing else to do but plan how he would win that meet. Our teams were even, nip and tuck, for five days running on dive bombing, skip bombing, strafing, and nuclear delivery—all except

Play These

for the banner. This was how he won the meet.

Surreptitiously, he developed a maneuver that was guaranteed to hit the banner. He started the pass by coming off the perch, pulling up parallel to the banner as close as possible without hitting it, throttling back suddenly and hitting hard left rudder. It would yaw the nose of the airplane so the pilot could squeeze off several rounds before spinning out. This maneuver would never work in real combat, but it worked for the competition: Bruce had forty-two hits for the first 100 rounds! We called, "Foul!" But his team won the meet.

I realized that there had to be something fishy because we all had the same equipment. Later in the bar we were mourning and he was giggling. I said, "Come on, Bruce. What the hell did you do?"

"Real simple, Gordy," he grinned. "We just yawed into the target." He took me up the next day and showed me.

The referees had questioned the tactic, but there was nothing in the published rules to bar this. The rules were changed for the next meet to disallow it afterward.

That was the last time the banner was used, but Bruce's maneuver was not allowed on the "dart," either, which was introduced that year into air-to-air training. The dart was invented at Nellis by Captain Dan Druen, now a retired general. Dan created and tested this device. It worked and was refined. The Air Force turned it out for contract and some outfit makes a mint now building them.

The dart was aerodynamically stable so that it flew steadily when towed, which made an enormous difference. The dart had a radar reflector on the nose cone. The airplanes had a radar-seeking gunsight. Finally, the tow airplane could make maneuvers to simulate air-to-air maneuvers in combat. One hit of the dart was a kill.

The William Tell Meet was held in late November 1958 at Nellis AFB, Nevada. Major General Maurice "Mo" Preston, the DO from Air Force HQ, was the Head Referee and Head of the Arbitration Board. I met him. He was looking for a replacement for Art Thomas, a classmate of mine who had the TAC Division in Air Force HQ under Mo. Slippery old Art had learned that I would be at Nellis and suggested my name to Mo.

By this time, I had secret orders telling me that the 31st was going to be inactivated and the number designation sent to George AFB.

Play These

Turner AFB was to be turned over to the Military Air Transportation Service (MATS). I had to buy a house when I was assigned to Turner. It would have been unethical and possibly illegal to try to sell that house based on my knowledge of the orders. I fully expected to take a bath on it when the news came out officially and I did.

After the Meet ended there was a banquet. Mo asked me to come to work for him in the Pentagon.

I said, "No thanks, sir. I put my tour in there and I am no longer eligible."

He laughed and said, "Art Thomas tells me that you ought to be his replacement."

I thought to myself, that son of a bitch! He's done it to me.

I thought I was out of it. My main concern then was finding jobs for all the fighter pilots and transferring the base. This took place in February 1959.

I received orders to go to the Pentagon to replace Art.

CHAPTER 11

I'LL TAKE ONE
HQ USAF: DCS/OPS

General Mo Preston played a large role in my destiny. He arranged for me to go to the Pentagon in February 1959.

I was not happy about having to come to the Pentagon. These orders meant that I had to give up National War College. I announced that I needed a few days to find a house.

Major Bascomb Neal was Mo's Exec. Bascomb said, "Colonel, I'd hold off a bit on that if I were you. There's some question about whether you're going to work here."

I asked what he meant.

He said, "Do you know anything about the POL business?"

I acknowledged that I knew "a little bit."

The SAC Director for Logistics while I was at Turner knew that I had solved a fuel filter ice problem in Alaska. He had concluded that I was the world's greatest petroleum engineer. He had been promoted to major general and was head of Air Force logistics in the Pentagon. Because he knew of the change at Turner, he knew I was available. He put in a bid for me to be the Air Force representative on the Defense Petroleum Agency. Their offices were on the Washington side of the river. If I were to buy a house on the Arlington side, Neal feared I might make a mistake. I thought he was kind to tell me of this but I was madder than ever. I didn't see Mo, so I waltzed up to the logistics office. I cooled my heels there for about an hour, but I did talk to him. He told me the whole story.

The chairman of this board, a two-star billet, was rotated among the three services. It was the Air Force's turn. The best they could come up with was a colonel and I was that colonel. This was the source of the controversy.

I was in limbo for two weeks. Mo Preston won, so I went to Ops as Chief of the Tactical Division. I was more than grateful. I inherited Art's secretary, Betty Mae, who came trotting in with some papers that Art had left. She suggested that I look them over. Practically on top of the pile, in Art's handwriting, was a note, "Remind me to talk to Mo about getting Gordy to replace me."

♠ ♥ ♦ ♣

I began as Chief of the Tactical Division, DO. I moved up to become Deputy Director of Operations for Operational Forces, DCS/Ops, HQ USAF, where I stayed until February 1962 supervising the TAC Division, SAC Division, Air Defense Division, and Transport Division.

While I had the TAC Division, Colonel Bill Crum had the Strategic Division. Bill and I were great friends and hunted and fished together. Lieutenant Colonel Dave Jones was his deputy. He had been General LeMay's pilot, executive officer and protégé. Bill left and Jones took the division.

We conducted a thorough study on putting ICBMs on railroad trains. As part of the research, I myself rode trains for a week. The conclusion was that it was feasible and inexpensive, but vulnerable to sabotage. Our guidance systems were less sophisticated then and, to ensure adequate guidance, would have required an enormous investment in geodetic surveying and reference point location.

Jones became the project officer for the B-70. Soon after that, General LeMay called me to his office. The Chief of Staff did not call me often. I couldn't figure out what in the world he would want with me. He quickly improved my mind.

"Jones is working for you," LeMay began, "but he's my B-70 project officer. He'll report to me. His job is totally the B-70, but you write his report card. Before you submit it, I want to see it. That's all."

Later, in early 1965 while I was DO at TAC, Jones was up for

I'll Take One

promotion. Probably at LeMay's behest, General Sweeney, the TAC Commander, undertook to paint a stripe called "fighter pilot" on Jones. I was given the paintbrush.

I sent Jones to Luke AFB, where he went through the full ten-month fighter training program. From there, he went to Nellis AFB for two months. He was assigned Commander of the 33rd Wing at Eglin AFB, which had been newly-equipped with F-4s.

After he had been there for the minimum interval, less than a year, Jones was promoted to BG and went to Europe as Inspector General. He worked his way up to Chief of Staff of the Air Force.

♠ ♥ ♦ ♣

When in the Pentagon, as Deputy Director for Operations, I practically lived in the command post during the Stanleyville rescue effort because it was a TAC operation. It was an absolute success. The Air Force was in a terrible dilemma about that time. They had no fighter base within striking distance of that whole area. By default, it became a Navy operational area because only a carrier could come close enough to provide offensive air. Senior Air Force leaders were tearing out their hair. Tankers could be put on station all over the hemisphere but it would still have been operationally infeasible. Fortunately, the crisis came under control swiftly.

♠ ♥ ♦ ♣

The invasion of Cuba at the Bay of Pigs happened in April 1961. The Joint Chiefs recommended unanimously and articulately against the invasion. Besides being ignored on the decision, they were not even consulted for a military recommendation on accomplishing it.

The invasion was managed by the CIA and was very highly classified. We in TAC Ops knew what was going to happen because we had to provide maps, charts and photos. We knew that training was occurring.

The air staff had minimal participation in planning and none in executing the operation. The Air Force should have been smarter, based on the experience in Korea. When one reads the details, one wonders how the U.S. could have committed such a grievous military blunder. The experience was similar to the way President Johnson ran the Viet Nam War and to the way President Carter ran the aborted rescue

I'll Take One

operation later in the Iranian desert. The major elements were common to all, starting with micromanagement by totally unqualified people.

♠ ♥ ♦ ♣

During the Berlin crisis in 1961, General LeMay flew in a KC-135 with a group of ten, including me, to Europe. The KC-135 was an operational tanker in the tanker stream. Some KC-135s had been equipped with drogues, instead of booms, to be phased into service for TAC. However, several National Guard units had F-84Fs with boom receptacles, so there was a mix of boom- and probe-equipped tankers, boom- and probe-equipped receivers, and some with both. A lot of National Guard units were recalled to active duty for the Berlin crisis.

There were four tanker Air Forces: SAC had KB-50s, then KC-97s, then KC-135s. TAC started with KB-29s, which were inherited from SAC, then went to KB-50s. PACAF and USAFE did the same thing. All SAC tankers were boom-equipped. TAC went the "probe and drogue" route, beginning with refitting the KB-29s.

There were three refueling stations on the modified KB-29: one on the tail and two out of the wing pods. It worked, but it wasn't 100 percent successful. We deployed using them. At top speed for the KB-29, the fighters were falling out of the sky trying to refuel.

Air-to-air refueling was a quantum step forward for fighters, which always had short legs. We always said, "We only have a forty-minute ass and we don't want any more fuel than that in the airplane." With deployments and more sophisticated airplanes, it wasn't possible to carry enough drop tanks to complete the mission. Some experimenters, namely Dave Schilling and Bill Ritchie, pioneered fighter refueling efforts. Dave and Bill flew the first flight across the Atlantic. Bill couldn't get fuel on one of the refuelings and punched out over Greenland. He was rescued. Dave made it all the way. The solution was fabricated by hand.

On the flight to Europe, General LeMay was monitoring the traffic. Our route was from the U.S. to Goose Bay, Newfoundland, to Lages, Azores, then on to Europe. Refuelings were after Argentia, Newfoundland, and just before Lages. We lost a couple of airplanes because they went to the wrong tanker. They either had a boom tanker with a probe or vice versa. LeMay promptly decreed two things: (1) there would be a single manager tanker force, namely SAC, and (2) it

I'll Take One

would be receptacle-only. As an interim measure, we would convert airplanes by putting systems on them. This was the reason that the F-105, which started with the receptacle only, was given a probe (because there were still some probe tankers in the world). It was two or three years before all went through the system, particularly in Europe and the Far East. TAC thereby lost its tankers.

♠ ♥ ♦ ♣

General "Doc" Strother was Deputy Chief of Staff (DCSO) in the Pentagon while I was there (1959-1962). What a super person. "Deke" Childs was his exec. I went to brief Doc often. He had a great sense of humor and his head was really screwed on straight. He was thoroughly practical and pragmatic, a fighter pilot who was not bomber-oriented. I went up with a plan for a no-notice composite air strike force deployment to Europe, which had never been done before. We wanted to see if TAC could do what it said it could do. It took me forty-five minutes to plow through this. It involved deploying fighter squadrons, refueling en route, landing at three different bases on the continent, conducting a couple of weeks of exercises, and then coming home. I finished and he sat back. He was a tall, thin man.

He said, "Gordy, that's a collar-and-asshole operation if I ever saw one."

I said, "I'm really disappointed. My people and I have really worked on this, coordinated it with everybody in the Pentagon. General, I don't understand your dissatisfaction and I'm particularly nonplused by your expression."

"Gordy, where I grew up in Mississippi, we had mules for plowing. In order to plow a straight furrow, you lined up the mule's asshole with the end fence post and collar and plowed toward it. This proposal of yours wanders all over."

♠ ♥ ♦ ♣

I was the Air Force project officer in the Pentagon for Operation CROSSFEED. The Air Force invited the Secretary of the Army, the Chief of Staff of the Army, the CG of the 18th Airborne Corps, all the big names and a lot of lesser colonels of the Army, but important people, to come to Nellis AFB and ride in an F-100F against targets, lines of communication, tanks, fixed gun emplacements, to see what one could see. The Army claimed that one reason the Air Force was so ineffective

I'll Take One

when attacking ground targets was that pilots were flying so fast that they couldn't see these types of targets. By the time a pilot acquired a target, he had passed it and wouldn't come back because he didn't want to be shot up.

The Army accepted. Bob Gates, in requirements, gave his briefing. I was the Master of Ceremonies and briefed for Air Force Operations. We took them out and gave them rides at various speeds, at various altitudes, in F-100s. We asked, "General, can you see that column of tanks down there at ten o'clock? We're at 5,000 feet and 300 knots." The column of target tanks was immobile.

"Yes, sir, I have it."

"OK. We're going down to 300 feet and 500 knots. See what you can see." Of course, it was a blur and gone.

"Now, General, we are going back up to 5,000 feet. I'll slow the airplane, we'll make an orbit, and you will see how easy it is to acquire a target."

We completed the orbit, made a nice, comfortable dive bomb run, and splattered the tanks. "Now, General, is there anything that you can see that makes that so difficult that we can't do this, consistently and continuously?"

"What about when it's a dark night or bad weather?"

"Then we have a ground-vectored system, admittedly not what we prefer, but it works. But the Army doesn't fight much at night, either."

After a couple of days of this, the Secretary of the Army and the Chief of Staff of the Air Force talked. Decker told LeMay, "You pick the airplane."

♠ ♥ ♦ ♣

TAC was faced with acquiring another airplane and planning for thirteen wings. There was a conglomeration of airplanes, mostly F-100s, in the stables worldwide. There was nothing on the horizon.

The F-105 test squadron was at Eglin AFB, under Colonel Bob Scott. I went down and flew an F-105B. My first ride was on June 24, 1959. It was hot. Advertised speed was Mach 2+. I planned to do that on the first ride. I took off. Jim Bean, one of my squadron commanders at Turner and one of the five individuals I had nominated for the F-105 program, was chasing me. Jim was Scott's number two. After a few maneuvers to check out the airplane, we climbed to 37,000 feet in a

I'll Take One

sixty-mile supersonic corridor between Eglin AFB and Tyndall AFB and opened her up. Mach 1.8 was as fast as it would go. It was too hot. The supersonic time is limited in that hog because it has so little fuel.

I told Jim I was going to zoom up to 40,000 feet and dive back down. I believed that I could reach Mach 2 that way, then level off and hold that speed. I made a turn, leveled off, and started to pull the nose up to pick up 6,000 to 7,000 feet so I could dive back.

The F-105B's oil gauge is the size of a quarter. The gauge promptly went to zero. Jim was riding my wing about 100 to 200 yards away. He called me and said, "You just pulled a hell of a contrail for a second!"

I said, "That was no contrail. I have no oil pressure."

He said, "Oh."

I came out of burner right away. We were pointed at Eglin and Jim was with me. The airplane had very little operational experience. A flameout landing pattern, procedure and parameters had been developed, but no one had informed me because I wasn't supposed to practice that the first mission. I throttled back to about eighty percent and was losing altitude but I was comfortable. Over the field, I asked Jim, "What's the high key for flameout in this bear?" "High key" is where a pilot begins a flameout landing. He flies right over the place that he will set down and makes a 360 degree turn until touchdown.

He answered, "16,000."

I said, "I'm at 23,000 and I don't think I'll have any trouble losing altitude in this." I came around. Everything was going great. If an airplane actually flamed out, the pilot would need 225 knots on final. I was holding a good 225, but I was still getting some power from the engine.

I came back, had the speed brakes out, the gear down, and flaps OK. About thirty feet in the air, the engine seized. The torque was so powerful that there was an abrupt change. I compensated properly, landed and coasted to the end of the runway. The chute worked. I used the manual brakes to stop and didn't need the barrier.

The cause of the incident was that a common B-nut fitting on the 3,000 psi oil line had ruptured. The oil had spewed out instantaneously. A jet engine doesn't use oil like a piston engine, so there isn't much there to start with.

In sum, I made the first actual successful F-105 flameout landing on my first ride in the airplane!

♠ ♥ ♦ ♣

I'll Take One

The Air Force looked at the Navy A-3J, the Navy A-4D, and even an AD-6, which became the A-1E. Of course, follow-on models of the F-105, the F-104, and the F-101 were considered, as well as, almost by accident, the Navy F-4H.

I flew the latest version of the F-104, "G," that we had. This was the German version, with an inertial system.

Bob Scott and I went down to Oceana Naval Air Station, were checked out in the A-4D and had the "ten missions or twenty hours" evaluation opportunity.

We did the same thing with the A-3J at North American, both at Columbus, OH, where the plane was produced and at Palmdale, CA, where it was flown. The A-3J was a twin-engine, Mach 2 fighter bomber, atomic delivery, which carried two weapons internally in a bay between the two engines. These weapons were delivered using the Low-Altitude Bombing System (LABS) maneuver, except that they were kicked out the stern instead of thrown over the shoulder. This was a unique and innovative system, but it wasn't a fighter, and certainly wasn't an interceptor. Major General Spike Momyer, who was then Director of Operational Requirements at Air Force HQ, was pushing hard for this airplane.

One morning, I flew with George Laven in a T-33 to Columbus. There, Lieutenant General Joe Moore, then DO at TAC, joined us. At nine-thirty, Zeke Hopkins began a two-and-a-half-hour briefing. Then we broke for lunch. One of Zeke's assistants, their chief test pilot, came running in to report, "We're all set to go for the first flight at one o'clock."

I looked at Laven, then at Zeke, and asked, "You mean we're supposed to fly this airplane? We haven't even seen it yet."

We thought we would be there a few days to be checked out in the airplane. Afterwards, we would proceed to Edwards AFB, at Palmdale, CA, to fly operational tests. By contrast, they expected us to fly there, that morning!

Zeke said, "We'll take care of that right now. I'll give you a cockpit check and you can launch."

I asked, "What are we going to do?"

He replied, "We've already made up your mission profile cards, right here!"

I stalled. "I'd like to look at the communication systems, then emergency procedures, and some other things. I want more than to kick the tire and start the fire!"

I'll Take One

"We have no time for that. The program is very condensed!"

I started to feel less comfortable about it. I could tell Laven and Moore were feeling equally nervous, but we went out and flipped for first ride. I won and took off at about two o'clock. Everything went according to the transition sheet I had been given. The airplane was good and behaved about the way it was supposed to. For a big airplane, it was fast, responsive, and maneuverable. It had great acceleration. I took it down to the supersonic corridor from Columbus to Louisville at 38,000 feet to open it up. It had what was described as an "oil can" effect: at altitude, at high Mach number, the airplane structure would compress and expand, making a popping noise like that of a squeezed oil can. What a sensation! No one had told me about this and it scared me to death when it happened. I came out of burner, throttled back, and called on the radio. Zeke reassured me that there was nothing wrong with it.

I came in at 240 knots, at 1,500 feet, and set up to land. This was the first airplane with essentially a "fly-by-wire" capability, although it was not called that at the time. The stick did not move. The pilot applied pressure to the stick, which sent an electrical impulse to a rheostat. The harder the pilot pulled, the higher the rheostat response and the greater the response from the control surfaces. I turned downwind, dropped the gear and flaps, and immediately went into an unprogrammed roll. I screeched, saw I couldn't regain control, so I dished out. I bottomed out at around 400 feet, immediately stroked the burners and threw everything into it. Then I sucked up the gear and flaps and climbed up to 20,000 feet to find my wits.

Zeke had seen the whole thing. He didn't know what had happened. It had never happened before. I told him I had had nothing to do with it; as soon as I had dropped the flaps, it rolled.

"The flaps must have been asymmetrical." I disagreed; it didn't show on the flap indicator. Later, when I had regained altitude, I flew a landing pattern and nothing happened.

I told him I was coming back down. I did, only the second time I didn't put down the flaps.

They found the problem. A spurious signal, when the flap circuitry was activated, told the airplane to "use full right aileron."

That first day, all three of us flew our first flight on the same airplane. Then we climbed into our airplanes and flew to Edwards. We expected to stay overnight, rest a little, and then begin receiving briefings. Instead, we were scheduled to fly the next morning at daylight.

I'll Take One

I put my foot down and declared, "I won't fly another sortie until I have some rest and more experience learning the systems." We didn't fly that day.

The following morning, we had to be on the flight line at four o'clock. It was pitch dark and cold. We were briefed. I had a simulated nuclear weapon delivery, dropping on the Edwards AFB, California range. Laven was to make an air intercept over Salt Lake City. Moore had something else to do.

Everything was set up. This time there were two airplanes. I climbed into a pick-up truck to be taken to my airplane. Instead of going out in front of Ops, we drove and drove, clear to the end of the runway. Finally, I asked the driver what was going on. He said, "Oh, we tow the airplane out here."

"Why?"

"To save fuel."

A truck with liquid oxygen (LOX) for filling an oxygen system had a blanket arranged to chill the fuel in the two external tanks. I asked the reason.

"If we chill the fuel, we can load another 800 pounds in there."

The air-intercept over Salt Lake City profile was the most fuel-critical. The manufacturers claimed that the pilot would have 1,500 pounds of fuel remaining on returning approach to land. In order to do that, we had to tow out, chill the fuel, strap in, hit the start button, and immediately take off. This really inspired my confidence in the contractor.

Even if everything else had been all right, I'd still have written a negative report. Thank goodness we didn't buy that airplane!

♠ ♥ ♦ ♣

I was standing in Ops at Edwards AFB in conjunction with the F-105 testing, when I saw an airplane, the F-4H, flying as part of the Navy test program. The airplane was very ugly, but it put on a pretty shiny performance. That evening, I inquired around to learn what it was and what it was doing there. I located one of the Navy test pilots, who gave me 2,000 well-chosen words on what a great airplane this F-4H was. He arranged for me to inspect it, but I wasn't able to fly it.

I went to Mo Preston and reported that this airplane should definitely be considered, notwithstanding that it was a Navy airplane and some modifications might be required to make it compatible for the Air Force. However, it was available, about to enter production, and its performance looked very good.

It bothered me that tactical fighters had such a low priority in the Air Force, compared to bomber development. It was understandable that the Navy should have developed superior fighters because they could concentrate all their resources on developing only fighter or attack airplanes. In addition, there were some pretty sharp people in the Navy business.

A couple of months later, some Navy friends Eddie Outlaw and Paul Pugh arranged for Moore, Laven and me to fly the F-4. They were interested in selling more of the airplanes so that the unit cost to the Navy would decrease. They gave us the standard Navy check-out, after which we were permitted to fly ten missions or twenty hours, whichever came first, to evaluate the airplane. My area of evaluation was weapon delivery; George's was interception; and Joe's was navigation and profile.

I wrote the report and recommended forty-seven changes to the airplane to make it useful for the Air Force and to correct some deficiencies. Eleven were significant and one was very significant. This last one was to remove the backseat pilot (including seat, oxygen tanks, instruments) and replace him with 2,200 pounds of fuel.

One example of other changes was the tires. They were the small, high-pressure type the Navy uses for carrier landings. These were totally unsatisfactory for Air Force runways. Making a larger, lower-pressure tire required that the wings bell out before the gear would come up and go in. This cut .2 Mach off the top speed of the airplane, however, because of the drag.

A second example was that it had to have a refueling receptacle rather than a probe because, by direction from General LeMay, we had nothing but receptacle airplanes and a single manager tanker force. The Navy still used the drogue. Other examples were Air Force-type ejection seats, with the ejection pull-handle (under the seat) versus the Navy type (overhead); the radios; the oxygen system (demand versus full pressure); an inertial navigation system versus a dead-reckoning computer; and so on.

General LeMay agreed on all the major changes except on the backseat pilot. In spite of all the evidence to the contrary (e.g., the F-105), he didn't believe one pilot could both (a) monitor the air-to-air radar and (b) fly the airplane/launch the missiles. That's how there came to be two seats in the Air Force version, the F-4C.

I'll Take One

When LeMay insisted on a back seater, we insisted that the "Guy in Back (GIB)" be a pilot. The rationale was that, while we had plenty of pilots, our training capability was limited. We foresaw that we would need more pilots. After pilots graduated from combat crew training, they were ready to be assigned to fighters. Sticking a junior birdman in the back of an F-4 was one good way for him to learn to fly the airplane and prepare to upgrade to the front seat. It avoided the need to buy a separate trainer, like a T-33 or a two-seat F-100F or F-105F. We already had a trainer! To that end, we installed a speedbrake switch, rudder pedals, afterburner switches, and additional instruments in the back seat so that the GIB could fly the airplane. The GIB could not fly the Navy version. I was the chief architect of this solution. I was Gabe Disosway's DO when this surfaced. He took a strong position, with McConnell, the Chief of Staff, about two pilots being the way to go.

That was successful for about a year. Then, at about the time of the Viet Nam build-up, this dropped out of the picture. First, Viet Nam generated an increased demand for pilots. Second, too many sons of senior generals ended up in the back seat of an F-4 when their classmates in flying school went directly into single-seat F-100s and F-105s as single seat macho jock fighter pilots. For example, Joe Schmoe, son of General Schmoe, goes to F-100s. Bill Zablotny, son of General Zablotny, goes to an F-4 and is assigned to an ignominious back seat. He is a second-class citizen. He talks to Dad; "Joe Schmoe has his own airplane. I'm sitting in a back seat and I don't like the guy in first class. I want an airplane for me, too. Why don't you do something about it?"

They argued that being in the back was unfair. A navigator could do the job. It didn't cost as much to train a navigator. Besides, the GIB in the reconnaissance RF-4 wasn't a pilot, so we didn't need it in the F-4. As a matter of fact, there was a big difference. The RF-4 back-seater had a hell of a job to do because all the radar and photo controls are in the back seat only and require special skills to operate. Of course, these were not needed in a fighter F-4. But, in a stroke of the pen, we had radar system navigators in the back seat of the F-4. I still think this was a dumbbell mistake, but all those senior officers with screeching kids prevailed. Later, there was a difficulty placing all the navigators when their flying days were done. They ended up in missile silos, intelligence jobs, and what not. There are no navigators now on C-5s or C-141s, thanks to the inertial navigation system. On the positive side, many of the F-4 navigators flew a tour and then went through

I'll Take One

pilot training. I'm sure they were better pilots for the F-4 back seat experience.

George Laven and I were in the Pentagon in the spring or summer of 1961, soon after MacNamara became Secretary of Defense. I vividly recall that MacNamara brought out 100 issues immediately, almost overnight. Some were silly, like "Why do we need fighters?" Everyone was in a turmoil and all four services were standing on their heads trying to answer these dumb questions from these so-called "whiz kids." For every answer you gave, they would think up fifteen more questions! MacNamara was briefed early on the Air Force, Navy and Marine programs for fighters and fighter development. The Air Force was very straightforward. A fighter was designated "P," for "pursuit," until after the start of the Korean War, during which we were flying P-51s and P-80s. I don't remember exactly when during the war it changed to "F." A bomber was a "B" and cargo (transport) plane was a "C."

The Navy, however, had an arcane system for designating airplanes, such as "F-4H1" or "SB-2C." One of the letters stood for the contractor's plant, but the letter didn't always match the contractor's initial. While MacNamara was being briefed, he halted the show to ask, "What is this insane numbering system for airplanes that you military minds have developed? I want it changed immediately!"

The instruction was, "If it's the same kind of airplane, it has the same number, whether it's Air Force, Navy, or Marine."

One month earlier, George and I had taken delivery of the first two F-4Hs (which became the Air Force F-110) on loan from the Navy. We had flown them, with the "F-110" designation painted on the side, from St. Louis to TAC HQ at Langley AFB, Virginia. With the dictum from MacNamara, all the planes instantly became F-4Cs, from whence flowed the Ds, Es, Fs, etc., in the model series.

The Northrop N-156 became the F-5. The attack versions were up to A-70 or something. We started from scratch; the Air Force A-1E, which had been the Navy AD-6, became the "A-1." The A-4 was a Douglas version. The A-5, which had been an A-3J, became the RA-5. The A-7 was furnished to both services. The A-8 and A-9 competed in a fly-off and the winner became the A-10. The A-11 I've forgotten. The A-12 was developed for Air Defense but never procured. The strategic-reconnaissance version of the A-12 was the SR-71.

♠ ♥ ♦ ♣

I'll Take One

The Air Force wanted to put a Vulcan (Gatling) gun in the F-4. First, we went to McDonnell Douglas (MDC) and said, "You must put a gun in the airplane. You said you could when we bought your airplane." They showed us the engineering drawings; the airplane would give up one Sparrow so the gun could be put in the right aft Sparrow well. Very inexpensive. I strongly believed all this stuff, so I went trotting up to Air Force HQ and assured them it would work. I was shoved all the way up to brief MacNamara on it.

MDC quoted a price tag of $15 million for the project, including tech order kits and everything, to equip the fleet and incorporate it into the airplanes still on the production line. Old MacNamara nodded his head. All of his wizards around him were taking credit for it, of course.

Soon after, I received a frantic call: "Hey, Gordy, you have to come out here. We're in trouble." They had made the most elementary mistake imaginable: they had not calculated the shift aft in the center of gravity. This shift was due to the increase in the weight of the pod over that of the Sparrow, which weighed about 3,000 pounds. This made the plane dynamically unstable. I had the joy of undoing all the persuasion that I had accomplished!

MDC initiated a crash program to put a pod on the F-4 model, which we used early in Viet Nam, but continued efforts to put the gun inside. I obtained a gun from an F-105 that had crashed into Mobile Bay immediately after takeoff. At Nellis AFB the gun and the original YRF-4 model (which was between the X and the production models) were married. The radar dish had to be shrunk to twenty-two inches to accommodate the gun internally. The current dish was twenty-seven inches, so the radar was removed to provide space for the gun. I flew the system for the first time (with no radar) and pinged the dart with the first burst. This established the feasibility and alleviated concerns that it would blow up in our face or that the exhaust gases would be ingested by the intakes, etc.

I had some trouble persuading Westinghouse to shrink that dish. Shrinking it five inches meant losing about ten miles on acquisition range and about three or four miles on lock-on. But it wasn't that much—less than twenty percent. So a prototype was built and everything worked like a charm. That became the F-4E. We beat the drum for funding ninety-six F-4Es in that year's budget. General Gabe Disosway was a strong supporter.

♠ ♥ ♦ ♣

I'll Take One

The A-7 was attractive to MacNamara's whiz kids, who were always trying to invent something more "cost-effective" —read: "cheaper." Alain Enthoven was one of the leaders of the pack—the "Guru of Cost-Effectiveness." He had a crowd of system analysts who forced the Air Force to perform innumerable, needless, expensive studies which were trashed if they didn't support the analysts' preconceived ideas.

The A-7 was a warmed-over F-8U "Crusader," made by Chance Vought, before LTV bought Vought.

When the Navy A-7D was produced, it was a subsonic and underpowered attack airplane. It was not purported to be a fighter. Whereas the Air Force calls all of its airplanes "attack fighters," from a C-47 to an F-15, the Navy makes a profound distinction. DoD thought this was the greatest airplane in the world; this subsonic airplane could carry an enormous amount of ordnance and deliver it with a highly accurate bomb delivery system with the "Heads-Up Display."

I went to the Navy's old Hensley Field in Dallas, Texas, right next to the LTV factory, to fly the standard ten flights or twenty hours, whichever-came-first, in the A-7. A systems command pilot went out also. He was a "stick force per g" type, concentrating on all the technical parameters.

I flew the operational profile to see whether the damn thing would deliver. It was underpowered and I almost augered in on the first flight. They loaded it with 8,000 pounds of ordnance, which it was supposed to carry comfortably. I put the flaps down and took off. The 8,700-ft. runway ended short of a lake. At the end of the runway, I was still stuck on the concrete! I finally staggered into the air and couldn't retract the flaps because I wasn't high enough to bank. The flaps had two positions: full down or full up. I staggered around and flew the flights. On one, I took it up to 35,000 ft. and rolled it over, leaving the throttle at eighty-five to eighty-eight percent, pointed it at the ground and let her go. It reached about .8 Mach, bucked and snorted, and stayed there.

I had not very kind things to write up about it. Furthermore, I blew my mouth off all over the Air Force about what a dog this airplane was and that a bunch of dum-dums were trying to persuade the Air Force to take it. McConnell called Disosway and told him to "tell that Graham to keep his mouth shut or he will be strangled!" Gabe called me in and told me. I confessed my guilt; I'd said some bad things at symposia and in speeches.

I'll Take One

The Air Force was told, "If you want ninety-six F-4Es, then you must take 324 A-7s." I wrote a list of fixes as long as my arm. This led to the A-7E, the Air Force version. The Navy then thought so highly of those fixes that their later contracts called for the A-7Es!

The Air Force did receive the ninety-six F-4s and the A-7s. Only one or two wings of A-7s were flown in Viet Nam, beginning in 1969.

♠ ♥ ♦ ♣

The F-111 was already in concrete when MacNamara became Secretary of Defense; all the technical orders had been written on it. It would have cost an enormous amount of money to change that. That was the last to be named that way, except the F-117, which is the Stealth fighter. That tells you how long ago THAT program started!

Every SECDEF in my experience has thought he could invent an airplane. Each one accepted that he could not invent a carrier or a battleship and that it was too hard and profound to invent a bomber, so he usually settled on a fighter. MacNamara blunted his pick on the F-111.

After three or four F-111s had been built, I went to the factory at Fort Worth and flew one. What a monstrosity! One band-aid after was another was applied to that airplane. On my first flight, there was a terrible compressor stall problem. If I pulled anything over three g's, or a forty-five or fifty-degree bank, the inboard compressor would stall and I'd have to cut the power off on that engine. It was so riddled with bugs that it would have been better to shove it in the bay and start over. There must have been fifty people monitoring the radio downlink with my telemetry and voice transmissions on that flight, hanging on my every word and scribbling frantic notes. I say that because I arranged for General Gabe Disosway to go down there and fly it, while I stayed on the ground and observed the reaction of that crowd.

Historically, the airplane had started out as a "Tactical Fighter," but it was basically an attack bomber/nuclear delivery vehicle. Then it grew. MacNamara had the brilliant idea that it should be a Navy airplane, too: "All of you can fly the same airplane. We'll buy them in greater quantity and pay a lower price."

The Navy protested that it wouldn't fly off a carrier, but found itself without an audience. They objected violently but couldn't afford to do it loudly. Two or three F-111Bs were built for the Navy; they just dragged their feet. Eight years passed while MacNamara was secretary. The day he left, the F-111B died. Grumman was standing in the wings

I'll Take One

with the F-14 and the presses were ready to roll. I greatly admired the Navy for the way they stuck to their guns, were polite and submissive, but had their homework done and were ready to move out when the prime obstacle was removed.

The Air Force wasn't that smart. They just kept trying. For example, the airplane was designed to have a gun in the bomb bay. When the pilot hit a button, the gun came out on a carriage like an accordion and, when the pilot hit the fire button, it was supposed to fire. There were so many problems that this was abandoned. One problem was that half the time, when the pilot pulled the trigger, the ingestion of gas from the gun caused a flameout and loss of an engine. Any aeronautical engineer, with any experience, could easily have predicted this from a quick look at the airflow.

A prominent feature of the airplane was that it had variable-geometry wings. Normally, an Air Force pilot wishing to go fast pushed the throttle and, at the same time, shoved the wing-retract handle forward. To slow down, he jerked the power (throttle) back and pulled the handle, so the wings would go into a position normal to the fuselage. In the F-111, this was backwards. I'll never know where the human engineers were on this one.

One pilot was killed before this was changed. He was a good test pilot whose first ride in the airplane at Nellis was with an instructor pilot (IP) in the other seat. He was making an approach with the wings in the halfway or midpoint position, at thirty degrees (sixty degrees was total sweepback), and needed more lift. Instead of adding power, he pulled the wing handle back and the wings went into sweepback instead of going normal to the fuselage. He went in before he could slam the power to it. That caused a hullabaloo.

Another big problem was meeting the specific requirements for range and fuel consumption. One cause of excessive drag was the joint where the wing came together at the hinge point on the fuselage. A big sleeve was built over this joint. It was a monster to behold, added a lot of weight and did little good.

There are still some in the inventory, in electronic intelligence (ELINT) versions. Some that were in the fighter-bomber configuration were used in the attack on Libya. I don't know how many times the price of that airplane has been plowed into it to make it do something useful. In every fighter-qualified pilot's book, it was an expensive, unmitigated disaster and failure.

♠ ♥ ♦ ♣

I'll Take One

I used to go to Alaska to fish, sometimes with Mo Preston. Usually, I would go in a T-33 with a fighter buddy over the Fourth of July. We could stuff our boots, fishing rods and a spare shirt in the nose deck. The two of us would take turns flying to let the other snooze in the back seat. We would go as far north as King Salmon. On July 4, 1961, now-retired Brigadier General Bob Spencer, who was working for me in the Pentagon, went with me. I was totally unaware that I had a bad ulcer that had developed over about four years. I had never felt the need to see a doctor or obtain medication. Looking back, I can recognize the symptoms.

On the way to Alaska, we lost the radio and had to abort into White Horse. We made a penetration and let down to 1,500 feet on a low-frequency beacon about five o'clock in the evening. Up there, it was still broad daylight. White Horse sits in a valley with 12,000-ft. mountains on each side. I was a good pilot, I have to tell you!

I called my buddy in Alaska. He conned a pilot up there to fly a B-57 in to come down and escort us back. I flew back on his wing. Then that pilot turned around and went his way.

As soon as our airplane was fixed, we went on to King Salmon. Because of the time of year, one could fish twenty-four hours a day. The first day, I didn't feel too well. I thought I was just tired. The Yukon River was unbelievably swift and the fishing was indescribably good for twenty-pound King salmon. We came in every four or five hours to eat and rest for a couple of hours. By the second day, I had severe nausea and an excruciating headache. I drank a bottle of 7-Up, thinking that would settle my stomach. It bounced right back. After three days, I couldn't stand it any longer.

They had a medical detachment there, with an airman to hand out aspirin. He told me I had a severe case of flu that was going around there at the time. He gave me a bottle of aspirin, which was the worst thing I could have taken for an ulcer.

We took off and flew back to Anchorage. I was really sick. I had originally planned to leave the following day, so we didn't miss much. We stayed in Anchorage about four or five hours and then took off for Calgary. We refueled there and proceeded to Minot, North Dakota. I had been flying in the front seat and was making the approach at about five o'clock in the evening when I realized I couldn't see the airspeed indicator. The figures were dim. But I landed the airplane. We had planned to go straight on to Selfridge AFB, near Detroit, and on to Washington, but I told Bob that I was going to have to rest up a bit.

I'll Take One

Something was wrong with me. I was weak and had not been able to keep anything solid or fluid on my stomach for three days. We went up to the BOQ and I bought some bread and tomato juice. Neither would stay down. I lay down. About eleven o'clock in the evening, I arose and walked around awhile. I was really sick. I went back to bed. Around three o'clock in the morning, I woke Bob up, told him I wasn't getting any better and we might as well leave. I told him I would go to the mess hall, get a cup of tea and some fruit juice or something and meet him down at the flight line. He could file the clearance and we would be off.

I went to the mess hall, managed to swallow some tea and tomato juice, but felt them starting to come up and rushed for the latrine. I made it into the latrine, but that was all I remember. I must have been out for forty-five minutes. Old Bob couldn't figure out where the heck I was. He'd gone back to the BOQ and been to the mess hall, but no one there had seen me. I managed to stand up, but I was covered with blood. I took off my flying suit and washed it in the basin. I cleaned myself up as well as I could, then went looking for a car to take me to the flight line. My original driver had tired of waiting and taken off. Finally, I found a car and drove to the flight line. I found Bob and said, "I ain't going to make it. I have to see a doctor."

There was a flight surgeon on duty but the only doctor around was at the Veterans Hospital, downtown. The doctor diagnosed me as having the flu. Fortunately, he gave me no medicine. He said, "We're going to hold you. Your blood count is way down and you look like hell. After a couple of days in bed you'll be all right."

I protested that I would catch hell because I was only authorized to take the plane for a maximum of four days, including a day out and a day back. I would be two days late returning! The air base group commander at Andrews was a first class S.O.B. I'd already clashed with him a couple of times and knew that, if I didn't return that airplane on time, he might never permit me to take out another one. Moreover, he had a policy that one pilot could not fly a two-place airplane because it would deprive someone else of some flying time.

I said, "Bob, you take the airplane back. I'm going to have to wait here a couple of days. I'll find a way home. Don't worry." So Bob took off alone. We both caught all kinds of hell.

Meanwhile, I went to the hospital. I only made it part way up the steps. The driver saw me starting to fall and he jumped out, ran around and helped me inside. They put me in a room and I lost consciousness again.

I'll Take One

I woke up about four hours later. I had an IV in each arm, with glucose in one and blood in the other. Soon, the flight surgeon came in. I was already feeling a hell of a lot better from all the fluids that had been pumped in.

I asked, "What the heck kind of flu do I have? This is the first time in my life that I've been this sick."

He said, "I have some news for you. You do not have the flu. You damn near died. You have a hemorrhaged ulcer and almost bled to death. You were just released from the emergency ward a few minutes ago. Do you feel all right now?"

I said, "I feel fine! I have to go home and return my airplane" (even though I knew it had already gone).

He said, "You aren't going anywhere." He was right; I was there three weeks, then I was air-evacuated to Andrews AFB, where I spent an additional three weeks in their hospital.

Finally, I was turned loose. A board met and decided to ground me permanently, per some Air Force regulation written in 1926. Any gastrointestinal bleeding or internal bleeding was justification for automatic, permanent grounding. There was no recourse, no waiver, no reexamination.

By then it was September. I was really unhappy about the prospects. That month, a group of us went fishing and moose-hunting with Mo in Newfoundland. I told him my situation. He was pretty familiar with it, since I had just returned to my job in the building. I said I didn't think I had any recourse except to retire. I had twenty-two years' service and was forty-three years old. I told him I really didn't want to retire, but I wouldn't stay in the Air Force if I couldn't fly fighters. He advised me not to make a rash decision.

He had nominated me as his number one choice for the National War College, but I didn't know this and he certainly was not going to tell me. The list came out in early November, before I had done anything, and I found myself on the list to go to the war college.

About that time, I received a call from a First Lieutenant Joe Blow in personnel. He wanted me to come to his office for "reclassification."

I told him, "If you want to talk to me, you come to my office." He came with his little portfolio and we went over my personal history statement. I was able to be reclassified as intelligence officer or entry level administrative officer. My fighter pilot Air Force Specialty Code (AFSC) was being deleted and my commander's AFSC, were all wiped off. I ordered him out of my office. I didn't want to talk to him. He left in confusion and resentment that I was making his job so difficult. I heard nothing more from him. I later learned that he had complained to his boss, who had complained to Mo's exec Bascomb Neal, who had mentioned it to Mo, who had said, "Punt and put him off," meaning until the war college decision was made.

I started thinking, after war college, I'll be stuck in some stupid ground job, since there is no way I'll be given anything else. I shall have lost another year. Charlie Blair wants me to come down to St. Thomas and run his Antilles Airboats, which sounds good to me. There isn't much money in it, but there is a lot of good fishing, and living there would be pleasant. I decided to retire.

I didn't talk to Mo. I expected he would call me. Meanwhile, I went to personnel and obtained all the forms I needed to request retirement. I hand-carried my request to old Neal, who read it. He shook his head and said, "Mo is not going to like this."

I told him, "I've thought about this a lot."

Mo received the paper and said nothing. I went in a week later, December 10, as I recall, and asked, "Bascomb, I need an answer. I have been offered a job in the Caribbean and have to start making plans. The kids are in school and I need to make some arrangements."

"I'll talk to the old man."

Two or three more days passed. I went to personnel to try to find out where the papers had disappeared into the system.

Traditionally, the list of general officer promotions was posted in the Pentagon the day before the Christmas holidays. About ten o'clock that morning, the list went up. I didn't even bother to go look. Then friends started to call to congratulate me. Finally, I jumped up and ran up to the fourth floor to look at the board in personnel. There was my name, bigger than hell, on the list for BG!

I couldn't run fast enough to old Mo's office to ask him to call back that letter! When I finally was able to talk to him, I reminded him of the letter. Then I said, "I have tried to find it, General Preston, but it's in the system somewhere and I'm afraid some jackass will pass it on and it will get some action now!"

Mo reached into his drawer and pulled out an envelope. "Is this what you're talking about?" He'd been sitting on that letter all that time!

He laughed and eventually, I did, too.
But I was still grounded.

♠ ♥ ♦ ♣

I didn't expect to pin on my star before June and was pretty confident that I wouldn't be reassigned or moved until then. My top priority was to be put back on flying status. I had just accepted the Board's decision as irrevocable and had not attempted to challenge it.

First, I read the regulation. I contacted the Federal Aviation Administration (FAA) to find out what regulations applied to commercial airline pilots. They had no regulation like the Air Force's. I went to the Surgeon General Ollie Neiss and requested their case histories. I went around and explained my situation to people who knew me (Momyer, Holloway, LeMay, Randy Holzapple).

All of them took my side and succeeded in persuading the Chief of Staff to appoint a board to look at this regulation. The Surgeon General was on the board; his was the only opposing vote to the board's recommendation that the regulation be amended to apply to the "whole man." This meant that the pilot's past record and potential should be considered in a decision on flying status.

The regulation was changed and I regained flying status in late February. There was a caveat; the Surgeon General managed to require that I fly in a two-seat aircraft because of the possibility of a recurrence. I could have flown in a T-bird with anyone. Ollie was a good friend with whom I used to shoot skeet, but he didn't think gastrointestinal bleeders should be on flying status.

♠ ♥ ♦ ♣

After I succeeding in obtaining an amendment to the regulation and was returned to flying status, I opened the door for over 200 (possibly 212) other officers. They came through right behind me. Three of them, Bob Purcell, Ed Burdette, and Larry Guarino, were close friends who later became Prisoners of War (POWs) in Viet Nam. At the time the regulation was changed, Burdette was working with me in the Pentagon and Purcell had worked for me in the 31st.

Burdette died in POW camp and was promoted posthumously to brigadier general. He was the only one in that category.

♠ ♥ ♦ ♣

I'll Take One

A new BG in the Air Force is woefully mistreated. He is fair game for any shabby job that has to be filled.

My first assignment was to be Deputy for Operations (DO) of Fourth Allied Tactical Air Force (ATAF), NATO, at Ramstein, Germany. This was a real plum. Those orders were canceled.

Then I was assigned as Director for Plans, Military Assistance Command Viet Nam (MACV), under General Harkins, who preceded General Westmoreland. All the key positions were Army. Plans was an Air Force role, to which Brigadier General Benny Putnam had been assigned. He was a naturally controversial figure who managed to cross wires with old Harkins in three months. Harkins fired him. I was the available to-be BG and had to take it. I regrouped. I had a T-33 and a "seeing eye" lieutenant and I flew almost daily so I could become current again.

On one trip, I flew to George AFB during the annual DESERT STRIKE exercise. Brigadier General "Big John" Dunning, a good old friend, was the division commander there. Major General Carl Truesdale was the Commander of Twelfth Air Force. Dinghy Dunham was also there. I landed after the exercise was completed that day, about half-past five in the afternoon, climbed out of the airplane and found a car John had sent for me. I was driven to John's office, where everyone was having a beer and sitting around in their "Sweeney-greenies," combat fatigues worn with blue scarves and blue background insignia and name tags. We were chatting when the phone rang. It was the Deputy for Personnel (DP) in Washington, who informed John that he had to saddle up and head over to Viet Nam immediately to be Harkin's Deputy for Plans.

I had just finished telling John what had happened! John covered up the receiver, turned to me and accused me of lying to him. I asked, "What is it?"

He said, "They're sending me over there for that job!"

I said, "I don't understand that."

On the telephone, Big John said, "Gordy Graham's sitting here and he thinks he has that job. Why don't you just give it to him?" After a short response, John covered up the receiver again and said to me, "Harkins doesn't want any Mexican generals!" This was a reference to the fact that I had not pinned on my star as a BG. I grinned to myself and said, oh, man!

The second half of the telephone call was, "Tell Graham that he is replacing you." Big John hit the ceiling. He figured that I'd

I'll Take One

engineered the whole thing! I convinced him later that evening that I had had nothing to do with it.

John went. He was only there a few months and died on the operating table at Clark AFB, Philippines, during a minor back operation. Something went wrong.

I returned to Washington and was jumping up and down with glee. It was one of the very posh jobs in TAC. Moreover, they had two-place F-104s, so I could continue flying there. Two days later, I raced back out there with $5,000, a huge sum, from General Sweeney to refurbish the quarters and build another bedroom to accommodate my whole family. Everything was going my way! I put $500 down on a $3,000 house trailer and was going to take thirty days leave to drive with the three kids across country, up through Canada, down through Seattle to see the World's Fair, and finally to George, where I would sell the trailer. My wife did not enjoy camping and was going to fly out.

The movers came and went. At eight o'clock Friday evening, while we were sitting in the trailer, the phone, which had not yet been disconnected, rang. We had rented the house and were leaving the next morning. Gabe Disosway, Sweeney's vice commander, asked, "Gordy, when are you going out to George?"

I replied, "In about twelve hours. I've cleared out the house and the furniture is en route."

"You'd better come down here and talk to the boss before you leave."

I thought, oh, God, I know what's coming and it's going to be bad!

I was up early Saturday and drove down to Langley AFB. I met Sweeney on the doorstep. He was a tall man. I could almost walk under his arm. As we walked into his office, he put his arm on my shoulder and asked, "Gordy, is there any compelling reason why you can't be down at Seymour Johnson tomorrow morning to take over the Fourth Fighter Wing?" Seymour Johnson AFB is near Goldsboro, North Carolina.

I said, "Yes, about half a dozen!" I told him my situation, which he brushed off with, "You can work that out! I haven't heard anything important."

I brought up as one compelling reason that Seymour Johnson had only single-place F-105s, which I was not allowed to fly. Sweeney called the Surgeon General and straightened that out immediately over

148

the phone, so that I was back on full flying status.

My $500 on that trailer went down the drain. I had a dog trailer for my seven dogs and had planned to tow the dog trailer behind the Air Stream trailer. I regrouped and we drove down in the station wagon with the dog trailer to Seymour Johnson the next day.

Chapter 12

I'LL UP THE ANTE
Seymour Johnson AFB, NC: Fourth Tactical Fighter Wing and Nineteenth Air Force

I arrived at Seymour Johnson AFB, outside of Goldsboro, North Carolina, around two o'clock on a Sunday afternoon in July 1962 in a station wagon with three hungry kids, seven bird dogs in a trailer and a distressed and disappointed wife. She had planned a month's worth of visits. It was hotter than hell.

I pulled into a shaded parking place in front of the club so we could eat lunch. The space was marked "Reserved for the Base Commander." Actually, I took up more than one place because of the trailer.

The club was preparing a Sunday dinner buffet so they had stopped serving lunch. My tribe and I sat down. I asked a young woman to bring some sandwiches. She said, "I'm sorry, we're not serving."

I asked her to bring the NCO in charge. She found a sergeant who was less than eager to please. I was wearing a sport shirt, so he could not know my rank. I said, "Sergeant, I just came in to take over the Fourth TAC Fighter Wing. I'm hungry and tired. My wife and kids are hungry and thirsty. I want something to eat. If you want to get it for me as fast as you can, fine. If you don't want to do it, then find a new job." We were served.

Afterwards, we went outside to find a military policeman writing

I'll Up the Ante

a ticket for my station wagon. He was extremely polite. He wanted to see my identification. I showed it to him and asked what was the matter. He said, "You're parked in the base commander's parking spot."

I asked, "Is he complaining?"

He said, "No, sir. He's not here."

I said, "Well, I wanted to park the dogs in the shade."

"I know, but you can't do that, sir."

I informed him who I was and he was immediately apologetic.

I asked him to contact the Base Commander, if he was around, so I could talk to him. He managed to transmit a message to the Base Commander, Colonel Dave Alexander, who was on the golf course.

We drove over to the BOQ. I thought the BOQ or some interim quarters had been set up because I had called ahead. No one knew anything and there were no rooms or spare quarters. I contacted the command post and talked to Alexander on the phone. I ordered him to come over immediately or start looking for a job.

It was silly of me because no one had informed these people of my arrival. I was overreacting.

Alexander was furious when he came and told me, "I'm not sure I believe you." I didn't play golf then, so I did not appreciate how serious interrupting a guy's golf game was.

I introduced myself, "I'm Colonel Graham and I'm taking over the Fourth TAC Fighter Wing from Colonel Evans."

He finally grasped that I wasn't bullshitting him. He found a place for us to stay. That marked my grand arrival as a selected BG!

The Fourth Tactical Fighter Wing was the only wing in TAC that was commanded by a brigadier general. As a rule, a wing commander held a colonel's rank. There was a reason for this unique case: Seymour Johnson had a SAC bomb wing; a KC-135 refueling squadron; an Air Defense F-102 squadron; the Fourth Fighter Wing; and HQ Nineteenth Air Force, which was commanded by a major general. The Fourth TFW Commander was responsible for all base administration and support, which justified a brigadier general. The Fourth was assigned to Ninth Air Force, under the command of General Richard Coiner, at Shaw AFB, South Carolina.

When I first took over the Fourth TFW, I found the wing a little lacking in military professionalism, but became really concerned when

I'll Up the Ante

it didn't pass an Operational Readiness Inspection (ORI). A relatively small number of individuals had to be dismissed for the word to spread and for the remainder to shape up. Before I left, the unit did pass the ORI.

I had the first "Wing Parade of the Year" in August 1962. I started the first "Officer/Airman Once-a-Week Inspection" in February 1963.

In addition, I organized the unit's first reunion. The unit, originally the "Eagle Squadron," later the "Fourth but First," had a great reputation as the highest scorer in Europe, in World War II, and in Korea. I flew with them in Korea. It was difficult to understand why the unit had slipped so.

We invited former pilots from World War II and Korea for this reunion. I was in a quandary when it came to selecting those to be seated at the head table. I wanted all the senior pilots from World War II and Korea who came to receive recognition. In the end, the head table extended the full length of the dining room!

General Sweeney was the speaker at the formal banquet. I don't think General Sweeney had ever addressed a group of fighter pilots before. He said nothing startling, until he moved to how progressive the Air Force had been, how TAC was now in the ascendancy, and declared that everyone who was now doing a good job would be recognized. He dwelt on this far too long. People started to squirm. Finally, he sat down.

The next topic on the program was recognition of the former pilots at the head table. I began by introducing some lieutenant colonel from World War II or Korea who was sitting next to me and asking him to say a sentence or two. This went on down the table. Most of them expressed appreciation for being present and satisfaction that everything was going well for the old Fourth.

The last person on the end was Jim Kasler, who was a fighter ace, had received a spot promotion to captain while in the Fourth in Korea (which he lost when he left Korea, as usually happened), and was then in my wing. He was later shot down in Viet Nam and was a highly decorated POW.

When his turn finally came, Jim had had a couple of boozeberries. He rose to his feet and spoke very slowly and deliberately—totally unlike the way he flew an airplane. "General Sweeney, I heard your remarks about how progressive we are, that TAC fighters are in the ascendancy and that everyone's going to be promoted. I'm Captain Jim Kasler. Ten years ago, in 1952 in Korea, I was Captain Jim Kasler."

I'll Up the Ante

Then he sat down, with a silly, vacuous grin on his face. It brought down the house.

General Sweeney leaned over to ask me in a whisper, "Who the hell is that dumb shit?"

♠ ♥ ♦ ♣

General Sweeney told me that a major reason for my assignment to Seymour Johnson was that, as at Turner, there was no range within striking distance of the base for us to deliver ordnance. Sweeney told me that my job was to complete the Air Force's acquisition of some property near Matamuskeet, on the coast of North Carolina, for this range.

Matamuskeet happened to be a prime place for goose hunting on the East Coast. It was comfortably distant from the base and only mattered to goose hunters. I had some torn loyalties, since I was a goose hunter. However, all the wildlife data supported our position that a bombing range would cause minimal or no disturbance to the game, fish and bird populations.

The whole Matamuskeet area was peat bog and marsh. From time to time, a fire would break out which was almost impossible to extinguish. It would burn for months to a year. The population of the county was 5,000 people. The representative for their congressional district sensed that the local people didn't want a bombing range there, so he took up their opposition as a crusade.

I invited all the civic and community leaders in the area to observe a demonstration at the base of what would occur if we opened the range. First, some airplanes made low-level passes and simulated strafing runs, then some made dive bombing runs. All were dry runs, without ordnance, since it was on base.

I had also built a pit, about four feet across by eight feet deep. It was deep enough for a twenty-five pound practice bomb to detonate harmlessly. The twenty-five pound practice bomb had the trajectory and ballistics of a regular bomb, but had only a five-pound smoke charge to enable the scoring counters to mark it. In the bottom of the pit was some straw, along with some other flammable material. The purpose of the pit was to demonstrate that the smoke charge on the twenty-five pound bomb was not hot enough to ignite anything. To make damn sure that nothing did ignite, I had soaked the materials in water beforehand. For the demonstration, I had two one-gallon pitchers, one

I'll Up the Ante

with gasoline, which I'd invite anyone to smell. Then I switched the container for one that was water with just an odor of gasoline. When the bomb went off, a big white smoke cloud would rise, but everyone looking in the pit could see there was no sign of fire. I couldn't know whether it would cause a fire or not, but I was damn sure going to prove that it didn't!

We gave them a tour of the base, souvenir ash trays, lunch, airplane rides. The bombing range was approved within four or five months.

♠ ♥ ♦ ♣

BLUE CHIP ONE took place at Ft. Bragg. It was a big exercise, including an air demo and air drop by the Army and weapons delivery by the Air Force. This was generated by President Kennedy because of the interest in TAC air and conventional rather than nuclear forces. This was Sweeney's initial exposure to an Army/Air Force joint demo: he'd never seen or done one of these before but he was going to do it right. I, as Commander of the Fourth Fighter Wing, was put in charge since Seymour Johnson was only sixty miles from Ft. Bragg.

All the preparations were peachy-keen; every single airlifter in the U.S. Air Force was on Pope AFB, North Carolina. This included everything from Military Airlift Command (MAC) and TAC that could carry a trooper or cargo.

The exercise was to start with weapons delivery, what we called Landing Zone Preparation (LZP). Minimum weather conditions for a normal delivery were 3,000 feet altitude and five miles visibility; for flyby, it was 2,000 feet altitude and three miles visibility. If weather was worse than that, we didn't do anything.

The day of the big exercise, the weather was stinking. I put up a T-33 with an airborne weather observer, which was on station beginning at daylight; when flight time limit was reached, it was relieved by another one. The weather observer radioed in every fifteen minutes on ceiling and visibility. I was on the ground at Pope. All the guests were there. Flatbeds with observer seats, like mobile grandstands, were to be towed around to view all the ground displays, which covered acres. A sample of every piece of gear that the Army and Air Force owned was on display!

Ceiling was 200 feet and visibility was half a mile. The forecast was for no improvement. A static display preceded the air demo. Nobody expressed any concern, except for those of us involved in the air part. Finally, the first flights had taxied out at Seymour Johnson, ready to go airborne, and someone had to decide whether the demo was a go or no-go. I said, "No way. Cancel it." They taxied back in and shut down.

I went to General Sweeney, who was sitting on one of the stands next to Secretary of Defense MacNamara. All the wheels in the world were there. I had to crawl up the back of the flatbed, like a fence, shinny down the side, and tromp on numerous dignitaries' feet to reach Sweeney.

I said, "Sir, I just aborted the air demo." He told me not to go away, so I trailed around behind him in a Jeep. He waited until that particular circuit was completed and then excused himself and stepped off. We went into Ops. He was furious.

"Why didn't you ask me?"

"Sir, I was in charge. Why did I have to ask you? Weather was way below minimums."

"Haven't you an alternative show?" he inquired.

"No, sir."

General Sweeney gave me a strong going over: "Graham, you have set the Air Force back twenty years."

Overnight, we created a 5,000-footer, a 3,000-footer, and a 200-footer air demo. We ran an air demo the next day, but by then a lot of the big wheels had left. It was a howling success when it went off, became embedded as an annual affair and grew each year. I only ran the first one.

♠ ♥ ♦ ♣

Sweeney wanted to be very close to the Army. Someone informed him about the Forward Air Controller (FAC). A FAC is a combat-ready fighter pilot, an Air Force lieutenant or captain, who is the key person working with the Army at battalion level, particularly troops in contact on the ground. Two FACs are authorized for every infantry battalion and equivalent combat unit.

From long-standing Army-Air Force agreement, two FACs were authorized per maneuver battalion. Until Sweeney's tour, these slots were filled only during exercises or war (in the case of Korea). Sweeney decided to assign permanent FACs to all the Army units. This was a hellacious drain on fighter manpower. We weren't given replacement pilot slots; they came out of our hide. Moreover, even though a FAC

I'll Up the Ante

tour was an abbreviated tour, less than two years, the job was not regarded as a choice assignment; pilots were out of the stream of flying unless they were near some fighter wing that would accommodate them to keep their skills up. To make it worse, Sweeney ordered that we assign our best pilots, no goof-offs, to enhance our image with the Army!

This decision affected the whole bloody Air Force. The FAC officers were directed to go to jump school and earn their airborne wings. Concurrently, wing and squadron commanders and the ops officers were informed that they had to be out in front and become qualified, also. A couple of my good Army buddies thought this was funny. They accepted this as part of their job, to lead the troops. They couldn't fathom why people like me were jumping out of airplanes. We called it "falling out of airplanes."

I was the first Air Force brigadier general to attend jump school. I went to Ft. Bragg, North Carolina. I was forty-four years old, in good physical condition, but I decided I wasn't in that good condition! They treated me like a buck sergeant; I was up at five o'clock and ran five miles in boots and full gear every morning. After five jumps, we were given our wings.

We had to jump periodically afterwards, for which we earned "parachute pay," which was similar to flying pay. I earned both for three months, as dual hazard pay, until some finance officer and legal eagle tumbled to the fact that one couldn't be involved in these two hazardous acts simultaneously. As far as I know, I was the only officer, certainly the only general officer, who drew hazard pay in both departments. At least I didn't have to give back the three months' jump pay.

Major General John Hester, DO, USAFE, was killed on a bad jump in Europe. John was a first lieutenant at Craig when I graduated. John's death slowed the emphasis on jump training for senior officers.

I jumped a total of thirty-four times, including all over the U.S., in Greece, Turkey, Iran, and Viet Nam. I jumped out of helicopters, C-123s, Gooney birds, C-130s, and a C-141. Our minimum practice jump altitude is 1,200 feet. Combat jumps are 500 feet. I never saw anyone killed, but whenever a number jumped, from two to seven were always injured. Usually, they fractured a leg. The Army wrote it off as part of the program.

I had a few bad experiences.

On a big joint exercise at Ft. Bragg, another jumper drifted under me just before I was into ground effect and "caught my air," as we called it, in the Drop Zone (DZ). My chute collapsed and I came down on top of him. He should not have allowed his chute to get under me. I wasn't injured, however, just badly bruised.

On one night practice jump at Eglin, there was an overcast sky and no moon. Throughout the Eglin complex, there are numerous winding streams and asphalt roads, which look virtually identical at night. The border of the DZ was not far from a stream. But it also was not far from a road. The jump master kicked us out short. I was the first one out in the "stick" of jumpers and thought we might be 100 yards short of the DZ. To avoid the trees, I decided the smart thing to do was go into a little stream. It turned out to be an asphalt road. I drove my legs clear up through my ears! I didn't break anything, but I damaged two vertebrae that never healed properly.

Later, I made a bad jump in Iran at dawn, in the dark. I was with the Combat Control Team (CCT), which is the first unit to go in. The Army Assault Team (AAT) goes in with our CCT to protect it while the CCT sets up communications to bring in the main assault force. The first stick landed in a part of the DZ that was littered with boulders six feet high. I hit hard on a boulder. I slid down it and executed a parachute landing fall (PLF), but I reinjured my back.

The Fourth TFW at Seymour Johnson had the only F-105 wing, two squadrons each of B and D models, in the Air Force. The B models had old-fashioned round instruments; the D models had newer vertical instruments.

The F-105 "Thunderchief" (also called a "Thud") was a Cadillac of an airplane. It was superb for the mission it was designed to perform—nuclear weapon delivery. It was big and heavy, more of an attack bomber than a fighter, but a pleasure to fly; it had all the thrust a pilot needed. It was a mistake ever to treat it as a fighter, even though it had all the trappings of a fighter, such as a gun and gunsight, single engine and single cockpit.

However, we had all kinds of difficulties with the F-105. There was a rash of training accidents from the day the F-105 began to reach the Fourth TFW in late 1960 and early 1961.

Some of the problems were due to design deficiencies. The "B" model, in particular, had a control system that was a nightmare. It incorporated a "Swedish cam." When a pilot applied pressure to the stick, there wasn't a direct stick-to-force ratio. In other words, the harder one pulled, the greater the transfer of rotation one should have had in a vertical maneuver. It didn't work that way. There was a flat space on the cam so that, when one pulled the stick to come out of a dive, it would start to respond—and then there would be no further equivalent translation into a more vertical plane no matter how hard one pulled. At the end of the flat spot, all that pressure was being applied so that the translation was suddenly excessive. This resulted in a porpoise effect from over-controlling—called a "J.C." (for "Jesus Christ") maneuver—on dive bomb runs. In a short time, three pilots died. After the third accident, we had enough information to determine the cause of the problem. There were no more accidents like those, but we also avoided that regime.

The "D" model had a very different flight control system. That system was never a problem.

More problems were due to quality control in manufacturing and production, like finding a bag of nuts in a fuel cell. There was one modification program after another, at the plant, the depot and on the base. For example, all the original hydraulic lines in the bomb bay had to be replaced. They curved around the perimeter of the bomb bay and, as the lines had bent, kinks had been created, which restricted the fluid flow or resulted in leaks.

In another case, we found a crack at the main hinge point on a wing. The wings were bolted to the fuselage through enormous holes, in a forging. All the airplanes were inspected and some more flaws turned up. Effectively, the whole fleet had to be grounded; fifty-seven of the seventy-two F-105 aircraft in the TAC Fighter Wing were in the modification program.

By this time, a wing in Europe and one in PACAF had been equipped. A massive program had to be undertaken to fix the airplane. Logistics (now Materiel) Command set up modification lines in Europe, PACAF, at the depot at Brookley AFB, and at Seymour Johnson AFB.

Because there weren't enough people to do this, Logistics Command subcontracted the line at Seymour Johnson to Lear-Sigler. The company was based in California and was not a very large outfit then. Yahoos off the street from California showed up. Some of them had never seen a wrench before. The few supervisors tried to teach them and watch them but it was a real nightmare. My own blue-suiters (Air Force personnel) were looking over their shoulders the whole time

I'll Up the Ante

to assure that we had a satisfactory product.

The commander at Brookley, Major General Emmet Cassidy, and I were on the telephone at least twice a day, it seemed to me. The TAC Director for Materiel, Brigadier General Bill Hipps, didn't like my raising hell. He wanted to mastermind the process. We had several bitter exchanges.

I received a letter of reprimand from my boss, General Coiner, Commander of Ninth Air Force, for interfering and not following channels. This was traceable to General Hipps. I didn't care one way or the other, really, because I accomplished what I needed to do. We didn't lose anything and we obtained what we needed from the program.

There were several configurations of airplanes because of the numerous modifications that were put into the field to match the ones being incorporated in airplanes coming off the factory line. Project LOOK ALIKE was quite simply that, to make them all look alike—a drastic mod to ensure that an airplane in one unit would be the same kind of machine as one in another unit. We spent more than the cost of the airplane on modifications.

♠ ♥ ♦ ♣

One day, the F-105 Standardization & Evaluation Chief from TAC HQ came down. He had been a pilot in the wing before Sweeney pulled him up to HQ for his current assignment. He was going to give some no-notice check flights. One pilot had made it all the way through the list to the last item, a simulated flameout landing. He started one but was going to be short of the desired touchdown spot.

The Standardization & Evaluation Chief told the pilot to take it around. He did so and tried another one. He was long and would have overshot. The third try, he was short again. It was too hazardous to risk continuing. However, he had slowed it up too much. He gave it the throttle and there was a four-second lapse of time, during which the eyelids open, the afterburner lights and the nozzle closes. When you go into burner, it feels as if you wait forever! He waited too long, went too low and too slow. Then the burner caught and he did what we call a "saber-dance" down the runway. He almost crashed into the hospital and was killed.

I was unhappy for two reasons. The Stan. Eval. inspector should have caught it earlier and sent him around again or aborted the run. Secondly, I thought it was a dangerous and stupid procedure to practice

I'll Up the Ante

in a swept-wing aircraft with the sink rate of the F-105.

I did some research. I went over our training curricula for situations involving night flying, instrument flying, navigation, weapons delivery and others. In the first place, a pilot needed 16,000 feet of altitude to start a flameout landing. The pilot had to have complete control of the system, meaning no hydraulic failures. It had to be in daylight and not under instrument conditions. There had to be at least a 10,000-foot runway and a barrier available, because one was going to take the barrier. There were some additional conditions. Analysis revealed a probability of two-tenths of one percent that all the necessary conditions would be present across the spectrum of the training curricula and actual operations. I put all this together and went up to brief the accident to Sweeney. This led to stopping simulated flameouts (SFOs) in the F-105 and, soon after, other Century series airplanes such as the F-104. I felt I had struck a blow for common sense.

♠ ♥ ♦ ♣

In September 1962, the Cuban Missile Crisis began. General Sweeney was overall commander for Air, under Strike Command, as well as being commander of TAC. By a conference call, General Sweeney invited all of the wing commanders to come immediately to TAC HQ, at Langley AFB, Virginia.

First on the agenda was an intelligence briefing. The Deputy for Intelligence was Brigadier General Rockly Triantafellu, one of several SAC imports by Sweeney. I had known him in the Pentagon, in Targets. Sweeney's Chief of Staff, Major General Pop Arnold, was directly from SAC. The Director for Plans had also come from SAC. The Director for Operations, General John Eubank, had commanded Nellis.

This briefing gave us our first inkling of the missile build-up in Cuba. There was recce photography from U-2s and RF-101s that showed very distinct surface-air missle (SAM)-2 signatures—the Star of David emplacement pattern. The missile batteries were arranged on a six-point configuration and the connecting roads made a perfect star. Of course, the meeting was very highly classified. We were instructed to say nothing when we returned but to prepare to deploy.

General Sweeney had been Director of Plans at SAC when he was a brigadier general, which was probably the first time I met him (while I was at Turner AFB). He was very highly regarded by General LeMay and was very capable in many ways. His staff was already

I'll Up the Ante

fully engaged in planning for deployment before we had a directive to do anything.

All of the TAC force that was combat ready was deployed from Eglin AFB south to Key West and on up the East coast, at Homestead AFB, Jacksonville, McDill AFB, and Orlando. The Navy was at Key West.

My Fourth Wing went to McCoy AFB, in Orlando, Florida, under John "J.J." Burns. McCoy was a SAC base. Only one F-105 wing went in there. I was given command of the Provisional Division, with directions to move over 200 fighters (F-100s) and some Air Defense F-102s to Homestead AFB.

Homestead was a big SAC base. Brigadier General Jack Catton was the commander. The whole bloody base was saturated with B-52s and KC-135s—and SAC. Catton had not received any instructions to deploy his airplanes elsewhere.

I was the first deployed senior officer who showed up on the scene. Jack and I began to butt heads. One evening, there was a showdown.

I called General Sweeney to say, "I'm helpless. I can't bring any airplanes in here because there is no place to park them." Sweeney flew down. Catton, in turn, called General Nazzaro, who was CINCSAC, who also flew in.

The four of us, Nazzaro, Catton, Sweeney, and I, met in my command trailer at about ten o'clock at night. The two four-star generals were arguing about who was going to own that base and operate out of it!

General Nazzaro refused to budge: "The Chief of Staff is my boss. He hasn't told me to deploy any airplanes out of Homestead. I'm not moving any."

I had a red phone, a direct scrambler phone to TAC HQ and to the command post in the Pentagon. They called the Chief of Staff of the Air Force on the telephone. Catton and I couldn't hear the other end of the conversation but the result was that Nazzaro seemed about to explode, gritted his teeth, slammed the phone down, and ordered Catton, "Move your airplanes to Wurtsmith right away."

I grinned and slapped old Jack on the back and said, "See, Jack, I tried to tell you in a nice way! And by the way, when you and Jo Beth move out, I want to take over your quarters." I thought he was going to slug me. Of course, she didn't leave while he was deployed. Jo Beth was a wonderful person.

The crisis ended in the first week of October 1962. Before we

I'll Up the Ante

left, Jack Catton returned. One night, we demolished the Homestead Officers' Club. We threw all the potted plants in the swimming pool, and maybe him, too. Jack gave me a certificate about "Graham's Raiders."

Throughout the crisis, target folders were made, crews were briefed, and then we waited. It seemed that every hour, on the hour, the ordnance load would change. Everyone was out on the flight line at all hours of the night reconfiguring the planes with napalm or rockets or whatever.

This activity resulted primarily from changes in planned missions and targets, which ranged from supporting an amphibious or airdropped invasion by ground troops to only bombing surface-air missile (SAM) sites (without an invasion). I never discovered whether these changes were emanating from the Secretary of Defense, Air Force HQ or TAC HQ. Maybe it was a combination. But we were at the tail end of the whip and we were snapped every time they wiggled a finger.

In former years, each fighter squadron possessed one napalm mixer. Over the years, with the emphasis on nuclear weapons and lack of emphasis on conventional weapons, the Table of Equipment had been reduced to authorize only one mixer per fighter wing. JP-4 aviation fuel went in one end and the dry napalm mix went in the hopper. The mix was swirled in a machine and then spewed out into a napalm can. At best, the machine could produce two napalm cans every forty minutes. Then they issued larger napalm cans, which took twice as long to fill! Half of these machines had been dormant in storage and didn't work. When we went racing off to war, I ended up with one operational napalm mixer for over 200 airplanes.

Once, in order to fill the napalm tanks on the strike airplanes by takeoff time, we had to work all night. I arranged for the supply officer to open the warehouse. We took all the brooms available, cut off the handles and issued them to GI cooks, bakers and anyone else around to stir the napalm by hand. We made it. After everyone was buttoned up to go, there was no launch. Less than twenty-four hours later, we reconfigured into something else, like bombs and rockets. Once mixed, however, the napalm had a shelf life of about six months, so the napalm cans went into storage.

♠ ♥ ♦ ♣

President Kennedy, Secretary MacNamara, General LeMay, and

I'll Up the Ante

the whole hierarchy from the Puzzle Palace (Pentagon) came down after the crisis to visit Homestead AFB. Sweeney was going to make certain the President knew he should be Chief of Staff. He came roaring down from HQ TAC, Langley AFB, to supervise this visit personally. He decided what decorations would be handed out by Kennedy, ordered a parade in honor of the President and scheduled a briefing. The whole program was to last about two hours. We had a dry run, then another dry run, then two thousand more.

The decoration ceremony occurred first, on the flight line. Kennedy hung the battle streamers on the flags and handed out some Distinguished Flying Crosses (DFCs). These were well-deserved by the reconnaissance crews of RF-101s.

Next was the parade. Sweeney had arranged for a cavalcade of cars to drive from the flight line around the base. Sweeney was sure to be in the lead car with his right hand on the President's arm. Every six feet along the parade route, on each side of the road, there were to be, alternating, an airman and a soldier. I ran a quick calculation; we would need all the electricians, plumbers, cooks, bakers and everyone else in all the units on the base to cover the route. I reported this to Sweeney, whose reaction was, "Call them out! We have to do this and do it right!"

It came to pass, somewhat short of perfection; hats were on crosswise (possibly the first time they had been worn) and uniforms and shirts didn't fit. After a while, it was funny. Sweeney didn't see the humor of it.

Last, the honored guests were escorted to the briefing room and seated in the front row. I opened the briefing with a five-minute, thumbnail sketch of the size of the operation and an overview of the key events. Then I introduced Captain McQuillen, an F-100 pilot, to give a ten-minute briefing on his mission and how he would have executed it. I had culled Captain McQuillen from among twenty-five or more top candidates nominated from each squadron. What an actor! He was about my size, young, good-looking, and extremely articulate. We had worked on his briefing, polishing it to the point that it was flawless. He spieled it off. I was really proud of this young man. When he finished, he asked if there were any questions.

Kennedy leaned forward a little and asked, "Captain, do you really believe that you could have done all this?"

Without batting an eye, McQuillen replied, "Of course I do, Mr. President!" with an unspoken, parenthetical "you dummy" at the end.

I'll Up the Ante

That brought down the house. Even LeMay smiled. The briefing then broke up, they boarded their airplane and took off.

♠ ♥ ♦ ♣

After the crisis, a cadre of people, including me, was retained at Homestead to write the history and close things down. Also, we started flying normal operations. There was a mountain of napalm cans to be expended because their shelf life would expire before they could conceivably be used in a war.

I obtained permission to expend the leftover napalm on demonstrations. One demonstration on a deserted stretch of beach was put on for the Army troops still at Homestead.

The first flight came in and dropped. It went poof-poof-poof, with about the effect of snapping a Zippo lighter. It didn't make enough of a flame or an explosion to justify a photo. I thought something was wrong with the fusing. We went out and detonated a number of them on the edge of the base and they were just as bad. That napalm hadn't mixed at all. There were big clots of dried napalm mix in the bottom of the cans. There would have been a real fiasco if we had had to drop that stuff in combat.

♠ ♥ ♦ ♣

Tony Hagemann, who had brought in his 522nd Fighter Wing from Cannon AFB, at Clovis, New Mexico, was one of the last to depart. It was a pretty spirited outfit, befitting a fighter group, of course, but requiring a strong hand occasionally. After the crisis, while awaiting departure, his group was looking for things to do. One midnight, they strung out all the firehoses and started a fight in the BOQ. Someone woke me up to tell me that Spot Collins was calling to say they were destroying the BOQ. I jumped in my car and raced over there. They immediately turned the hose on my staff car! Then they recognized the front plate and the fun was over. Tony assessed everyone in the wing five dollars to pay for all the damage and cleanup.

For his next stunt, Tony's squadron cleaned out the base's supply of all the packages of toilet paper sheets and filled their speed brake wells with them. On one of the demos for the Army contingent on the beach, they planned a low pass during which they would flip their speed brakes and rain toilet paper all over the Army. Everything would have gone smoothly except that they had a dum-dum lieutenant in the squadron. After firing up on the ramp, a pilot routinely checks hydraulic pressure, flaps, and other things. This lieutenant popped his speed brakes, which he was supposed to do, and which resulted in his jet exhaust's blowing that toilet paper all over the community. What a mess! Hagemann's boys were out there all day long picking the stuff up.

♠ ♥ ♦ ♣

In October 1963, after sixteen months as Commander of the Fourth TFW, I was transferred to the job of Vice-Commander, Nineteenth Air Force, still at Seymour Johnson, under General Mo Preston.

General Preston had had a heavy hand in force structure decisions three years earlier in the Pentagon when he had been the Deputy for Operations (DO). The Air Force was then closing bases and inactivating units. Nineteenth Air Force, called the "suitcase Air Force," had fifty-five people and was scheduled for inactivation. Lo and behold, Mo was sent down to command the Nineteenth. He called me in and asked what I thought about it.

I said, "General, that's not exactly a job with a lot of future, if you want my candid opinion." I explained the rationale for disestablishing it. But the Air Force had not reckoned on the Strike Command/Kennedy resurgence of tactical air-ground support and all that. Thus, within a very short time, Nineteenth Air Force emerged as one of the most active organizations in TAC!

Nineteenth served a useful purpose in that it provided a permanent, professional planning and executing organization for continuing exercises with the Army. The lowest ranking officer was a major. Likewise, the NCO complement consisted of all technical and master sergeants. This arrangement avoided disrupting regular Air Force units because people didn't have to be pulled out of their units or TAC HQ to man temporary staffs for individual exercises.

Nineteenth Air Force was a very interesting part of my Air Force career. I wouldn't go so far as to say that it was great or enjoyable, but it sure as heck was interesting! All I did was pack, go somewhere, return, and repack. I went on temporary duty (TDY) to India, Iran, Greece, Turkey, Saudi Arabia—wherever an exercise was held or trouble flared.

♠ ♥ ♦ ♣

I'll Up the Ante

The Chinese came across the border at Ladakh, India, in 1962 and carved off a sixty- to eighty-kilometer salient on the north border of India, which they occupied for about six months. They didn't attempt to expand or consolidate it but just hung on and then pulled out. The U.S. State Department wisdom was that this was merely a demonstration to the Indian government that the Chinese could really smash through if they wanted to.

At the time, the Chinese and the Russians had had a falling out. The Russians were vigorously supporting the Indians.

The Indians appear to have requested U.S. aid after the Chinese action. The Indians didn't want a Military Assistance Group (MAG). That was too military-oriented. The selected designation was "Military Supply Mission to India," to be commanded by an Army two-star. The plan was developed in the Joint Staff, not in the Air Force, and the mission was given the name SHIKSHA.

A small number of Army and Air Force officers were assigned to the military mission under the command of Admiral McCain, then CINC-Eastern Atlantic and Mediterranean (NELM), the senior Navy billet in Europe. This added Navy fingers in the pudding. Army STRIKE Command tried to muscle in, even though it wasn't in their area of responsibility. India had managed to fall between the lines, so nobody really had responsibility.

In August 1963, I went with a survey team on my first mission to India. The survey team included a number of agriculture and economic experts, in addition to the military, but I never saw them. I was still in the Fourth TFW at the time. The job of the survey group was to figure out how to help the Indians.

Alert to every opportunity, General Sweeney jumped on the wagon. As a relatively new brigadier general, I was designated chief of the Air Force element. I returned to India in November 1963, with the joint Army-Air Force group.

We arrived in my command airplane, a C-130, on a Saturday at Palaam, the international air field outside Delhi, where we were supposed to be met by embassy people, cleared through customs and immigration, and taken to our cantonment. There wasn't a soul there to meet us. No one knew anything about our mission. We were just a bunch of googan guys who had debarked from a military airplane wearing flying suits with insignia. We were contained in a corner for a couple of hours with our hand baggage. I tried to obtain permission to call the embassy for help. Finally, a flustered embassy peon showed up and apologized.

Next, the Indians attempted to impound any imported electronic

I'll Up the Ante

item, such as a commercial hand-held tape recorder, which I had, or hi-fi tape set that one of the others had; my shotguns, rifles and pistols. I had obtained clearance before launching with all this stuff, but the word had not been passed to the customs people. We were there from morning to dark, arguing. It was hot and miserable. We finally were allowed to leave the airport.

Nothing was ready. The first night, my team had to be put up wherever rooms could be found in downtown hotels. All of this was supposed to have been planned, coordinated, and prearranged. The next day, we sorted ourselves out. On Monday, I went to see the ambassador, Bowles. I wore my uniform.

The ambassador was wearing a sport shirt, hanging out of his trousers. He looked like a Coney Island tourist. He frowned when I entered. After I sat down, he said, "General, you can't wear those clothes here. This [pointing to his attire] is our uniform and I want your people to dress in this fashion. Sports shirts are totally acceptable everywhere except at formal affairs. We're trying to downplay the military establishment. The Indians are very sensitive about the military image."

I responded, "Mr. Ambassador, nobody told me this. Consequently, my people didn't know this and they only brought uniforms with them. They came to work in a military environment, putting up a military project, and I am not going to do anything about it unless I receive an order from my commander in London. I don't think there is any point in discussing it further because that's my position."

He fumed and sputtered, but could do nothing. This was the high point of our relationship. From there it went swiftly downhill. But he did stay out of our project.

The first night in Delhi, and frequently afterwards when I had occasion to visit, I stayed in a big, beautiful old hotel with about 500 half-bald Russian technicians. They were conspicuous by their rolled-up shirt cuffs, big thick glasses, and shirt pockets crammed with slide rules and a minimum of five or six pencils. They were accepted by the embassy people, but we were barely tolerated!

I had one fighter squadron. We were quartered about one-hundred miles north of Delhi at Ambala, a huge Indian Army cantonment with a large air base collocated. It was one of the three headquarters of air defense regions and commanded by an air commodore. He was interesting but not much of a pilot. Colonel Joe Kruzel brought a squadron from Cannon AFB, where he was the division commander.

I'll Up the Ante

He was a fighter ace, an old friend, later a vice commander with Fifth Air Force who retired as a major general. They were quartered at Palaam, where they had eighteen F-100s.

The Air Force's job was to install five air defense radar sites and then to conduct a joint exercise to train the Indians in air defense procedures. I selected sites facing China, of course. When I returned, after the survey visit, the Indians had reoriented all but one of them to face Pakistan! I had a real challenge to change that around. There was a lot of resistance from the Indian Air Force. The chief was a Sikh, Arjan Singh. Later, after he retired, he came to visit me in Japan once. He was not much of an airman but very nice, well-educated, low-key, deliberate, and probably a pretty fair administrator. I never heard any of the lower grade Indian officers exactly cheering for him, but they didn't criticize him, either. His Deputy for Operations (DO) Barker was married to a Russian woman.

Singh's vice commander was Air Vice Marshal Pinto, a good fighter pilot and, highly unusual in India, a very devout Catholic. Pinto and I worked extremely well together, right from the start. He was about my age, maybe a year or two older. Most of my association was with him, even though I should have dealt more with the DO. Pinto informed me about the DO's political persuasion right away and advised me that anything of political or military significance or interest to the Russians would be transmitted by Barker immediately. He had virtually a direct line to Moscow! This was a good alert.

We built the radar sites. The Indians built the control center, using an existing facility. This was as primitive as you could imagine. They didn't want us involved in their internal security.

We also held the air defense exercise, which was not very good. The people had not held an exercise like it for so long that they couldn't remember or had never learned how to do it. They had a stable full of real trash for airplanes; Hawker-Hunters and Folland Gnats. Folland was a British engineer who had invented the airplane. The Gnat was an 8,000-pound airplane with a range of only seventy miles, a point defense fighter that was like a sports car. You put it on like a suit of clothes, not like entering a cockpit. The British had probably fobbed it off on them. I can't believe that the Indians would have decided to buy the plane; it had two .50 caliber guns but no missiles. The Hunter was a second-generation, subsonic British jet. It had an engine that canted down in the aft end. The Indians also had twelve MiG-21s at one highly secure air base.

I'll Up the Ante

I checked out Pinto in one of the two F-100Fs that we had, out of the total complement of eighteen. If I tried to do that today, I would be court martialed before I could climb into the airplane. Pinto rode in the back seat and I took him for an hour ride. We landed, refueled, and I put him in the front seat and let him fly. He was a good pilot. He loved it. I took Group Captain Devasher up, too, and a couple of others. Devasher was the senior operational officer on the scene. He and I became very close friends. We went tiger hunting together. I didn't bag a tiger, but I enjoyed trying!

♠ ♥ ♦ ♣

I wasn't able to fly often because of being based at Ambala, not being handy to the airplanes, and being constantly on the road in my C-130 to check out the radar sites. I had carte blanche flying that airplane; the Indians had no air traffic regulations requiring Ground Control Intercept (GCI) or Identification Friend or Foe (IFF) and no navigation aids, apart from a few low-frequency beacons. It was like flying in the U.S. in the thirties! Palaam, alone in the country, had an Instrument Landing System (ILS).

I did discover one thing while flying around in the C-130: I found three Indian surface-air missle (SAM) II sites, all on the west Indian border and oriented toward Pakistan. There was no doubt about that Star of David signature. No one had told us about them. I took some pictures, using a hand-held 35 mm camera, of the first one I found and went smoking into Delhi to ask our air attaché if he knew about this. He had no evidence of any and clearly didn't want to know anything. Nor did he want the ambassador to know anything. He was a non-person who, other than this one meeting, had nothing to do with us while we were there. Of course, he worked for the ambassador and had his orders, I'm sure, to stay away from us. I held no grudge; that was his situation.

I sealed the photos about seventeen ways and sent them, via the embassy pouch, to Rockly Triantafellu, the Deputy for Intelligence (DI) at TAC. This caused a sensation. They hustled up to Air Force HQ with the information. It was the first knowledge the U.S. had that India had SAM sites.

♠ ♥ ♦ ♣

I'll Up the Ante

The Army's job was simply to supply gear, which involved supply types and logisticians but no technicians or training personnel. The senior Army officer, a major general, was a logistician. He was the Commander of the Military Supply Mission to India but exercised no command or control over our operations or personnel.

Besides providing technical assistance for the installation of the air defense sites and the exercise, the Air Force job boiled down to trying to dispose of all the equipment that kept arriving on scene. The supplies arrived by air, in C-124s and C-133s, at my cantonment at Ambala. One C-133 had to make a forced landing at an airfield near Acra, where the Taj Mahal is. It was there for the duration. That airplane had a history of engine problems and was not in the USAF inventory very long. The crew had a ball for weeks there.

There was a lot of equipment. As you know, when good ol' Uncle Sugar starts pouring that stuff out, he doesn't know when to stop. Poor Indians! For example, the survey mission had discussed with the Indian counterparts how important air conditioning and refrigeration were for U.S. military. The Indians had no refrigeration in the field at all. It was virtually nonexistent in the cantonments and camps. The Indians made out their wish list and it was clear that we had made an impression. The Indians couldn't buy imported refrigerators because the duty was astronomical. I don't remember what the duty was, but it was probably similar to duty on a foreign automobile, which was over 200 percent. Their goal was to equip every senior military officer in the Indian Army and Air Force with refrigerators, which would not be needed after the exercise. They did it.

There were so many refrigerators that there was no place to store them. One was in each six- or eight-man enlisted tent and every one-man officer's tent, each of which was erected on a concrete pad. I used to call living in my officer's tent "practicing being miserable with the Army." The poor enlisted men had so many refrigerators in their tents that they were severely overcrowded. They couldn't turn around! They were using them for closets.

Communications to TAC and the U.S. were almost nonexistent. I mentioned earlier that I had use of a C-130. It was a brand new C-130E that I really used and loved. A very competent major came with the aircraft as the aircraft commander. He taught me how to fly the airplane, under supervision. It was a great airplane! I could nip down to Delhi to the embassy and use their communication system, either by telex or letter. Of course, it was all reviewed by the embassy staff or

I'll Up the Ante

ambassador and screened for compatibility with their positions. Alternatively, I had a single-sideband set, suitcase size. With this, I could talk to TAC HQ at two o'clock in the morning, although not well. This made Sweeney jump up and down for joy; if he wanted to tell me something, he had to call me at that hour. Reception was impossible at any other time.

In the midst of the radar site development activity, General Sweeney came over in a KC-135A to inspect. This was his first and last such visit. Before my transfer to Seymour Johnson, Sweeney had requested that I nominate a fighter pilot to be his aide. He wanted someone smart who understood the TAC lingo. I had given him the names of Skip Stanfield, Bill Creech, and one other. He interviewed them all and selected Bill.

Someone decided that Sweeney could fly nonstop from a SAC base at Torrejon, Spain. I looked at the map. I didn't know much about KC-135As, but it looked like a pretty respectable geographic leap to me. Sweeney wanted everything to be tickety-boo when he arrived at 12:15 p.m., so I made arrangements with the chief of the Indian Air Force, who was to be present with several of the senior officers. There was to be a ceremony and honor guard appropriate to Sweeney's rank.

Creech miscalculated the time difference by one hour. I was at the airfield at 11:05 a.m., a little over an hour before the announced arrival time, when word was brought to me that Sweeney was ten minutes out, "exactly on schedule." They were throttling back so that he would not arrive earlier than expected. I frantically called Creech on the radio and said, "Bill, you were supposed to be here at 12:15! You're an hour early!" There was a deep silence. Obviously, he was talking to Sweeney. At first, Sweeney decided he would come on in and forgo the protocol. The Indian officers were on the scene waiting for the airplane to land, so I relayed this to them. They came hustling out, putting on their turbans.

Sweeney reconsidered. He decided that, if they stayed at altitude and pulled back to minimum cruise, they had enough fuel to orbit for an hour, so the Indians went back inside and dispersed.

Then Sweeney changed his mind again. The airplane was nearly down to fuel minimums when it began to descend. They landed about fifteen minutes early. The Indians assembled hurriedly. I'm sure they had a great appreciation of the yo-yo thinking of the American mind.

The visit did not go smoothly. I took Sweeney up to Ambala in

I'll Up the Ante

the C-130, where we had a short inspection of the cantonment. The first enlisted men's tent he entered was filled with six cots and three refrigerators. I observed that he noticed them, but he said nothing. In the next tent, it was the same story. Outside, he turned to me and asked, "What the hell gives with all these refrigerators? What are you doing with all of them?" I tried to explain, but I know he didn't believe me. He was always skeptical about everything. By the time he had made the rounds, however, he had seen a refrigerator standing in every corner of that cantonment.

Sweeney only stayed for lunch, then left to go back to Spain. He didn't like anything about it; there was an Army two-star while there was only an Air Force one-star; he had nothing but contempt for the Indian capability; he hadn't been spectacularly welcomed by an ambassador throwing his arms around him; and it didn't make him any happier that I was taking orders from the Navy. Sweeney had never thought of going through London, which was the HQ, to pay his respects to CINC-NELM.

♠ ♥ ♦ ♣

I almost flew a MiG-21 in India. My buddy Pinto took me to the base, about fifty miles from Ambala, where their twelve MiGs were kept. Pinto and I had been flying each other's airplanes and I had the brilliant idea that I wanted to fly that MiG. I asked him and, although he hesitated, he said he would look into it. God bless him, he did. He briefed a couple of cohorts well. I was carefully shielded from virtually everyone and transported in an Indian officer's uniform to the base, as an "Exchange Officer." The pilot officer who checked me out in the airplane was probably a protégé of Pinto's and sworn to secrecy.

I was in the cockpit and would have been airborne in another five minutes when some blabbermouth figured it out and blew the whistle. The pilot officer came running out and apologized and said, "I'm sorry, sir, but you have to leave right away."

I asked what the matter was.

He said, "We just had a call from Air Vice Marshal Barker alerting us to the fact that you are on the base and that you are not allowed here." He didn't say anything about flying the airplane, but I'm sure that was part of the conversation.

I climbed out of the cockpit and they practically ran with me to a car, which drove off fast. I had taken my helmet up there with me,

I'll Up the Ante

thinking I might be able to use it, and didn't have time to pick it up. They brought it back to me later. There was no repercussion. I fully expected old Ambassador Bowles to exploit it, but nothing was ever said. Pinto apologized later for any possible embarrassment to me. He said he had tried to keep it close but someone had found out. I assured him that I had not been embarrassed, but rather, was afraid he might be in trouble. He just shrugged it off as another example of how he and Barker were never going to agree on anything!

Tragically, Pinto died in a helicopter accident. He and four senior Army officers were flying near the western border, snooping, when their helicopter hit a wire strung across a canyon. I received word soon after the wreckage was discovered, before they had been able to recover the bodies. The Indians lost a great person and we lost a great friend of the U.S.

About an hour later, I was in our cantonment area in Delhi, taking a snooze on a hot afternoon under mosquito netting. My aide, Lieutenant Bill Grieger, came in and woke me up. He said, "General, I wanted to make sure you knew about the death."

I replied that someone had told me about it an hour earlier. He asked if I wanted to do anything about it. I assured him that we wanted to pay our condolences in some fashion. I asked him to go find out what the procedure was and start working on it.

He looked at me kind of funny and said, "I think that's all going to be handled by the embassy."

I said, "No, Bill, you're all wet. We don't go through the embassy on this. It's a military situation." I could see that he thought he wasn't communicating or that the old man was still half asleep. Finally, he succeeded in telling me that the radio had just reported that President Kennedy had been assassinated.

The funeral for Pinto the following day was quite an event. After the service, there was a wake, just like a Catholic one in the U.S. The widow, wearing black, was present, along with all the family members and everyone who had known him and wished to pay his respects. I stood in line for three hours to give my condolences in three minutes. The next day, he was cremated on the bank of the river and his ashes were sprinkled on the water. I never asked, but assume reasons for his cremation were hygienic and custom.

♠ ♥ ♦ ♣

I'll Up the Ante

Three or four months before I arrived in India, Jackie Kennedy had stopped in India en route to Cambodia, where she visited Angkor Wat. While she was in India, the government presented her with a rare white Indian rhinoceros, an endangered species, for the National Zoo in Washington, which had none. The animal was a big hummer—about 2,000 pounds.

The zoo sent a curator to Gauhati, India, close to the border of then-East Pakistan (now Bangladesh), to make arrangements for bringing it to the U.S. Gauhati had a facility for holding wild animals, located at some distance from a 3,000-ft. airstrip. The poor curator spent several months looking after this rhino while he tried to find some transportation.

Someone in the State Department had the brilliant idea that, since I was over there with a support airplane, I was available to assist in this most delicate mission. A telex arrived at the embassy directing me to go over to Gauhati, put the rhino in the C-130, and haul it to the U.S.

I didn't know how to answer the doggone message and immediately began to explore alternatives. By some miracle, I managed to place a telephone call to the curator. Transmitting a message by telephone in India then was like sending smoke signals.

My C-130 major and I flew over to Gauhati. The curator was frantic to take his rhino home. He was licking my hand from the minute I stepped off the airplane. First, we went to look at the animal. I had never seen one. It was pretty impressive!

We decided to build a cradle and fashion a couple of big slings to hoist the beast onto a flatbed, which we expected to find somewhere in that part of the world, and trundle her to the airstrip. She was not cooperative.

The major was exceedingly proud of his C-130E. It was clean and brand new, one of the first in the Air Force and right off the production line. I could see him gritting his teeth while he pitched in to build the heavy slings and cradle. Finally, he said, "General, I'll do this, but I want you to know that I'm taking a dim view of a bunch of rhinoceros shit in my 130!"

Altogether, I made three trips over to Gauhati. A round-trip took a whole day. At some point, the curator revealed that the rhinoceros was pregnant. I gave that as the primary reason for telling the curator that I could not take the risk of transporting her. The curator was at his wits' end.

Meanwhile, at the other end, I kept making excuses for the delay.

I'll Up the Ante

Eventually, I left without the rhinoceros. I assume she gave birth safely.

Months later, someone sent me a clipping from the *Washington Post*. The rhinoceros had been flown back in a C-124 by the Air Force and was in the Washington zoo.

♠ ♥ ♦ ♣

We buttoned up Exercise SHIKSHA and came on home. The exercise was supposed to be repeated one year later. This did not happen. It collapsed completely for reasons I do not know. Perhaps the Indians had all the supplies they needed to last them for a few years and did not care. Perhaps our relations with Russia deteriorated and that caused them alarm.

♠ ♥ ♦ ♣

Immediately after unpacking from SHIKSHA, we started on Exercise DELAWAR, in Iran. This was the most massive exercise, by an order of magnitude, that had ever been planned or conducted in the Middle East. There was an Army major general in charge of the Military Assistance Group (MAG) in Iran. Air Force Brigadier General "Rock" Brett was assigned to the MAG.

General Paul Adams was STRICOM and DELAWAR was his baby. Old Adams was one of the most irascible people I ever worked for. I never saw him crack a smile and he was the most competent person to chew me out that I ever met. I was the on-scene Air Force commander for the exercise, but Major General Clyde Box, on Adams's staff was the senior Air Force officer. He was a troop carrier. The airborne commander was Colonel Bill Moore, a wing commander at Sewart AFB, Tennessee. He had jumped with me at an exercise in Washington and on a couple of other exercises in the States. I knew Bill knew his business.

This was a 1,000-man drop, with associated equipment such as tanks, armored personnel carriers (APCs), 155 mm guns, etc. The force staged out of Incirlik, Turkey, and flew 800 miles to the drop zone. It was too simple to take them up in a C-130 from the Iranian air base at Vahdati and drop them right back there; they had to come all the way from Turkey!

The weather information was about as primitive as going out in

I'll Up the Ante

the back yard and letting go of a toy balloon to learn the wind direction. There was no weather station between Iran and Turkey. There had never been a program to exchange weather information in that part of the world because no one trusted anyone else. Bill and I took the forecast, insofar as we could, from the commercial airlines. This was not very reliable, but at least it was superior to that of local Iranian weather forecasters. Dust storms can be very bad there, so Bill and I had a go/no go condition in terms of visibility and ceiling that we used for practice drops with a few airplanes. We had checked the route and timing to make sure everything would be right.

For the big drop, a reviewing stand was erected by the Iranians for the Shah, General Adams, and all the dignitaries. There was no Iranian unit participating in the drop and no one making the spectator arrangements had ever seen a drop. I reviewed the plans and objected that the stand was on the downwind side of the drop zone (DZ). Their excuse was that it was facing away from the sun.

The day of the drop, I was talking to Bill in Turkey, three hours away by air, on the single sideband radio. He was ready to launch. The weather was OK, but a little iffy. This was insufficient reason to abort an operation on that scale. We launched. By 8:30 or 9:00 in the morning, I had jumped with the Vahdati-based Combat Control Team and was on the ground, in my jeep with my radio at the DZ, talking to Bill when he was sixty miles out. All the dignitaries were filing in to take their seats. Visibility was slowly dropping due to dust and haze. It settled right on the minimum, which was two miles for that kind of drop. Minimum ceiling was 1,500 feet, but there was no overcast and this was OK. By the time the units arrived, visibility was below minimum, down to about one mile.

I didn't have time for a staff meeting with General Adams to determine a course of action. There were standard plans with minimum conditions required before a mission could be executed; if the minimums weren't met, the mission was aborted or a contingency plan was selected.

I called Bill and said, "Make one pass and see what you think."

He led that entire stream over the DZ and reported, "I couldn't pick up the DZ until it was almost drop time. I know I have soldiers who aren't good enough. It's too risky. I'm heading back to Incirlik. So long!"

By then, the spectators had seen the C-130's roaring overhead for a half an hour and were certainly wondering why nothing had happened. I jumped in the jeep and drove over to General Adams, who was sitting

I'll Up the Ante

by the Shah. I leaned over and whispered, "I've just had to abort the drop." His face turned white, red and then blue. I left promptly.

General Adams soon sent word that he wanted to see me in his quarters. When I arrived, he was sitting backwards in a kitchen chair with his arms crossed over the back. He was tapping his leg with an Army swagger stick that he always carried. It is a picture I will never forget. He ran up and down my backbone by the numbers. After three or four minutes, he asked me a question. I started to answer but he interrupted and began his speech all over again. This pattern repeated several times. I soon shut up and eventually he ran out of gas. I left.

The following two days, the weather was clearly below minimums and there was no question of a drop. We dropped the third day and everything was quite satisfactory. I recall that five soldiers were hurt, but not seriously.

However, there was a stronger surface wind than we would have liked, which affected the heavy equipment. The result was predictable. The heavy equipment was scattered from hell to breakfast at the end of the DZ. Some of it was half a mile off the DZ. One 55 mm howitzer landed only inches behind the reviewing stand. General Adams never had anything unkind to say about it, but he recognized that the potential for creaming the Shah was there. We picked up the pieces and the troops recovered back to Adana.

The Shah then conducted a big inspection of Vahdati. I have a large collection of gorgeous photos of the Shah and Graham trotting around, most with Graham's arm extended to point out things. Some remarkable aspects weren't in the photos.

For instance, the highway and roads over which the Shah traveled were always swarming with security guards equipped with submachine guns. These guards were extremely trigger-happy. They surrounded my office and command post when the Shah came inside. When they couldn't see through the windows, which had been closed to simulate a blackout in a combat environment, these guards just broke the windows with the butts of their guns. Then they leaned in and kept an eye on their Shah.

General Adams left after the inspection and we then swiftly closed out and returned to the U.S.

♠ ♥ ♦ ♣

General Khatami (accent on the first syllable) was the chief of

I'll Up the Ante

the Iranian Air Force. He had married the Shah's sister, which may have contributed to his career development. He was a great person, as wealthy as every Iranian in the upper circles that I ever met was. He wanted to fly an F-100. I took him up and checked him out. If I had been caught doing that, I'd have been in the pokey for the rest of my days. He was a good pilot and, also, a good helicopter pilot. We became very good friends. He was later killed in a hang-glider accident, which had been sabotaged by someone who cut his wires.

♠ ♥ ♦ ♣

Soon after, we planned a CENTO deployment exercise. The Turks, Greeks and U.S. were to play major roles; the Brits and Italians had minor ones. We were to stage from Adana, Turkey, and drop in Thessaloniki, in northern Greece. I parachuted in myself to check it out. The drop zone (DZ) was far better than the one we used in Iran, but it still wasn't very good.

I also made an inspection tour of Adana in preparation for this exercise. I was amazed to discover mountains of supplies there, on the other side of the base from our cantonment area, that had been brought in five years before, during the Lebanon crisis in 1958. There were tons of drop tanks, 55-gallon drums, tents, and everything you could imagine.

A final planning briefing was held in Izmir, Turkey, at the HQ for NATO Sixth Allied Tactical Air Force. All the senior military officers from Turkey and Greece were present. After the briefing, everyone was to return home and prepare to leap off at the end of thirty days.

Before the meeting had completely broken up, a major, one of my intelligence officers, came running in to tell me that a crisis was developing in Cyprus. There had been some incidents. The Greeks were about to send in a contingent. The U.S. State Department was in a total dither about this exercise, involving Turks dropping into Greece in a parachute assault. So the decision was made to abort the whole thing.

An immediate concern was that the Greek officers who had attended the meeting were in danger of being thrown in the Izmir slammer. I surreptitiously boarded the Greek officers in my C-130 that afternoon, sat in the airplane until dark, then took off and flew them back to Athens. I'm convinced the Turks knew about this, but preferred not to make a big splash.

♠ ♥ ♦ ♣

I'll Up the Ante

There was another operation, HARD SURFACE, held in Saudi Arabia in 1963. What an apt name. It was approved when, for some obscure reason, our State Department decided that the U.S. should send a message to the Middle East that we were prepared to go in with force, if necessary.

North Yemen was our friend; South Yemen was not. We were supporting the Saudis, who were backing North Yemen. Egypt was backing South Yemen. The Saudis had a few F-86s. We had trained their pilots. They had no air defense system or ground-controlled intercept (GCI) capability.

We took an F-100 squadron to Dhahran and forward-based ten airplanes 620 miles away at Jidda, on the west coast. A flight surgeon was with the team in Dhahran and a corpsman was with the team at Jidda. The corpsman could hand out aspirin, but that was about all. We were there almost six months.

For this small, super-secret mission, we became non-persons; our mail was directed through Wiesbaden, Germany, using a phony Army Post Office (APO) address. Someone would fly it down to us. We weren't allowed to meet or talk to the Saudis and we couldn't communicate to anyone where we were, what we were doing, or the nature of our mission.

But we really weren't doing anything. The F-100D was a day-fighter/bomber, with no airborne radar or night-intercept capability. We believed that, after a suitable interval, say thirty or forty days, we should be sent home. Finally, we began to feel that someone had forgotten we were there! Whenever I was back in the U.S., I would beat the table and plead with Sweeney to bring the force home.

Then a seriocomic incident occurred. Every five days, two airplanes with their pilots rotated in each direction between Jidda and the main establishment at Dhahran. There was absolutely nothing between the two bases except Bedouins and desert. One of the pilots at Jidda became sick. Based on the radio conversation with the corpsman, the flight surgeon thought it sounded like appendicitis and decided he should fly over there. So we stuffed the flight surgeon in the back seat of an F-100F and it took off. Right in the big-ass middle of Arabia, the engine quit. They stepped smartly over the side and floated down. They landed not far apart and had no difficulty getting together.

The communications gap was such that, when airborne in the middle of the peninsula, a pilot could not communicate with either base. This was where they were. Before takeoff, we always radioed our takeoff time to our destination. When the downed pilot and the flight surgeon hadn't shown up at Jidda by ten o'clock, we sent a two-ship flight, which soon found them by their smoke signal.

Using their handheld escape and evasion radio, the two assured us they were uninjured but had noticed a group of men on horses and camels coming toward them for a couple of hours. They were probably homing in on the smoke.

Everybody was presumed hostile. We had no way to help downed airmen because we were not allowed to arm our airplanes and had no airplanes for dropping relief supplies. We did keep a relay airplane over them. About two o'clock in the afternoon, the riders reached them; they were extremely curious, but friendly. We breathed a big sigh of relief.

I requested a couple of choppers from USAFE. It took the Hueys five days to fly in from Wiesbaden, Germany. They had insufficient range to make a round trip to the downed airmen, so we had to establish a staging point for fuel stock. It took some time to set this up. The pilot called in daily but spoke as few words as possible to conserve the radio batteries. They did complain that they were bloody tired of rice and dates.

I had an interpreter and flew him out in the back seat of the "F." He was terrified. Before we took off, I briefed him to tell the sheik on the ground that we were planning to come in choppers, that we were friends and they should not be alarmed. This was duly communicated during one hell of a palaver.

The interpreter and I made a second trip out to the accident site to ensure that all was arranged. During this trip, we were invited by the sheik to a big farewell party. The interpreter and the sheik's people spoke different dialects, but could communicate. I directed the interpreter to tell the sheik that we would have to leave by 2:00 p.m., because we had to stage in time to return to base before dark.

In addition, I wanted to give the sheik a special present for caring for my airmen. Giving a present is a custom throughout the Middle and Far East. I asked the interpreter to find out the sheik's name, rank and air speed so I could have it engraved on a brass plate, which would be mounted on a Nineteenth Air Force plaque. I wasn't proud of this choice of present but plaques were all I had in my locker.

Before dawn on the day of the rescue mission, we arrived at the staging point. I brought my lieutenant and the interpreter. I couldn't take many because we had to have room for the pilot and flight surgeon.

I'll Up the Ante

We kept one Huey as a spare at the fuel point, which required that we have a security force there, too.

When we arrived, the Bedouins put on a magnificent show. Two or three games were particularly interesting. One involved a pole with a cross-arm, from which was suspended a ball (smaller than a basketball). They rode horses at full gallop toward it and tried to hit it with their spears. When a rider hit or punctured the ball, there was a big hurrah.

They were forever shooting their bloody guns! They would toggle off a round for no reason. They had the greatest assortment of antique firearms you ever saw. I didn't examine them all but I'm sure some of them were muzzle loaders and equally sure there weren't any Winchester repeating rifles.

Under a big tent was spread the feast, featuring a barbecued lamb surrounded by rice and raisins. Some of those raisins were walking. I knew that, as the honored guest, I was supposed to dig the eye of the lamb out with my right forefinger and eat it, smack my lips, and rave about how good it was. Of course, there was no alcoholic beverage of any kind. The interpreter had fully explained the complete protocol that I was expected to follow. I sure wished I'd had a couple of shots of booze to stiffen my spine on that eye business, but I ate that sucker and crammed in a handful of rice to keep it down.

In all, we were about twenty men under the tent, squatting down on our haunches. The women, with their faces veiled, were hanging around the background. Including them and the children, the whole tribe was probably around a hundred. They had goats, sheep, a few donkeys, horses, and camels.

I kept checking my watch as the deadline approached. Finally, I decided that we had to leave. I stood, pointed at my watch, and made some apologies. We formed up outside near the chopper and I hauled out the plaque. Through the interpreter, I told the sheik what an honor the Great White Father in Washington was bestowing on him. It meant nothing to him. He probably didn't even know there is a United States. He accepted the plaque, turned it upside down and inspected it. He couldn't figure out what it was for. Finally, he nodded his head and handed it to one of his henchmen. I could see that I hadn't made any points.

I was wearing a chrome-plated .357 magnum pistol with ivory grips. We had sidearms back in camp and the pilot had one when he bailed out, but we normally didn't display them. I also had a beautiful,

I'll Up the Ante

leather Army officer's belt with a silver buckle.

The women standing behind us had some small bowls, slightly larger than baseballs. I took one from one of the women, put it down on the ground, then walked about twenty yards, pulled out the pistol and fired. It flew all over. I handed the pistol to the sheik. One of his men put out another bowl. Although he knew how to point a rifle, I don't think he'd ever fired a pistol before. By God, he blew it apart with his first shot! He grinned from ear to ear.

I flipped the cylinder, kicked the two empties out, took a couple of rounds out of my belt, refilled it, and put the gun back in my holster. I took off the belt and put it around him. It didn't fit, of course, but he held it until one of his men came up to hold it on him. Then he took out the pistol and looked it over. I showed him how to load it. Through the interpreter, I told him it was my present to him. Mentally, I was asking myself how the hell I was ever going to explain this, because it was a general officer's issue weapon! The Air Force allowed a brigadier general to pick his own sidearm, but I had had my standard .357 dolled up with the chrome and grips. Then I thought, Now is the time to exit—FAST!

The last thing I saw and heard was the sheik firing in the air as we blasted off. He had only a few extra rounds, but I don't think he knew or cared where he would find more.

We never had another accident. In accordance with TAC regulations, however, as commander, I had to report to General Sweeney explaining the circumstances and appoint an accident investigation board.

Naturally, the first duty of such a board was to visit the accident scene. This was not practical, so I manufactured a board report out of whole cloth. I submitted a phony accident investigation board personnel roster; I prepared the twenty-four hour report, the forty-eight hour report, subsequent progress reports, and the final summary report on the findings of the board. The board found that the accident occurred because the "engine quit due to malfunction or unknown materiel failure." Nobody ever questioned it.

I think that accident may have contributed to a decision soon after to terminate our activity there. I'll never know if we achieved some objective. No one ever said, "Thank you for the good job." The only question was, "How soon can you be ready for the next exercise?"

A Photograph Album

Left: One-year-old Gordon M. Graham in Ouray, Colorado, 1919. Right: "Mammy" who lived next door to the author and took care of him and his brother while his mother worked, circa 1920, Ouray, Colorado.

Dodge touring car which the author's mother drove from Taft to Colorado and back in the summer of 1926; the author and his brother, Jay, are in the back seat.

Down for Double

Sixth grade Lincoln Grammar School, Taft, California in May 1928. Left rear: teacher Miss Marie Thomas and at right rear Principal Miss Sarah Grey. The author is in the front row, third from the left.

Major Gordon M. Graham with P-51 D "Down for Double" and "Yank", English bulldog mascot of the 354th Fighter Squadron Bulldogs, Steeple Morden Air Base, England in November 1944.

Down for Double

Major Gordon M. Graham; Captain Lee Mendenhall, Operations Officer; Captain Brady Williamson, Flight Commander; Captain Elldred Speck, Adjutant, 354th Fighter Squadron.

Return from mission in "Down for Double." Crew chief, Staff Sergeant J.J. Murray standing on the wing with his back to the camera, Sergeant Mike Simon, Gordon Graham's armorer, on the ground with his back to the camera. The other men are refueling the aircraft.

Down for Double

Staff Sergeant J.J. Murray, crew chief of the author's airplane "Down for Double" and the author, Steeple Morden Air Base, England in January 1945.

P-51D WR-F the second "Down for Double" before nose painting on take off January 1945, Steeple Morden Air Base, England.

Down for Double

Lt. George Kemper was flying "Down for Double" when he was shot down by ground fire while strafing. He bellied in and German troops apparently moved the wrecked P-51D into a bombed out hanger near Gutersloh, where it was found by Lt. Col. Roberts in April 1945. Roberts photographed the aircraft and contacted General Graham in January 1996 and sent him this photograph.

"I was scheduled on the mission (February 22, 1945) but was pulled off. Lt. George 'Monk' Kemper (right), aborted on the hardstand so I told him to take my aircraft. It was the one and only time I let anyone fly my ship. He was shot down strafing, bellied in and was captured.

After the war, 'Monk' contacted me in the U.S. and sent me this beautiful chrome-plated, ivory gripped German Luger pistol. He had led an uprising in the POW camp about the time it was to be liberated, had a tussle with the camp commandant, got the Luger away from him and killed him."

354th Fighter Squadron in March 1945 in Steeple Morden, England. Back row from left to right: Captain Stan Silva, Lt. Joe Mellen, Captain Al White, Lt. Fletcher, Captain Jim Duffy, Captain "Jabby" Jabara. Front row: Lt. Todd, Capt. Bud Fortier, Gordon M. Graham, Lt. "Gabby" Heaton and Lt. "Long John" Stanton.

354th Fighter Squadron, 355th Fighter Group, Steeple Morden, England in April 1945.

Down for Double

Dorothy Brunel, American Red Cross, and the last of five "Down for Doubles," Steeple Morden Air Base, England in May 1945.

F-100D landing accident (wheels up) 31st Tactical Fighter Wing, Turner Air Force Base, Albany, Georgia in March 1958.

Down for Double

Gordon M. Graham administering reenlistment oath to Master Sergeant Duran who served as his enlisted aide-de-camp. Turner Air Force Base, Albany, Georgia in May 1958.

F-100Ds refueling in flight over southeastern U.S. from a KB-50 tanker aircraft, 31st Tactical Fighter Wing, Turner Air Force Base, Albany, Georgia in May 1958.

Down for Double

The author preparing to taxi out to give Air ROTC cadet an orientation ride in the F-100F, 31st Tactical Fighter Wing, Turner Air Force Base, Albany, Georgia in June 1958.

31st Tactical Fighter Wing weapons team, Tactical Air Command, at "William Tell" the first World Wide Gunnery Meet at Nellis Air Force Base, Las Vegas, Nevada in November 1958. The football being held in the center is a 25-lb. practice bomb. From left to right: 1st Lieutenant "Bud" Homan, Major "Chuck" Horton, Colonel Gordon M. Graham; Major Art Johnson, Captain Walt Bruce. The 31st team took second place honors in the five day event.

Down for Double

F-100D 31st Tactical Fighter Wing, Turner Air Force Base, Albany, Georgia on skip bomb run delivering practice bomb at World Wide Gunnery Meet, "William Tell," Nellis Air Force Base, Las Vegas, Nevada in November 1958.

31st Tactical Fighter Wing maintenance, armament and pilots of the team. "William Tell" World Wide Gunnery Meet, Nellis Air Force Base, Las Vegas, Nevada in November 1958. Graham is in the first row, center, Team Captain.

Down for Double

Sanford "Sandy" McDonnell, Corporate Vice President, McDonnell Aircraft Corporation presenting the "keys" to the first USAF F-110 at St. Louis, Missouri on January 24, 1962. The F-110 was short-lived. Secretary of Defense MacNamara directed that it be designated F-4C. Colonels Graham and Laven ferried the aircraft to HQ Tactical Air Command, Langley Air Force Base.

Brigadier General Gordon M. Graham (date of rank, July 1962).

Down for Double

Dawn jump, Ft. Bragg in 1962, training. Ranking officer was first in the "stick."

Graham, Commander 4th Tactical Fighter Wing, Seymour Johnson Air Force Base, North Carolina, with F-105D Republic "Thunderchief" (also known as "Thud") in July 1962.

F-100Ds randomly dispersed at Homestead Air Force Base, Florida in October 1962 during the Cuban missile crisis.

Brigadier General Graham completing final jump to obtain paratrooper wings at Ft. Bragg, North Carolina in January 1963.

Down for Double

Brigadier General Graham being awarded paratroop wings by Major General Throckmorton, U.S. Army, at conclusion of last qualifying jump in January 1963.

Delegation from city of Ambala, India welcoming the author and contingent in August 1963 at arrival to conduct Joint Air Defense Exercise "SHIKSHA" with Indian Air Force.

Down for Double

Brigadier General Graham talks with Lieutenant General Mohammad Khatami, commander-in-Chief, Imperial Iranian Air Force, after his arrival at Vahdati. IIAF officers, Brigadier General Naimi Rad, left, and Colonel Naderi, second from right, also greeted their commander.

Major General Gordon M. Graham, Vice Commander Seventh Air Force, Tan Son Nhut Air Base, Saigon, South Vietnam in September 1966.

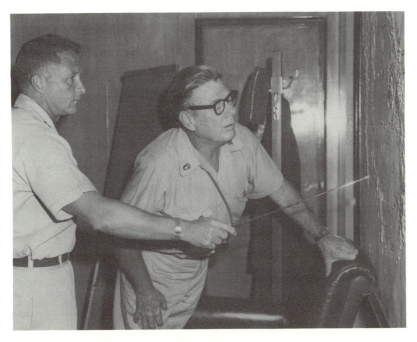

Arthur Godfrey being briefed by General Graham on a visit to the Seventh Air Force HQ, Tan Son Nhut in September 1966.

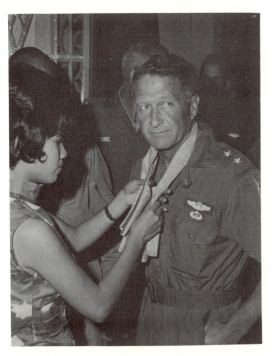

Welcome party for USAF officers by General Ky, Commander Viet Namese Air Force in September 1966, Tan Son Nhut Air Base, Saigon, South Viet Nam.

Down for Double

Colonel "Heinie" Aderholt welcoming the author to Nakhon Phanom Air Base, Thailand in November 1966.

Getting ready to take off on recce mission in RF-4C, Tan Son Nhut Air Base, Saigon, South Viet Nam in December 1966.

Down for Double

Picture showing MiG-21 kill by F-4C over North Viet Nam in February 1967. Photograph taken with the gun camera.

Down for Double

Pre-departure on reconnaissance mission in RF-4 with "GIB" (guy in back) Major Jerry West, Tan Son Nhut Air Base, Saigon, South Viet Nam in March 1967.

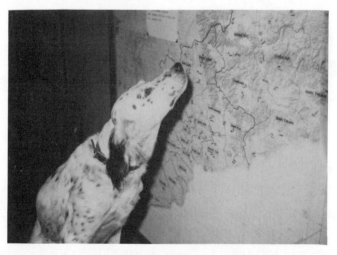

Patsy, English setter, mimicking Lieutenant General "Spike" Momyer, Commander Seventh Air Force, Tan Son Nhut Air Base, Saigon, South Viet Nam March 1967. She went with the author from North Carolina to Virginia to Viet Nam to South Carolina to Virginia to Japan to Turkey and finally died in Japan in 1974—a tremendous bird dog and companion.

Down for Double

Visit of Billy Graham to Tan Son Nhut Air Base, Saigon, South Viet Nam in May 1967. From left to right: General "Spike" Momyer, Commander Seventh Air Force; Billy Graham; Major General Gordon M. Graham, Vice-Commander Seventh Air Force; Brigadier General Thompson, Director of Materiel, Seventh Air Force.

Rocket damage to enlisted quarters by Viet Cong, Danang Air Base, South Viet Nam in August 1967.

Down for Double

Major General Graham, Vice Commander Seventh Air Force, Viet Nam welcoming General Howell Estes, Commander, Air Force Logistics Command to Tan Son Nhut Air Base, Saigon in May 1967.

Lieutenant General Chang, Republic of Korea, decorating General Graham with Korean Order of National Security Merit, Saigon, Viet Nam in July 1967.

Down for Double

Major General Graham at reception for Governor and Mrs. McNair, Sumter, South Carolina in October 1967.

General "Spike" Momyer, Commander, Tactical Air Command and Mrs. Graham pinning three stars on Gordon M. Graham on the occasion of his promotion to Lieutenant General and assignment as Vice-Commander to General Momyer in August 1968.

KC-135 refueling an F-4C in flight, 1968.

Down for Double

Flight of F-4C Phantoms in August 1968.

Lieutenant General Graham, Commander U.S. Forces, Japan and Commander Fifth Air Force 1970-72, Fuchu Air Station, Tokyo, Japan.

Pre-departure in F-4C, Yokota Air Force Base, Japan in March 1970.

Down for Double

Lieutenant General Graham greeting President Pak, Seoul, South Korea in August 1970.

Defense Minister of Japan Yasuhiro Nakasone conferring with Lieutenant General Graham in March 1970.

Down for Double

Lieutenant General Graham and Mrs. Graham, Fuchu Air Station, Tokyo, Japan in June 1972.

General Hayao Kinugasa, Chairman, Joint Staff Council, Japan Defense Agency congratulates Lieutenant General Graham at award of Japanese Order of the Sacred Treasure First Class, Tokyo, Japan in October 1972.

From left to right: General Hayao Kinugasa, Chairman, Joint Staff Council, Japan Defence Agency; Lcdr Toshihaya Baba, Aide to General Kinugasa; Lieutenant General Graham, Commander, USFJ, Fifth Air Force. On the occasion of presentation to General Graham of the Japanese Order of the Sacred Treasure in October 1972.

Lieutenant General Graham, Commander Sixth Allied Tactical Air Force, (NATO) Izmir, Turkey, visiting First Tactical Air Force (Turkey) under his command in June 1973.

Down for Double

Lieutenant General Graham, Commander, Sixth Allied Tactical Air Force, Izmir, Turkey, visiting Greek unit under command Sixth ATAF in March 1972.

CHAPTER 13

I'LL TAKE TWO
LANGLEY AFB: HQ TAC

I left Seymour Johnson in November 1964. From then until August 1965, I was the Assistant Deputy for Operations (DO), TAC HQ, at Langley AFB, Virginia, and from August 1965 to July 1966, I was the DO.

On December 1, 1964, I was promoted to major general.

At TAC, General Sweeney had a staff that tried to imitate General LeMay's SAC staff. The result was a command run by fear, oppression and tyranny instead of loyalty, responsibility, and cooperation. Mistakenly, General Sweeney's senior people interpreted his brusqueness, drive and insistence on perfection and professionalism with harshness and intolerance. They weren't as smart as he was and didn't understand how to do it right. Regardless, his staff's philosophy of command was accepted as characteristic of Sweeney, himself.

♠ ♥ ♦ ♣

SAC had begun imposing its "Management Control System (MCS)" while I was commander of the 31st at Turner AFB. The MCS, like many SAC policies, eventually seeped into every corner of the world. The MCS was a report compiled by the comptroller that reflected every single reportable item in a command, such as number of flying hours, number of maintenance man-hours per flying hour, number of people on leave versus number of people present for duty, and every other thing one could think of. General Sweeney's comptroller retinue was enough to man a full wing. It required hours of staff time to track and compile the data. At TAC HQ, it was mashed together with every other unit's. This was presented to General Sweeney once a month. Pity the poor bugger who had a fighter wing that was color coded red. Yellow was marginal; green was OK; and blue was exceptional — a color coding never achieved by anyone I knew.

Sweeney was obsessed with reports, papers, analyses, and reviews. Ninety percent of it was excessive and unnecessary. But it kept everybody grinding. There was so much of it that it was not possible to distinguish between the valuable and worthless. But Sweeney was smart: he recognized that the wave of the future was tactical air-to-ground operations, limited war, and counterinsurgency. South Viet Nam was just beginning when he took over from General Frank Everest.

♠ ♥ ♦ ♣

In December 1964, my wife and I invited Sweeney and his wife to a Christmas party. He said they couldn't come because he had to go to the hospital at Andrews AFB, Maryland, for a physical checkup. He was a very vigorous person but he hadn't been feeling well. Thirty days after the first trip to Andrews, he went back. Then the word went out that he had cancer.

Sweeney was totally ineffective from about March or April 1965. He would come to the office for perhaps an hour. He was still trying to run TAC and wouldn't turn anything over to his Deputy, Lieutenant General Westover. When Sweeney became ineffective, I, as DO, and Bob Worley, my assistant DO, ran TAC operations.

The Dominican Republic crisis occurred that spring. At first, this crisis called for a total airlift operation, beginning with an airdrop. Then the State Department decided it wasn't going to be a hostile environment so we should land the aircraft. A monstrous stream of a couple of hundred C-130s and C-141s configured for airdrop received orders after they were airborne to reconfigure for a landing. They stopped at McDill AFB, Florida, to reconfigure the best they could, and then proceeded.

Bob Worley and I ran the Dominican airlift out of the TAC command post: twelve hours on for me, then twelve for him, with an

I'll Take Two

hour overlap at the end of a shift, so that meant a fourteen-hour day for each of us. We flew down there at different times to see how it was going.

There was an enormous cantonment and bivouac area, with tents erected all over the place. The Dominican Republic Air Force had a squadron of twenty P-51s. It was feared that the pilots would be dissidents and attempt to strafe the U.S. contingent, so there was a big drive to hunt down the officers and encourage them to surrender or come over to our side—sort of a cops and robbers game. Nothing ever happened; they all turned themselves and their airplanes in.

♠ ♥ ♦ ♣

Sweeney retired in June 1965 and died in August 1965. Secretary of the Air Force Zuckert came down for the retirement ceremony for General Sweeney and to confer decorations on him. There weren't more than a dozen of us in the briefing room for the ceremony, which only lasted ten minutes because Sweeney was so weak he could hardly stand up.

Sweeney was replaced by General Gabe Disosway. Disosway was totally different. Responsibility was delegated back to wing commanders and numbered Air Force commanders. SAC regulations were torn up by the ton. The command was completely reoriented. Morale shot up off the scale. Training became more realistic, with emphasis on conventional, not nuclear, ordnance delivery. The air-ground operations became more oriented toward realism and practical execution, rather than show, smoke and mirrors for the Army. The Army LTG Howze Board and the Air Force Lieutenant General Disosway Board were notable for equipping and executing the Air Mobile concept with more intensive close support air and training.

♠ ♥ ♦ ♣

Of greatest significance was the gradual increase in involvement in Southeast Asia. The Tonkin Gulf incident occurred in August 1964, involving the destroyer, "Turner Joy." The majority of the Air Force units in Southeast Asia were on temporary duty (TDY), but there had been a couple of permanent change of station (PCS) units. We were still operating under the fable of providing "only instruction and advisory assistance, but not participating in combat."

I'll Take Two

There was a feeling in Pacific Air Force (PACAF) that they couldn't continue or augment their effort in Southeast Asia because that would jeopardize their command's primary nuclear mission. So PACAF requested help from TAC.

F-105s, TDY from the Eighteenth Air Force at Kadena Air Base, Okinawa, flying out of Korat, Thailand, in a sixteen-airplane strike, went to take out a bridge in northern Laos. They lost two airplanes. F-100s, deployed TDY to South Viet Nam, conducted a retaliatory strike and attacked targets in Dong Hoi in North Viet Nam, including an ammo storage dump. Some planes were also lost on this strike.

The loss of the airplanes reportedly came as a total surprise to Secretary of Defense MacNamara. How could jet airplanes be killed in that environment by those funny little guys in the jungle, given the aircrafts' speed and ordnance-carrying capabilities? There had to be something wrong with the pilots. He perceived that the Army and Air Force gave him unsatisfactory answers.

MacNamara directed an investigation. A team was formed under Lieutenant General Glen Martin, who was then deputy for plans in the Pentagon. I was named to the team for TAC. Brigadier General Rockly Triantafellu went for intelligence. Major General George Simler went for operations. Other members represented communications, armaments, and other areas. We flew over to study how jet airplanes could be shot down by natives with bows and arrows, literally. We picked up a couple of pilgrims in PACAF, including R.C. Franklin who was then in the DO shop there.

We visited the units, listened to briefings and scoured around. Some of us concluded swiftly that there was nothing mysterious about the losses. A pilot who repeatedly follows a fixed flight path when attacking a ground target will have a high probability of being hit eventually, even if the enemy has only small stuff, like 37 mm and small arms fire. This is exactly what was happening.

We spent a lot of time there, far longer than was needed. After we arrived, our charter was increasingly broadened to include organization, then structure, then units, and anything else that was of interest while we were over there. I was responsible for writing the report, which became the "Graham Report," and presenting the briefing when we returned. By then, it had grown to be voluminous.

First, I presented the results to the air council; then the Chief of Staff, General McConnell; the Secretary of the Air Force; and finally to MacNamara. MacNamara treated it as though we were just clumsy pilots who had too little useful information and too late; we should have had the answer to him long before; and we were embarrassing him by being shot down. Obviously, we were poorly trained and our tactics were worse.

My report changed nothing. Tactics weren't drastically revised. The obvious lesson was disseminated; don't make two passes, one after the other. If you make a pass on a particular heading and then repeat it, the enemy will hit you sooner or later. We were flying too many gunnery range tactics, using the wrong ordnance, like Bullpups against concrete bridges. Taken singly, tactics weren't stupid, but in combination, losses were bound to occur. The pilots were all experienced, but not in combat.

♠ ♥ ♦ ♣

The U.S. commitment in Viet Nam progressed beyond a pure military assistance group (MAG) effort and was assigned to Second Air Division, under the command of Lieutenant General Joe Moore. Major General Gil Myers became Joe's vice commander. Major General George Simler was sent back to Viet Nam as Joe's new DO almost immediately after our first investigation.

Gil was an experienced pilot and actually ran the war. Moreover, there wasn't a more tactically-qualified general officer in the Air Force than Joe Moore.

But Joe lacked the necessary strength in his staff. Until 1966, the staff was composed of cast-offs—TAC officers of whom a wing commander wished to be rid. The Viet Nam conflict was not viewed as important. The pilots were regular unit squadrons, but the non-operational staff and liaison people were expendables. It was infectious: the Secretary of Defense was unwilling to make a full commitment and was satisfied with diddling along. The Air Force leaders' attitude was that, if SECDEF thought it was unimportant, maybe it was.

The Air Force build-up started slowly but increased with that of the Army and Navy. The drain began to affect the TAC force structure. Constant and extended TDY was not a feasible solution. MacNamara and his cohorts rejected PCS actions as long as possible to deny the U.S. presence an air of permanence, but eventually they accepted this. Then, of course, the war was supposed to be concluded on their schedule in a matter of months!

This turned around in late 1965 and early 1966. The name of the game in TAC changed to PCSing combat units, building airfields and more elaborate structures; and PCSing support personnel. Over time, a pretty good manpower organization and structure evolved. Of course, this was increasingly objectionable to the OSD staffs because it demonstrated their inability to predict and control things.

Looking back, we underestimated how really bad it would be. At first, I shared the view that the U.S. was not fighting the counterinsurgency with the right kind of application of force or appropriate tactics. This resistance could be stomped out fairly quickly, at relatively low cost.

My feelings, which I think reflected those of the people in executive positions, were that this was an aberration and a pain in the neck that interfered with our training and real mission. It would go away soon. It was a jillion miles away, anyway, and PACAF should be handling it. We took it seriously, but I don't remember anyone saying that we should prepare for a prolonged effort.

After I went over there on the inspection trip, I started to analyze our behavior and the environment. My assessment changed; I concluded that it was going to be a long, painful experience, similar to the Korean fiasco, and for many of the same reasons. There was even greater micromanagement than in Korea and there was the drift to gradualism and escalation, based on an attitude of "Don't hurt them too much, just enough to send a message. They'll fold."

CHAPTER 14

HIT ME AGAIN

VIET NAM: 7TH AIR FORCE

The time came to replace the Second Air Division with Seventh Air Force. In June 1966, Lieutenant General William W. "Spike" Momyer was assigned as commander; I was assigned as the vice. Brigadier General "Dinghy" Dunham became DO. We lived on base at Tan Son Nhut, near Saigon.

The Southeast Asia theater was under the jurisdiction of the Navy when I arrived in July 1966 for my one-year tour. Captain Kuntz, USN, was the administrative head of base exchanges, POL, construction, supply, logistics and support. The Navy didn't have the resources to do everything to support a land war a jillion miles from Navy ports and facilities. Kuntz was better known as the Mayor of Saigon. He acted the part. He had a big black limousine with a driver, a gorgeous Viet Namese woman friend and spent money like water. Someone blew the whistle on him and he was court-martialed for misappropriating funds and taking kickbacks.

General Westmoreland, Commander of Military Assistance Command, Viet Nam (MACV), changed this when the Army took over everything. The Army Corps of Engineers contracted with Raymond Morrison Knudsen to build all our airfields, including runways and everything, except Tuy Hoa. They had far more work than they could

Hit Me Again

accommodate, so other, smaller contractors were brought in. The Army's airfields were always behind schedule and having problems, such as the matting would buckle or the water wasn't potable. The Army lived austerely, in field conditions, and never built any permanent facilities in Viet Nam.

The Air Force decided it would build Tuy Hoa to show the Army how to do it right. Tuy Hoa was built to Air Force specifications under OPERATION TURNKEY, with Air Force supervision, and was a show piece. The Air Force built long, concrete runways and acres and acres of buildings. The buildings were semi-permanent, of corrugated metal with air-conditioning, and about ten times above the standard in comfort, location and equipment of Army construction. It was called a turnkey operation because Seventh Air Force was given the key to the base the day it was operationally usable.

The U.S. built Phan Rang, Tuy Hoa, Cam Rahn Bay, Pleiku, Bien Hoa, Nha Trang, and greatly expanded Tan Son Nhut and Danang. In Thailand, we built Takhli, Korat, Ubon, Nakhon Phanom and expanded Don Muang, near Bangkok. We also built an enormous B-52 base at U-Tapao, Thailand. We built the runways and taxiways for another fighter base but never manned it; we decided we didn't want to put any more assets in Thailand. The Thais took it over.

We were never crowded, in the sense that we hadn't enough airbases to go around, but we had crowded conditions at all of them, particularly at Tan Son Nhut and Danang. This was partly because we had commercial air traffic at Tan Son Nhut and Marines at Danang, as well as intense Army aviation operations out of both bases.

Cam Rahn Bay was the largest base we had over there. It had been built under the supervision of the Army Corps of Engineers. We built a first class field there, with dual runways and facilities to support C-130s and the 12th TAC Fighter Wing (with F-4s). It was also close to an Army and Viet Namese Army (ARVN) Division. We put up all kinds of facilities, including a huge general hospital. This later was the Air Force/military detoxification facility. We had 10,000 soldiers and airmen who needed treatment before being flown home. It was bad.

The enemy Viet Cong (VC) never targeted or hit it. I'm not sure whether they had plans for it after the war. It was enormous, in a beautiful setting. I always thought that after the war, it would become the Cannes or Nice of the Pacific. The port facility itself was as good or better than anything in the U.S.

♠ ♥ ♦ ♣

We had a constant parade of important visitors. Most were civilians from MacNamara's groups in the Department of Defense. We had to escort them around the country to visit an air base or attend an Army briefing. I had some cards printed up for "Le Directeur du Tour." I developed a ruthless and cruel scheme.

There was a twelve-hour difference in time from Washington, DC, to Viet Nam. The visitors' plane would leave Washington around ten o'clock in the morning, refuel at Hickam AFB, Hawaii, and usually arrive around noon or one o'clock our time, after having been en route twelve to fifteen hours. I would usually greet them, particularly if there was any horsepower aboard. If I didn't, my alternate used the same pattern, so the agenda was very consistent. Every group invariably wanted to hit the ground running, starting with a "working lunch," so no time would be wasted.

Two rooms had window air-conditioners—the officers' mess VIP Room and our briefing room. We first welcomed them in the cooled VIP Room, gave them a couple of pops to loosen them up and then a big, heavy lunch. The food was excellent. Viet Nam was one of the few wars that I have been in where we had good food and lots of it. Some informal five-minute presentations would be given while they were eating.

Then they would be taken to the cool, dark briefing room for a very detailed, two-hour briefing with charts on operations, statistics, sortie rates, etc. The chap in the projection booth knew where the controls for the air conditioner were and would slowly turn the thermostat up so that the room gradually became unbearably warm. Almost always, there was a one-hundred percent casualty rate.

By the end of the briefing, the air would have been gradually cooled down again and the visitors would have awakened. The lights would be turned on and I would say, "I'll try to answer your questions, if anyone has any. If I can't answer, we have other experts here."

Someone would always ask a question that we had covered thoroughly. I would respond, "Well, we pointed all that out. Put slide twenty-two back on, please." There was seldom more than one question.

They were then rushed off to be flown to a base for a tour. There we kept them extremely busy. We would bring them back about eight o'clock at night, go through another debriefing, which was a condensation of the five o'clock Ops meeting. This was followed by a couple of drinks and a big, fat dinner again. Then they were hustled off to bed. At four o'clock the next morning, we woke them up so they

Hit Me Again

could see the "frag" going out. The "frag," short for "Field Order, Fragment," consisted of targets, weapons, sorties.

The visitors asked a lot of questions that had already been answered or were so silly that we had trouble avoiding letting them know how silly they were. An example was, "What is the rate of fire on the F-105 Gatling gun?"

"It is 6,000 rounds a minute."

"Why can't it be fired at 4,000? or 5,000? Why do you just have to use 6,000?" There were some real jellyheads.

Generally speaking, Westy and MACV took care of the congressmen. We saw only a few who wanted more detail on the air aspect.

♠ ♥ ♦ ♣

When the USAF arrived in Viet Nam in force, the first thing that had to be done was to set up a Tactical Air Control Center (TACC).

The Viet Namese Air Force (VNAF) had their own TACC. We had a VNAF officer side-by-side with the USAF officer in our TACC. They knew everything we were doing minute by minute and day to day. As a result, we were less than one-hundred percent effective in country; the enemy VC had ample warning continuously on strikes. Unless a strike was an unannounced divert, the VC were never caught by surprise. They might as well have been in the planning conference. Secondly, the ARVN couldn't execute anything properly. They had to be included in this exercise because it was in their country and they were very jealous of this. It was understandable. For this reason, no VNAF officers were ever involved in the out-of-country strike operations. Of course, we may have been penetrated but the security was much tighter in that than in the in-country part. The out-of-country TACC was completely separated from the in-country one.

♠ ♥ ♦ ♣

The defense of Tan Son Nhut was divided among the VNAF, the ARVN, the U.S. Army and the U.S. Air Force. Every day, there was at least one "Spot Intelligence Bulletin" on our desks with a report of suspected VC activity, usually about a newly-discovered plot to assassinate military officers or invade Tan Son Nhut. We became very calloused about this.

Hit Me Again

Every night, there was harassment and interdiction (H&I) fire, particularly 105 mm and 55 mm artillery by the Army for noise, and there were random bursts of small arms fire. So no one paid attention when they heard shots during the day or the night. Then, once while I was there, sappers did attack the base. It occurred around midnight on December 4, 1966.

Thirty-seven VC penetrated the ARVN sector between two guard towers, which had infrared scopes; crossed a minefield on the side of the base opposite Ops; and climbed down into and up out of a ditch that was about eighteen feet deep and about fifty feet wide. Moreover, they dragged 80 mm mortars and the rest of their arsenal with them a couple of miles or more, across the air patch to the flight line.

The command post called to report that there had been a penetration by an unknown force. I ran out and jumped in my car. I always carried an M-16 with a shortened barrel on a stand in the car. The gun was loaded, locked and hidden.

First I went to the security police HQ. In thirty seconds, I learned nothing from them. They were yelling into phones and everything was sheer bedlam.

I went back to my car. A sergeant in a "bread truck," a maintenance van with an open door that goes from airplane to airplane, roared across the road, slid into the ditch and out, and broadsided my sedan on the far side. My car was still functional, so I drove away and out to the main guard post at the edge of the ramp.

Guard posts were elevated about twenty feet and equipped with floodlights and M-60 machine guns. I jumped out of the vehicle and hollered at the sentry to ask if he could report on the status. I could see two airplanes on fire behind me and a firefight on the ramp.

The sentry pointed out where the sappers were, but yelled that they were out of his field of fire. I ran over to see where he was pointing. There were seven dispersed figures trying to stick plastic charges on choppers. I opened fire and hit every one of them.

It was clearly a suicide mission. They were well-equipped with weapons, including rifles, hand grenades, rocket-propelled grenades (RPGs), and plastic charges, but they were so busy trying to destroy airplanes that they didn't return my fire.

No one knew how many attackers there were or where. Fear was rampant that they were going to make their way to the compound and assassinate all the senior officers. Some people were still running around like chickens with their heads cut off and there was shooting in every

Hit Me Again

direction, but things started to come under control.

I drove to our command post. Some sensible reports were beginning to come in and I started to put them together. The command post had already called Momyer, but I called to update him with what I had learned. I told him, "We really don't have a handle on it, but I don't think there can be very many involved, probably not more than fifty. We're getting a bunch of them." I didn't tell him that I had shot some.

He said, "Keep me informed." He didn't want to come down and add to the confusion, I guess. But it wasn't his duty; it was my job.

In daylight, things returned to normal. They had destroyed five or six airplanes and damaged a lot more. With two exceptions, all airplanes were out in the open on the flight line. The rest were all revetted and were a lot more difficult to reach. They did damage one RF-4 in a revetment, however.

We took a couple of prisoners. Five or six attackers had holed up in underground crypts in an old Viet Namese cemetery on the base. It was three or four days before we dug out the last one. All thirty-seven attackers were killed in action, accidentally, or trying to escape.

Afterwards, nothing really changed. From prisoner of war reports through MACV, we learned of printed "hit lists" to assassinate military leaders. Killing a senior officer earned a VC soldier a promotion, a reward and other goodies. However, I know of no assassination of an officer or even of any attempt.

♠ ♥ ♦ ♣

General Momyer established a daily Ops Meeting, a staff conference which began at five o'clock in the afternoon and usually lasted about an hour. At this meeting, there was a comprehensive review of the day's activities, including reports of missions flown, accomplishments, accidents, and losses, and a description of activities planned for the next forty-eight hours.

Every afternoon, following this meeting, Spike would call to me through the door, since our offices were collocated. I would go in and we would talk about aspects that he thought were vital and should be entered into his diary. He would painstakingly record the significant entries. For example, one entry was: "This is the seventh time we have launched strikes against the Thanh Hoa Bridge. The bridge is still intact. We need better weapons and our tactics are not producing the results they should." He would note the date of significant weather events, such as the beginning of the monsoon.

The next morning, there was another meeting at seven o'clock, after the "frag" had gone out for the day's work. The morning meeting was considerably shorter but had updated intelligence and current weather. By then, it was too late to make any major changes in strikes. At most, bad weather might cause several strikes to be diverted from primary to secondary targets.

I kept a log book which was more of a detailed ops type, with data on the number of sorties, forecast and actual weather. I did it in previous wars, too. I still have them all. I don't know why. I think it was to remind me to not repeat mistakes.

Seventh Air Force managed two different air strike operations; "out-of-country" was in North Viet Nam and "in-country" was in South Viet Nam.

Offensive strikes into northern North Viet Nam were flown out of Takhli, Udorn, Ubon, and Korat, Thailand, and Danang and Cam Rahn Bay, Viet Nam. North Viet Nam was divided into six Route Reconnaissance Packages. We shortened the labels to Route Packs 1 through 6. Route Pack 6 was divided roughly in half; RP 6A was allocated to the Air Force and RP 6B, which was on the coast and included Haiphong Harbor, to the Navy. Thus, pilots in each service had a roughly equal shot at glory and expenditures in the north. Some in the Air Force disputed the equality and proposed swapping back and forth, but we did not. The Navy also had RP 5 and RP 3 and the Air Force, RP 4, RP 2 and RP 1. However, sorties could be diverted from one route pack to another so long as they were coordinated through the airborne command post.

For the in-country war, the standard procedure was for Seventh Air Force to coordinate each day with MACV on allocations of sorties to pre-planned targets for the next day. We always reserved some sorties for "immediates," which were unanticipated new requirements. We also had targets available for "diverts," if sorties had to be reassigned because primary targets were found to be non-targets or weather prevented them from being struck. This minute-by-minute decision-making was accomplished through the Tactical Air Control Center TACC).

In addition, we managed special operations in two areas in Laos, the northern one called STEEL TIGER and the southern, BARREL ROLL. Laos was considered in-country for planning and operations purposes. Route Pack 1, in southern North Viet Nam, was added later as a Special Operating Area, TIGER HOUND.

Target nomination in North Viet Nam was an obscure and complicated procedure. We could do it at Seventh Air Force; the units could volunteer; but basically, the targets came from a Joint Chiefs of Staff list of ninety-two that had been drawn up in 1965. CINCPAC, i.e., the Navy, had responsibility for nominating the targets for us. We always complained, but sometimes we disagreed violently. It made no sense for someone 5,000 miles away to be directing the operation. The Navy strike force in Viet Nam suffered the same fate because their carrier task force responded to the same types of directives.

A fighter pilot assigned to a wing flying missions other than into North Viet Nam flew a one-year tour, with a fixed number of missions, in Viet Nam. Seventh Air Force policy, which had carried over from Joe Moore's Second Air Division regime, was that, if a pilot flew an out-of-country mission, e.g., a strike against a target in North Viet Nam out of Danang or, occasionally, Cam Rahn Bay, then the pilot's tour was reduced by more than an in-country mission. However, an out-of-country mission also included A-1E Search and Rescue (SAR) and Rescue Combat Air Patrol (RESCAP) missions flying over Laos and southern North Viet Nam.

Forward Air Controllers (FACs) and Air Liaison Officers (ALOs) were rapidly being assigned to the ground divisions. Airborne FACs were being reequipped. A big FAC training program had begun back in the U.S. Because there was no existing source for FAC candidates, two fighter pilots were selected from each squadron. Additional SAC, MAC and miscellaneous pilots were "recruited" for the FAC system. These people saw the war firsthand and loved the job.

Momyer added a requirement that FACs fly over their designated areas regularly, so that each FAC would know every little trail, hooch, stream and crossing in his area. FACs would fly these missions almost daily, in addition to flying strike marking and fire suppression missions.

We discovered that the FACs in a squadron at Khe Sanh were finishing their assigned "one-year tour" in as little as three months. They were flying their area familiarization missions over the Demilitarized Zone (DMZ) in Route Pack One and earning credit every time for an out-of-country mission! A few thousand of those runs could be done in no time. Several of those FACs passed through the system before we discovered this and modified the policy. I thought they were pretty ingenious.

♠ ♥ ♦ ♣

Spike instituted a very disciplined staff operation, which was sorely needed. One of us always attended Westmoreland's staff meeting, which was held one afternoon a week. He went to one and he sent me to almost every one after that. It was a typical, ponderous Army staff meeting. The judge advocate would start. He would be followed by all the staff officers with reports of new cases of venereal disease, summaries of decorations for every category, the kill ratio, body count, etc. It was a painful hour and a half, especially to an airman. The air activity report was over in thirty seconds.

I flew 146 missions in Southeast Asia in F-4s and RF-4s. A regular line pilot would typically fly 200. General Hunter Harris was CINCPACAF when we first went to Viet Nam. In 1963 or so, he had sent out a command letter authorizing combat or combat training missions, which could be interpreted to cover missions I flew, even as a major general. I found a copy when I first arrived and licked my lips. I told no one about it.

Momyer was not aware that this was legal. I was current in an F-4 and soon became current in an RF-4. There were a few different switches in the RF-4 cockpit for the cameras, but the rear seater did that job, anyway. The RF-4 had a terrain avoidance radar, which was useful for night and bad weather low-level work.

We had virtually no intelligence coming out of North Viet Nam other than recce. We had to believe the bomb damage assessment (BDA) reports filed by pilots when they returned from their missions. Pilots weren't always accurate, but there was no way to authenticate a report by anyone on the ground or from any successful intelligence nets. CIA was a big zero as far as we were concerned. It wasn't their fault. They just couldn't function up there. But someone had to determine whether the Ho Chi Minh Trail needed more bombs, or whatever. We took miles of film, but one couldn't always have total confidence in that, either. So I went on a few strikes to see for myself. Then I started to fly some in South Viet Nam, more frequently.

There were joint meetings with Westy and his staff. Many times, they were held at the division level, like a division commanders' conference. All kinds of allegations would surface about commanders calling for TAC air when they had troops in contact and it was thirty minutes before there was a response. The system wasn't working. I decided that I would investigate firsthand. I started bringing in and reporting records of the time a contact report was received, the number of the sortie, the time it was over the target, and the type and quantity of ordnance expended. I always ended with, "I was there." This quickly put a stop to that.

There were some errors and some legitimate gripes. One was "short rounds," which was the term for ordnance expended on friendly forces. Almost invariably, it developed that it was a ground forces error; they had given the wrong coordinates or the wrong direction to the FAC. We almost always worked through a FAC. Only in a dire emergency would we drop without a FAC to mark the target.

I flew strikes up north for the same reason. I patrolled that Ho Chi Minh Trail from the border of South Viet Nam all the way up to Dien Bien Phu and on over. I don't know how many hundreds of thousands of feet of film I took over there. I was even named the "Recce Pilot of the Month" once.

I had been flying for about eight months and taking elaborate pains to conceal my activities. The DO, wing commanders and ops officers where I flew knew, but I wanted to keep it quiet because I thought I could be more effective that way. One morning, I flew out of Cam Rahn Bay with a wing man on a very successful sortie in South Viet Nam, for which I reported casualties and destruction of some hooches and an ammo dump I stumbled onto. This was sufficiently significant to be reported as a separate item that afternoon, in a routine briefing on activities. The new young intelligence lieutenant on the staff then blurted out that I was the pilot who had filed the report. Momyer went up in smoke. He immediately called me into a very private session, gave me all kinds of hell, and threatened me with a court martial if I ever did anything like that again.

I didn't say much. I was a lot more circumspect after that, but I kept on doing it. I found out later, however, that he had known I was doing it but had decided not to say anything as long as my name didn't come up.

Why? Because Spike was very disenchanted with our intelligence reporting, particularly on the Ho Chi Minh Trail, up north. One of the wing DOs, Lieutenant Colonel "Woody" Rousher, had worked for Spike in training command. Spike knew Woody well and had a lot of respect for him. Spike sent for Woody to come in personally, in an F-100, and set up a mission so Spike could decide for himself whether the information supplied by the intelligence community was good, bad or indifferent. I found this out when Woody came to me and said, "The boss wants to go on a little sortie up north and I'm nervous."

We didn't send F-100s up north, certainly never alone. I drew the mission up, plotted it all out, picked the places for him to go, and so on. It went off. He returned from the mission and went into the daily Ops meeting, still wearing his flight suit. Then we went into his office. He was grinning from ear to ear. He went to the wall chart and showed me what he had seen and told me how inaccurate the intelligence reporting was. At the same time, he spouted about what we needed to do to change it. He never did say that he had flown the mission, but hell, it was pretty obvious that he hadn't seen it all from Tan Son Nhut! So I had a horse on him.

I came home almost a year ahead of Spike to take Ninth Air Force, at Shaw AFB, South Carolina. When I left, he had a little farewell dinner party for me. Spike paid me a tremendous compliment, for him: "I really appreciate what Gordy has done. If I could have just kept him out of the airplane, he could have done more!" So I knew he knew that I never stopped flying.

Spike and I ran the war in two twelve-hour shifts, with one-hour overlaps at each end. Naturally, I had the night shift. Usually we were both there during the day. I didn't spend the night in the command post. I went back to my trailer and went to bed, but I was on call. There were a lot of administrative, paperwork chores, such as decorations, personnel assignments, materiel problems, airlift.

Spike and I worked together very closely as a team all the time. I rarely did anything independently without either telling him I was doing it or had done it, and vice versa. He was the final authority, particularly in policy or doctrinal matters. I knew where my turf was and where it ended.

Momyer had two hats. One was Deputy Commander for Air, under Westmoreland, a meaningless, non-functional chore. He had an office and secretary in MACV HQ, but I don't think he went in there three times in two years.

Momyer responded to Westmoreland in a reactive fashion. He did what he thought should be done. If Westmoreland was dissatisfied or had some special requirement, he'd do it. Westy ran the in-country air war exclusively, including the B-52 strikes, and left the war in North Viet Nam in the hands of the USN and the USAF.

Hit Me Again

There had to be some coordination with the Navy because of diverted strikes and to prevent overlap and duplication. This happened occasionally, nevertheless. I was flying with a FAC more than once when B-52s would start dropping bombs while a TAC air flight was working the target. We just had to pull the TAC pilots out. This would have been avoided under a single air commander.

Momyer's other hat was Commander, Seventh Air Force. Spike fought incessantly to become the single manager for air. He became the single manager during the Khe Sanh siege, even though the Marines and Navy fought it tooth and nail. He almost succeeded when there was active consideration of an Air Component Commander.

When we arrived, airlift was not consolidated under one manager. We changed that. We took over the CV-2 Caribous from the Army, C-130s and C-123s, and consolidated airlift into an air division at Cam Rahn Bay, under Colonel Bill Moore. We arranged for the C-130 units, which were on TDY from PACAF, to be PCSed.

I was in charge of the switchover of the Caribous in the U.S. Army to the Air Force. That was called Project REDLEAF. The Caribou transfer was actually caused by the Army shortage of chopper pilots. Army chopper losses in Viet Nam were appalling. The airlift force was a ready-made source of pilots to replace chopper losses. The Army airlifters were very unhappy because they were fixed wing pilots.

The Army had parceled out the Caribous to every level of command. Even a company commander could call for airlift. The Caribous hauled everything under the sun, vital or trivial, regardless of priority. Likewise, their maintenance effort was dispersed, which caused problems with spare parts.

We transitioned on the scene. We put an Air Force pilot in the right seat. Then, when he was checked out, we replaced the second Army crew member with an Air Force crew member. Simultaneously, we ran a ground training program. We took over the Army units gradually, one every two or three days.

It was a real achievement for one service to take over — smoothly, effectively, and without interruption — another service's day-to-day operational support in a combat theater, but we did it. Moreover, we almost tripled the sorties and tonnage rates within a month or two.

I was also in charge of the Flying Safety Program, but Spike gave direction and had a hand on it all the time. When we arrived, a pilot could do almost anything in an airplane. He could buzz the field, do a couple of rolls on the way home, or go supersonic over a bunch of

Hit Me Again

hooches and blow off their roofs. The FAC mavericks in the 504th Tactical Air Support Group, including those who were flying missions out of Khe Sanh for out-of-country credit, had a terrible accident rate. This was understandable; the FACs were scattered all over the country, very independent, operating out of Army strips. They took Army guys up all the time and did their jobs. It is particularly difficult to discipline and control groups like them because you have to depend on their judgment and initiative in combat situations. If one tries to hammer them, they will do zilch. We turned this around 180 degrees. The accident rate went from something like twenty per 100,000 flying hours to about three, almost overnight. We bruised a lot of feelings, but it had to be done.

I came to know Westmoreland fairly well. Westmoreland was very methodical and he had a talent for selecting good people for his staff. He was very loyal and protective of his staff, too. Some of them hurt him later. For example, his intel officer was a colonel there. Westy had that man promoted to two stars, finally. He turned around and did Westy a terrible disservice on the CBS investigation of Westmoreland's management of the Viet Nam War. This hurt Westy; he didn't believe someone would do something like that.

Westmoreland was not unique in his approach to the Viet Nam War. He shared the typically-Army views of the time but he was intelligent enough to realize that his World War II experience as an airborne troop had its limits and that there was still a need for groundpounders and heavy, supportable forces like tanks and armor. But like others in the senior Army leadership, he regarded with some distrust the rebellious element in the Army that was embracing new and cooperative interactions with the Air Force.

The Howze Board and the Disosway Board in the early sixties studied the "air-mobile" concept. Max Taylor and others developed the role for helicopters and the "vertical envelopment" strategy. I was no authority but I was able to observe all this because we participated in large-scale, elaborate exercises, such as INDIAN RIVER and GOLD FIRE in Florida, to develop all the doctrine.

Down deep, I think Westmoreland never recognized that there was a separate Air Force. He still looked on the Air Force as another arm of the Army. As one illustration, the Commander of Seventh Air

Force never, at any time, had control over the B-52 force or strikes. Force management, target selection and everything else were done by Westy and his Ops Officer, who happened to be a Marine general when I was there. Westy called an operational conference every Saturday morning. It began at eight o'clock and ran most of the morning. I can still see Westy standing in front of the map on the wall and saying, "Now, I'm going to withdraw *my* B-52s from the delta area and put them into the Khe Sanh area this next week." He considered the B-52s as merely an extension of his artillery force. The same went for TAC air.

The B-52s were on Guam. Later, some moved to U-Tapao, Thailand. They remained under the operational control of SAC, despite the fact that true operational decisions were made in Westy's DO shop at Military Assistance Command, Viet Nam (MACV) HQ. General Jack Ryan, Commander of SAC and, later, Commander of PACAF, supported this philosophy. The arrangement, oddly enough, was comfortable for SAC because SAC did not have to relinquish control of its B-52s to Seventh Air Force.

This violated the basic tenets of "single manager" and "a single Air Force commander in a theater." It stuck in our craw. Momyer probably still loses sleep when he thinks about it. But it was worse than this. The Navy, Marines, Viet Namese Air Force, and Army gunships were independently managed. The net result was that there were six "air forces" operating in one theater, sometimes in the same target area at the same time.

The Marines successfully resisted, on all but one occasion (in February 1968 at Khe Sanh), any use of their forces except in support of the Marine ground division. They refused to allocate sorties to Seventh to frag for in-country targets. The Navy also refused.

However, before or shortly after becoming airborne, when their primary targets were socked in, all airplanes were made available as "diverts," so we could put them on a target through a FAC when they checked in. This was considered all right and did not infringe on doctrine. They were glad to do it because they were given credit for flying the sortie and unloading the ordnance, which in turn filled the service's sortie allocation and ensured that the next sortie allocation would be higher.

♠ ♥ ♦ ♣

Hit Me Again

President Johnson and Secretary MacNamara decided each month how many sorties would be flown in Viet Nam. They communicated this figure directly to the Commander-in-Chief, Pacific (CINCPAC), who then allocated the number among the Air Force, Navy and Marines.

Hypothetically, let's say, the Air Force was allocated 8,500 sorties for one month. The number increased every month for several years. The same happened to the Navy and the Marines. Each service had to fly its assigned number of sorties, no more, no fewer. It didn't matter that there was no lucrative target or that there were more targets than we had sorties. If we didn't fly the number, due to weather or whatever, we had a terrible time explaining it. So we learned to fill the squares, even by flying sorties with ridiculous payloads, to make the Puzzle Palace happy.

The incentive to fly sorties exacerbated a severe Air Force and Navy bomb shortage in Viet Nam in late 1966. As the second in command over there, I was in charge of the daily bomb inventory. We were sending out F-100 sorties with a single 500-pound bomb on each side. Sometimes, we even sent out F-100s with only a pair of 250-pound bombs the Navy gave us. On two occasions, I ordered C-130s to ferry bomb casings from Phan Rang to Cam Rahn Bay, a distance of twenty miles, and return with bomb fins, fuzes and bodies to Phan Rang so we could make the next day's sorties, albeit with a reduced load. We even bought World War II bombs, at a price of $1,000 each, from Germany, which salvaged them from their bomb dumps, and then we paid to have them airlifted to Viet Nam. MacNamara insisted there was no bomb shortage, only a shortage of Air Force bomb inventory management skill.

We suffered from the target selection and ordnance selection at the Secretary of Defense level. The worst management decisions I recall involved targeting of surface-air missile (SAM) II emplacements.

We weren't allowed to attack a SAM site unless it was shooting at us. We lost a lot of good Americans as a result.

A pilot first reported seeing one in North Viet Nam on May 24, 1965. The trademark Star of David pattern, with the crisscrossing roads connecting the six positions of a SAM battery, was visible from miles away. There was a quantity of reconnaissance photography from airplanes that went up all the time.

Hit Me Again

We watched the development of these sites from the beginning. We pleaded constantly and in vain for permission to take them out before they became a real threat to our airplanes. We were backed up by CINCPAC, Admiral Felts. He never torpedoed us once. We were told that the North Viet Namese weren't serious and wouldn't use the SAMs. How they knew this, no one ever told us. We knew that when the North Viet Namese were ready, they would pull the trigger and hit us. They did.

We used one squadron of F-104s for eight or ten months for shallow penetration missions up north. It was the only F-104 squadron in Southeast Asia. The F-104 was an interceptor, but short-legged and limited in capability. It was a guided missile when it was at altitude and flying at full Mach. The highest I went in one was 80,000 feet. It had little, tiny wings. The F-104 carried a couple of Sidewinders and had a gun, but only carried about 4,000 pounds of ordnance, i.e., bombs and rockets.

Lockheed ran a tremendous promotion and sales campaign for it as a fighter-bomber and a lot of people were killed as a result. It was fun to fly but it could not survive: the F-104 was the only fighter that had no APR-37 radar warning device. Without the APR system, it couldn't detect enemy missile radar illuminating it. The warning devices were pretty neat but relatively primitive at first. They developed much faster and became far more sophisticated as a result of that war.

The F-104 squadron went on a mission up north and lost two airplanes that day to the SAM IIs. All hell broke loose back at the sewing circle in the Pentagon. We were directed to attack a designated SAM site with precisely sixteen F-105s— no more, no fewer—making a single pass, carrying 750-pound bombs, Cluster Bomb Units (CBUs) and napalm, between ten o'clock in the morning and two o'clock in the afternoon local time on Thursday. No ifs, no change due to weather, no delay. We sent a message back immediately to inform the Pentagon that it was a dummy site; we had flown over it and knew it wasn't active.

"Go!"

We executed the mission and lost four pilots. Someone must have leaked the information in advance. There was never a word said afterwards. No one apologized or acknowledged it was a mistake, or suggested that we pick the targets from that point on.

Hit Me Again

We were prohibited from dropping in specified areas in and around Haiphong and Hanoi. Circled areas where we could not drop bombs and/or where other restrictions applied were numerous. It was unrealistic to expect a fighter pilot to memorize and be able to recall at any instant all the specific rules of engagement. They were all different for STEEL TIGER, BARREL ROLL, Route Pack 1, and Route Pack 6. As fast as we could challenge and simplify, the gang back in Washington was creating new and more complicated ones.

Jack Broughton was a victim of the complex rules of engagement. Jack was the vice commander of the 355th Fighter Wing at Takhli. Colonel Bob Scott was the wing commander. They had F-105D Thunderchiefs, nicknamed "Thuds."

Jack was a West Point graduate and an unbelievably good pilot, officer and leader. He had been a leader of the Air Force Thunderbirds. He was marked for four stars. I knew Jack very well and was proud to know him.

Jack had flown 103 missions. He only needed 100 for his tour, but he wanted to fly 105 because that was the number of the airplane. On one of his missions, a strike up north, egressing out over the coast, he took some flak. Two majors peeled off and stayed with him all the way back. For this, he felt a keen loyalty and bond.

Later, after another strike, these same two majors took some hits egressing and thought the fire was coming from a vessel in Haiphong Harbor. They peeled off and made a strafing pass at the ship. Too late, they recognized it as a Russian vessel.

We were prohibited from firing on any vessel in Haiphong Harbor because we might strike a nonbelligerent. The two Thud pilots realized what they had done. They landed at Udorn and had their gun camera film removed. This camera is activated each time the gun trigger is pulled and remains on briefly after the gun ceases to fire. The guns were rearmed, the film replaced and the airplane refueled. They then came on to Takhli.

The F-105 also had a strike camera, which sweeps a seventy-degree arc with a five-inch panoramic lens. It is activated when any ordnance switch is depressed and so took photos of the strafing pass. Only the armament officer could remove that. He always put it on a courier to process it at Tan Son Nhut, from where it was transmitted by satellite to Washington. The Pentagon often saw strike photos before I did because they were rushed to process and transmit.

The pilots tried to talk the armament officer into letting them have

Hit Me Again

the strike film. "No, sir, it has to go on the courier." They tried in vain to persuade a sergeant to do it.

At the debriefing, the majors reported that they had expended no ordnance, so they were not obliged to complete the expenditure sheet. They were becoming nervous about the strike film. They couldn't talk the captain into playing ball, so they went to Broughton.

They leveled with him. Broughton called the command post on the radio to tell the armament officer to come to the officers' club with the strike film.

By this time, it was about nine o'clock at night. The captain drove up. Broughton ordered him to hand over the film. Then he walked out in front of the headlights of the truck and stripped it out, exposing and ruining it. He threw it back to the captain and said, "There's your film."

About twelve or thirteen people were standing around. They laughed. The incident was quickly forgotten.

About midnight our time, the Assistant DO at the Hickam AFB Command Post, Colonel Bernie Muldoon, called me. "Gordy, we have a lot of steam coming out of Washington about a short round incident."

I replied, "We have about one every hour. What is it now, at midnight, Bernie?"

He said, "This is a little different. The USSR alleges in the United Nations that we strafed one of their vessels, the Turkestan, in Haiphong Harbor. They want an investigation and some disciplinary action taken."

I tried to reason with him: "Come on Bernie. Hell, Haiphong, Schmaiphong. We don't do things like that. Must be some damn, clumsy Navy pilot. They're always doing that."

"No," Bernie said, "There's more to it than that."

But nothing happened. The Russians continued to claim that they had incontrovertible evidence that the incident had occurred and had involved USAF airplanes, but they never admitted that someone had had a camera that had taken a picture, and that the picture was clear enough to see the tail numbers of the airplanes.

Bob Scott was away on a three-day rest and recreation (R & R) leave in Bangkok. Spike was on R&R in Hong Kong.

I personally flew over there, examined the ordnance expenditure forms, quizzed the wing commanders, made sure they had debriefed every pilot, and conducted a thorough witch hunt. No one had reported expending any ordnance up there. I kept calling Bernie to tell him, in the words Broughton kept telling me, "General, we're as clean as a hound's tooth."

Hit Me Again

Two weeks passed. The turmoil had not died. I had to check all strike airplane reports for that day. There was still a demand for an investigation.

General Ryan came over for a visit. This was soon after he became CINCPACAF and may have been his first trip. Brigadier General Art Pierce, his Chief of Staff; John Vogt, his DO; and two or three others of his senior staff came first to Tan Son Nhut and then proceeded to Takhli, which was the farthest away and the start of the return loop.

Scott and Broughton had a dinner party for them. Everyone went to bed around ten o'clock that night except Jack and Art, who adjourned to the club with the fighter pilots for some drinks. About a half dozen were sitting around with their feet up on the table. The subject of short rounds came up.

Jack said, "Oh, hell, Art. That stuff happens all the time. We don't do it deliberately, but you can't prevent a pilot from misidentifying a target or whatever. Why do you worry so much about it?"

Art's attention started to focus. "Well, what about this one up there in Haiphong Harbor?"

Jack feigned indifference. "Maybe some of my fellows did that. I don't know. We don't pay that much attention."

This really sparked Art's interest. He went back, awakened Vogt, and told him, "I think these fellows know something." By then it was about two o'clock in the morning. They discussed it and decided to go talk to Broughton. Broughton had gone to bed. He did not like being awakened and gave them the idiot treatment.

Next, they found the armament officer who had had the strike film. He told them the story. Then they woke up Ryan. At six o'clock, Ryan was grilling Broughton.

Broughton steadfastly denied the event had occurred. Then Ryan called in the armament officer and said, "This captain said you destroyed the film."

So Broughton confessed that U.S. pilots had strafed the vessel.

Charges were preferred against Broughton and the two majors for violation of the rules of engagement, perjury, and false reporting. There was one specification (destruction of government property in excess of $100, meaning the film).

A general officer had to preside at the court martial. All except one of the general officers in the theater were involved: Ryan's whole group, Momyer and me. The exception was a BG on Taiwan. He was to be president of the court. Broughton's smart defense lawyer

Hit Me Again

peremptorily challenged him, which eliminated him. The president became Chuck Yeager, Commander, 405th Wing at Clark AFB, where the trial was held. Chuck was senior to Broughton.

It was a kangaroo court. I was a character witness for Jack at the trial. The last sentence in my letter was, "I would make an effort to have Jack be a wing commander under me any time, any place." Chuck later told me that my deposition had a great bearing on the decision of the court.

The trial led to the exoneration of the two majors. Broughton was convicted only on the specific charge of destruction of government property in excess of $100. That was all they needed. He was through.

Jack made a gross error in judgment. His error was not in destroying the film but in trying to conceal that destruction. If he had just admitted that his pilots had made a mistake, nothing would ever have happened, but he was very loyal to his people and feared they might be court-martialed.

Jack retired about a year later and went to work for Charlie Blair at Antilles Airboats. After Jack flipped one of Charlie's airplanes, they argued, and Jack quit and returned to Los Angeles. Not long after, he went to work at North American Rockwell on the B-1.

Jack was very bitter about the mismanagement and micromanagement of the war and the personal vendetta conducted against him. He wrote *Thud Ridge* and *Going Downtown*, which are classic descriptions of the ROLLING THUNDER operation. The tragic aspect was that the board for the Correction of Military Records overturned the court-martial conviction and expunged all references to it from Jack's records — after he had retired.

Spike and I had had enough experience in other wars, unlike some zealots in the Pentagon, to know that interdiction of trails by airplanes is impossible. In Korea, for instance, we controlled everything that moved and still couldn't stop a steady stream of peasants from coming down from the north with a fifty-five-gallon drum of gas on an A-frame on each back.

Our constant litany was, "Let us go smash the targets in the north. Turn us loose. We have the weapons and capability. We'll make short work of those targets around Hanoi and Haiphong."

Long after I left, when it was too late, they loosened the shackles.

Hit Me Again

Pilots finally were allowed to bomb the air bases. When I was there, we could watch the North Viet Namese MiGs take off and come up to get us, but we couldn't shoot at them until after they shot at us in the air.

I went on an AC-130 gunship (105 mm gun) interdiction mission. We only killed three trucks, but they were killed dead. Truck bomb damage assessment (BDA) was pretty reliable. Reconnaissance airplanes usually went in the day after a significant strike. The enemy just had a lot of trucks and kept pushing more of them down the trail. They exercised very good camouflage discipline to conceal them. They even hauled stuff on bicycles. The message is, if enough ants are all going in the same direction, a lot of stuff can be moved.

The idea of using the old C-47 Gooney bird as a gunship was originated by a captain at Eglin. I was horrified to find that the Air Force had designated this a fighter airplane, FC-47. "Sailor" Agan was DCSO HQ USAF. I wrote to Sailor, who was an old fighter pilot, protesting that one couldn't prostitute the term "fighter" by putting it on an ancient Gooney Bird! He responded, "You're right," so it was changed to AC-47.

The AC-47 pilots earned every dime they were paid: they were flying ancient, primitive, junky machinery; it was physically uncomfortable to accommodate the guns; and it was hazardous, with the expended ammo cases all over the bloody floor that could cause one to slip and slide, especially in turbulence. But they did the job and saved a lot of the Special Forces camps!

The AC-47 was soon followed by the AC-119 and AC-130. The AC-130s were very sophisticated. They had infrared sensors and radar. The sensors were tied to the gun systems, which included among other things a 105 mm gun. When that bear cut loose, it shoved the airplane about one-hundred yards sideways! I couldn't believe how accurate those gunners were. This was especially evident in Laos, on the Ho Chi Minh Trail.

Using the sensors, the navigators picked up truck traffic coming down the trail at night. They would loiter on the side, put the pipper on a target, and kerblooch! They could pick off the enemy like crows off a wire. The Army loved them, too.

Hit Me Again

In 1965, there were few F-4 units. In 1966, we had F-4 units with the 8th Fighter Wing, under Robin Olds at Ubon, the "Triple Nickel" (555th) Squadron at Udorn, and the 366th at Danang. These were followed by the 12th at Cam Rahn Bay. The F-4 was hampered because it had no gun. The F-4Cs had no pods, even.

The F-105 was totally unsuitable for air-to-air against a MiG because of maneuverability. The F-105 carried Sidewinders and a good gun, but no radar missiles because air-to-air was not its mission. This was a dubious disadvantage because one couldn't fire without a visual acquisition, anyway, but if you were that close, you used a Sidewinder. Nevertheless, the F-105 did manage to shoot down some fighters.

We had over 8,000 Falcon missiles aging on the shelf in Air Defense Command. These missiles were designed for air defense against attacking bombers. The Department of Defense decided to convert the F-4s to fire these instead of Sidewinders. After a pilot turned on the switch, it took two minutes for them to "warm up" so they would fire. When they fired, they were beautiful to behold. But they were very ineffective against fighters in air-to-air combat. This was the reason Robin Olds didn't kill five and make Ace status in Thailand. The USAF reversed this later and returned to Sidewinder.

♠ ♥ ♦ ♣

The first few QRC-200 electronic countermeasure (ECM) pods came to Viet Nam in the fall of 1966. These were put on the two F-105 strike wings. We didn't have enough for one pod per flight so we flew the pods from Takhli one night to Danang to have their F-4s simulate F-105 formations, altitudes and everything. The F-4's would bait the enemy to come up, thinking they would have a bunch of turkeys, and find they were in a hornets' nest with F-4s. Robin Olds led one task force and Skip Stanfield led the other, from Danang. It worked like a charm! In one day, we shot down seven MiGs. All of these were downed by the 8th Tactical Fighter Wing led by Robin Olds. It worked so well that we tried it again three days later and the damn fools came up again. We killed three or four on the second round. Then the enemy wised up.

We had jammer EB-66 airplanes ("Barracuda") in the north and snooper C-47 electronic intelligence aircraft that monitored conversations and relayed them to the ground station in South Viet

Nam. We had nothing to do with space-based intelligence sensors.

♠ ♥ ♦ ♣

All our heavy overhaul work on the F-4s, F-105s and F-100s was done at Clark AFB, Philippines. We ferried the airplanes the 750 miles across the South China Sea.

Practically always, the ferry pilot was someone due for a little vacation, perhaps because he had had a heavy time recently or was halfway through his tour. The pilot was supposed to drop an aircraft off one day and ferry another back the following day. We just winked and let the pilot rest and relax a couple of days. Pilots went solo until we had an incident.

A major and a captain took off in an F-4 from Clark to return to Danang. They aborted the first day because of a Tactical Air Navigation (TACAN) instrument malfunction. The last navigation aid on the way home from Clark was a TACAN station, about seventy-five miles west of Clark, on an island. From that fix, the pilot relied on the airplane's inertial navigation system and radar.

The following day, the two pilots took off and everything was peachy-keen. They checked in with the controller as they swung past the TACAN station. The heading was 278 degrees. They locked onto 278, set the autopilot, and nipped along at 30,000 feet. They noticed that the inertial system needle was starting to wander, but they didn't cross-check with the magnetic compass hanging on their windscreen.

At the usual time, they turned on the radar and were painting Danang Harbor, they thought. They called "Panama Control," on Monkey Mountain (Danang), which was the big controller for that part of the world. They reported that they thought they were one-hundred miles out and they had a good radar return. They asked what the weather was and the usual information. The information was passed so they pressed on. They decided it was time to let down, based on the radar return. They peeled off, went down to 8,000 feet, and broke out of the undercast. One look revealed no Danang, no air base, nothing.

They were over Hainan Island. They fiddled around for about ten minutes before they figured out that wasn't the right place, but they didn't know where they were. They finally decided they were north of Danang, so they picked up a southerly heading. About that time, the Chinese shot them down.

I was in the command post when the word came. Danang

scrambled some F-102s. They went roaring up there and found the pilots in their dinghy. There was a patrol boat approaching them. The F-102s weren't in great shape to do anything; they had only air-to-air missiles. They made a couple of passes and fired some missiles to scare the boat into turning around. It went back and joined another boat. In the meantime, the carrier on the scene, Task Force 77, scrambled some airplanes. They showed up and found the dinghy. We launched an SA-16 to pick them up and brought them back.

Afterwards, we obtained statements from the pilots and I led the team that reconstructed the sequence of events. The radar return from the bay they went into was precisely the same as for Danang. We hadn't known that there was an unusual radar skip distance effect there. They were 200 miles out when this happened. It was an extraordinary conglomeration of errors and events.

Immediately, we directed that planes go in pairs in case of a similar malfunction. We also put a "duck-butt," with a radio transmitter, midway for the pilots.

♠ ♥ ♦ ♣

I dealt with a lot of the DoD Whiz Kids. These people were there long enough to achieve reputations as experts. All they did was say the same thing over enough times that others came to believe them. They and other inventors were always trying to help us.

CAROLINA MOON was a weapon with a 10,000-pound charge and a sensor which was to be dropped on the river above the Thanh Hoa Bridge by a C-130 flying low at 105 knots. The weapon would float down the river and, when the sensor detected that it was under the bridge, would explode and overstress the bridge from the underside to destroy it. A C-130, which could normally carry 30,000 pounds of cargo, could carry two of these weapons.

We received the directive and objected on the grounds that it was suicidal. We were ignored. The first time we executed the mission, one airplane went out and did not return. The next day, reconnaissance photos showed that the bridge was intact. All we knew was that it was an unsuccessful sortie.

The lieutenant colonel in charge decided to send two C-130s, each with two MOONs, together in a second sortie two or three nights later. He was one of the "Be-boys," as in: "Go get them, boys. I'll be here when you get back."

Hit Me Again

There was no moon. The pilots were to fly right on the deck, out over the water, then turn in to make landfall and drop the weapons a mile or two upriver from the bridge and return home. Neither of these airplanes came back, nor was the bridge damaged.

A garbled VC POW report came in sometime later about a "massive charge of explosive found on the bank of the river somewhere in the vicinity of the bridge." That's all we knew about it.

♠ ♥ ♦ ♣

Ambassador Bill Sullivan ran the war in Laos. He was a graduate of the Naval Academy and fancied himself a real strategist in wars of national liberation. His nickname was "Field Marshal Sullivan." TAC provided the people and A-26 airplanes for Operation WATER PUMP, in Udorn, Thailand, to train Laotian pilots. The 56th Air Commando Wing was sent to Nakhon Phanom, Thailand, under Colonel Heinie Aderholt, a dedicated, energetic individual. Sullivan referred to Aderholt's wing as "my Air Force."

The wizards back in the DoD came up with an idea for interdicting the Ho Chi Minh Trail. Ambassador Sullivan heard of it immediately because we were directed to do it in Laos.

This particular scheme was to drop two or three 10,000-pound cylinders of Calgon, the hypophosphate detergent used in dishwashers, from a C-130. The composition of Calgon is such that it acts to decompose clay particles once water is added. These enormous cylinders could be rolled out the stern of the cargo bay and dropped on a major crossroads, one per pass. After the cylinders had been dropped, the rainmakers would come over, seed the clouds, and make it rain. The clay, Calgon and water would combine in a colloidal mix that would render the crossroads impassable, a sea of mud. Thus, the Viet Cong could not come down the Ho Chi Minh Trail and we would win the war.

I recommended to Momyer that we try it in a benign environment in South Viet Nam first, to see if it worked. We had so much rain that we didn't need to make that. We could just wait until there was a good rain forecast, then roll some of those bears out, and walk a ground party in the next day to see whether it was effective. We did this.

We executed three practice sorties near Pleiku and went in to see what it looked like. We discovered that simply dropping the Calgon cylinder did not result in splattering it all over an area. Some of it dispersed, but a pretty good-sized mountain of it was left. We recommended putting some charges in it so that, when it hit the ground, it would explode and scatter.

The crews discovered that plunking the Calgon where one wanted it and having it disperse over the area required a highly precise air drop, flying at 105 knots, which was as slowly as one could fly a C-130, at tree-top level. In addition, one had to make damn sure that it rained within about five or six hours or the stuff dissipated. This was really not our problem. We had only to deliver the goods.

Sullivan was impatient and no one wanted to put the time in on it to really check it out. When Sullivan heard of the test, he sent a long telex (which he was very fond of doing). His last line read, "Let's make mud, not war."

Three passes at 105 knots at one-hundred feet altitude over any trail in use was a sure recipe for extinction. We strongly pleaded that the idea be abandoned. Instead, we were directed to do it. One of the three airplanes made it back, but with a couple of engines shot out and a couple of troops hurt. The rain didn't cooperate. That was the end of that.

♠ ♥ ♦ ♣

One of the DoD Whiz Kids invented a program called RAPID ROGER.

MacNamara asked the question, "Why does the Air Force need so many airplanes? They don't fly twenty-four hours a day. Why don't they fly more than one three-hour strike sortie a day?"

One answer was, "They haven't enough air crews."

MacNamara's response was, "Give them more aircrews."

Next, the answer was, "They have insufficient maintenance people."

MacNamara: "Give them more maintenance people."

The name of the game was to "maximize the number of sorties that a fighter wing could make, with augmentation." The normal "frag" ordered 1.3 sorties per day over a month. This was increased to two per day, around the clock.

We threw up our hands. The 8th Fighter Wing, commanded in the beginning by Colonel Joe Wilson and later by Colonel Robin Olds, was designated the RAPID ROGER Wing. Augmentation proceeded. The program was to last six months.

An enormous quantity of statistical data was taken and entered into the base computer, which was practically overloaded. A team of fifteen or twenty analysts came over from the Pentagon to administer the data collection. The maximum sustainable rate we ever achieved was 1.6. The F-4s just broke down. One can only cram so many airplanes on a runway at one time; only recover in weather so many at one time. One can not augment around these things. They finally heard our plea and terminated the program just short of the six months.

We had a big termination party for the demise of RAPID ROGER. Robin, dressed in a black cloak, with a phantom hat, was executioner. We put a dummy ROGER in a coffin and dug a grave in front of the officers' mess. We photographed Robin driving a stake through the dummy's heart. That party went all night.

♠ ♥ ♦ ♣

A study by Lieutenant General Starbird, U.S. Army, led to a project to use computer technology to detect movement of supplies and personnel on the ground. It received a lot of attention. The technological aspect appealed strongly to MacNamara.

A mock-up was constructed at Eglin AFB. People were brought in and trained in what became the long-term training facility. The project came to be called IGLOO WHITE.

An operational facility was constructed at Nakhon Phanom, Thailand. The Air Force dropped sensors of various types on the Ho Chi Minh Trail in Laos. One sensor could sniff a human scent. Another could detect interruption of a magnetic field. Some could relay sound. For instance, we picked up conversations (in Viet Namese, of course) when the VC found the equipment, such as "What do you think this is?" Some conversations were hilarious. The follow-on aspects became very sophisticated. For example, if a sensor was triggered it would detonate explosives such as antipersonnel cluster bomb units (CBUs). It worked. In addition to VC, we found a lot of dead monkeys and elephants.

Sensors had to be dropped from airplanes because there was no way to push in there on foot. We embraced an externally-referenced long-range navigation (LORAN) system. It was highly accurate, not subject to weather, required little training, and all the sophisticated equipment was on the ground in our territory. We used this system to find the coordinates selected for the sensors and just automatically pickled them off [dropped them from airplanes using the switch for releasing bombs].

Hit Me Again

The next issue was bringing in air power when people were detected. This became very sophisticated. A signal was relayed to IGLOO WHITE, which transmitted coordinates to airplanes on alert, which took off and were on the target within minutes. This involved an enormous expenditure of time and effort.

This "Maginot Line" barrier ran across Viet Nam below the Demilitarized Zone (DMZ) and through Laos along all the trails there, in depth. MacNamara must have believed it would interdict the VC supplies or he would not have expended the effort on it. But it didn't stop the flow.

♠ ♥ ♦ ♣

Lieutenant Colonel "Earthquake" Titus ran Exercise SKOSHI TIGER. It was directed by MacNamara and the Air Force to put a squadron of F-5s in the theater and show how much better they could be because they were cheaper, required less training, and were easier to maintain. Northrop had been pitching this theme for years.

The F-5 had relatively little capability. A major deficiency occurred when the guns were fired: debris, composed of tiny slivers of metal, hit and pitted the windshield. This didn't cause a problem until the pilot had to fly through a thunderstorm or weather, then the windshield became opaque. The F-5 carried little ordnance. Our standard planning factor for range was seventy miles from Bien Hoa, where they were based. They had no legs and only fifteen minutes of loiter time. If they didn't contact a FAC and expend within fifteen minutes, they had to return to base.

They were in Viet Nam for over six months. They generated a lot of excitement and enthusiasm from the cheap-airplane proponents. Thank God nothing ever came of it.

♠ ♥ ♦ ♣

In 1967, General Jack Ryan was CINCPACAF. He was obsessed with the idea that we had a capability to bomb up north in all weather that we were not exploiting. The Air Force was stubbing its toes by comparison with the Navy, which had an all-weather capability in the A-6 and was equipped to do this.

The F-105 "Thud" had a ground-map mode in the radar that had been designed for dropping a nuclear weapon. Precision is less

Hit Me Again

necessary for nukes; the F-105 had a built-in 3,000-ft. CEP (Circular Error Probable, a statistical measure of accuracy for gravity bombs); the airplane moved forward 1,500 ft. as the strobe was moving across the scope.

Ryan came over to Viet Nam. One night, Ryan, Vogt, and some of his other people had dinner with us in Momyer's newly-constructed quarters.

Ryan said, "You don't know what you're doing. You are not professionals. You won't give radar a chance." He insisted that, by gosh we could do it; we just lacked enthusiasm, dedication and will. Momyer quickly became hot under the collar.

The Fourth Tactical Fighter Wing (TFW) with the F-105D was the first wing to have ground-map radar. If there was one person who knew that F-105 radar, it was I. I tried to explain to Ryan that, at 500 knots, the strobe covered 3,000 feet. The best average error (CEP) a pilot could achieve was 1,000 feet. He wouldn't accept that.

Ryan toured the bases, particularly the strike wings. He went to the 8th Wing first. Colonel John "J.J." Burns was DO at the 8th Fighter Wing, which had F-4s. John had worked for me twice, including as my DO at the Fourth TFW. He knew as much or more than I did about fighter radar.

Burns briefed him. Ryan and his group said they didn't like what they heard and accused Burns of making excuses. Burns as much as told Ryan how the hog should eat the cabbage. If Ryan didn't like it, he knew what he could do.

Ryan went livid and issued a direct order to Momyer to transfer and court-martial Burns. Burns had a negative attitude that was infecting the whole wing. Then Ryan and crew left.

Momyer called Burns to come tell him what the hell he had done. Burns did. Momyer ignored Ryan's order and told Burns to go back to work.

We received a lash-up modification to the F-105, which helped some, but we were never able to do what Ryan wanted until we received the first wing of F-111s. They had such a disastrous experience, however, for other reasons, that they were pulled out.

CHAPTER 15

HOLD THESE

SHAW AFB, SC: NINTH AIR FORCE

In September 1967, I became commander of Ninth Air Force at Shaw, South Carolina. I replaced General Marv McNickle. I was there for only eleven months. It wasn't very eventful, but it was one of the best jobs I ever had in the Air Force. I enjoyed the operational aspect and the flying, and the hunting and fishing were super.

The Pueblo crisis occurred in January 1968. I sent a couple of squadrons from Seymour Johnson to Korea, but I was not personally involved.

One tragedy marred that assignment. Bob Worley, who had been my assistant DO when I was DO at TAC HQ, replaced me as the vice under Momyer when I left Viet Nam. Bob was a highly qualified fighter pilot and a close friend for years. While egressing from Route Pack 1, his F-4 was hit and he was killed two weeks before he was due to come home at the end of his tour.

The F-4 ejection system allowed the pilot in the front seat to eject both people. The GIB (for "guy in back") has to go first, whether he does it on his own or is ejected by the front seater. This is because of the blast of the ejection rockets.

Worley and his GIB didn't know that the hit was in the liquid oxygen container area. The wing man was alongside and saw a bad fire. They were just barely over the water and north of Danang when the GIB punched out. The suction effect of the GIB's ejection pulled the flames into the cockpit and Bob never got out. The wing man saw him just crumple.

In my next job as vice commander, TAC, at Langley, a beautiful new HQ building was completed in late 1969. Most of the staff, including plans, personnel, and so forth, moved to the new building. The new one was opposite the old building, where the commander's office remained. I thought it would be fitting to name the new building the "General Robert F. Worley Hall." Other buildings there, such as Lawson Hall and Dodd Hall, had been named after people who had been killed.

I was again working for Momyer. I drew up all the paperwork to name a building after a deceased Air Force officer, which turned into a six-month chore. Approval had to be obtained from the Corps of Engineers based on research to prove there is no other "Worley Hall" somewhere else. The dependents all had to approve. It never occurred to me to ask Momyer; Bob had been his vice when he was killed. I just assumed that he would think it was a good idea.

When the package was complete, I put it on his desk with a note saying, "Spike, please sign this and we can start planning for the dedication."

He called me on the squawk box and I went in to see him. I could tell something was bothering him. He slammed the package down on the desk and said, "Gordy, who in the hell told you to do this?"

I said, "Nobody. I just thought it would be a good idea. Bob was a dear friend of mine. He was your vice commander. The building is just '802' right now."

He said, "If I had wanted to do something like this, I'd have started it."

The next commander was Bob Dixon. I wouldn't be caught in the same world with him, so I didn't approach him. After Dixon came Creech.

Creech was like Jack Broughton—an ex-leader of the Thunderbirds and a terrific person.

I went to Creech and reminded him that he owed me one. Here's a package for "Worley Hall." Creech said, "Gosh, that's a great idea.

Hold These

We'll do her." He was commander there while five years went by. I bugged him about twice a year. He never did sign it.

Jerry O'Malley replaced Creech. Jerry said, "Gosh, yes. It should have been done right away." He started to move it, then he was killed.

Bob Russ followed O'Malley. Bob had worked for me once, when he was a first lieutenant. I trotted over there after a suitable interval and told Russ the story. Bob said, "That's terrible! Unbelievable!" He called his chief of staff in and by gosh, he pasted that thing together. An airplane was sent down to pick up Bob's widow Bette and his four kids. They put on an absolutely super dedication, complete with a Missing Man Formation flyover. I gave a short talk. A big painted portrait was hung in the hall entrance foyer.

CHAPTER 16

I'LL TAKE THREE
LANGLEY AFB, VA: TAC HQ

When Momyer was preparing to return from Viet Nam, he called from Saigon to ask if I would leave Shaw and come to TAC to be his vice commander. We had strong mutual trust and respect, even though we differed violently in certain areas.

This meant a promotion to Lieutenant General. How does one say "no" to an offer like that?

I said, "Yes."

♠ ♥ ♦ ♣

Momyer decentralized some TAC functions to Ninth and Twelfth Air Forces. This reversed some of Sweeney's decisions. People who came after Sweeney were unaware that the centralization had occurred and that some functions were misplaced. Gabe Disosway began the job, but was unable to finish because they required more time. Momyer did a good job.

♠ ♥ ♦ ♣

The Annual Fighter Symposium was to occur at Nellis AFB, Nevada. Practically every general officer in the tactical fighter business attended this symposium. The symposium usually lasted five days. There were panels on developments, tactics, ordnance, and other matters.

Momyer didn't think too highly of that symposium, so he directed me to run it. While I was there, he directed me to run through the Thunderbird show and decide whether it was a go or a no go. Their first scheduled show was in five days.

I flew an RF-4 out from Shaw. "Earthquake" Titus, commander of the wing at McDill, was going out there, too. We rendezvoused en route and hit a tanker. Climbing back up to 37,000 ft., I leveled off and flipped on the autopilot. The airplane made a violent pitch-up. It was about a 6-g snap and I thought I had shed the tanks. After it peaked, the reverse occurred. In spite of my straps being locked, I went down so abruptly that I hit my head on the canopy. The "guy-in-back," was screaming bloody murder. We began to pull another pitch-up. At this point, I thought for sure the airplane would depart and spin, so I pulled the drag chute and, also kicked the stabilizer augmentation, which kicks off the autopilot. The autopilot went off and the chute stabilized us. We lost about 15,000 feet of altitude. I jettisoned the chute and recovered my wits. I said, "Earthquake, come check me. I might have lost my tanks." On the left pylon was a cargo tank, in which we carried clothes and gear. I had a shotgun, tennis racquet, and God knows what else in there.

He said, "OK. Gee, you didn't expect me to follow you through on all that, did you?" He reported that the tanks were all right and he saw no damage, so we went on to Nellis. I was a little short on fuel, but had enough.

We were at Nellis for four days. I checked the airplane and couldn't find anything wrong, signed it off and flew it back. However, I never turned the autopilot on and I never had my hand off that stick.

About four months later, I was reading the daily reports on flying accidents. An incident report came across my desk about an RF-4 from Shaw which described an almost identical situation. The pilots were flying at night, about 20,000 ft. I grabbed the telephone, contacted the command post to put me through to Shaw, track down the data on the airplane, and sure enough, it was the same airplane!

I called my buddy Bob Little at the factory in St. Louis, who had been the chief test pilot and later became corporate VP for McDonnell Douglas, and told him the circumstances. I said, "Bob, you just bought an RF-4 back! You can fix it. We've looked all over this plane and can't find

I'll Take Three

anything wrong. I want a new airplane."

They sent a team which found the malfunction. The artificial "feel" system in the F-4 has a bellows with a port fore and aft to make the feel resemble the actual pressure on the stick. The bellows opens and closes, together with the pressure on the stick. A piece of masking tape, which had been used to distinguish the hydraulic lines from other (fuel, etc.) lines, had adhered to the bellows and would periodically cover the bellows port, which sent a spurious signal to the airplane control system.

♠ ♥ ♦ ♣

The first night at Nellis, the old fighter gang was there; I was the only three-star; the two-stars included Willie P. McBride, George Simler, Al Schinz, Gordy Blood, and Zack Taylor. The DO at TAC, Moose Hardin, an airlifter, not a fighter pilot, was there, too. He was the senior two-star present. I called young Joe Moore, the head of the Thunderbird team, who came to the bar to find us. I told him that I had been given the authority to decide whether he would be permitted to put on his show.

I said, "The symposium doesn't start until tomorrow afternoon. Can you set it up with your guys to run through the show tomorrow morning? I'll ride with you, in your back seat." That was great, as far as he was concerned.

After we had thrown a couple back, I smugly announced to Gordy and Moose that I was going to "dust off the Thunderbirds" while I was there. Moose said, "Gordy, I'm the DO. How about my going along, too?"

I said, "I don't see any reason why not. There are more back seats."

Old Gordy said, "Well, jeez, there are five of them—four and the solo. Why can't we all do this?" This was a great idea. So, by rank, we picked five, including Gordy and Moose, of course. Willie P. McBride was outranked and didn't make the cut. He has never forgiven me for this.

The Thunderbirds are very publicity-conscious; when we arrived on the flight line, there were suits with the bomb-burst-with-stars insignia for us, a photographer and all kinds of Thunderbird trinkets. Before we left, they had prepared an album for each of us.

Someone evidently cued the tower. While we were taxiing out

for the show, the tower operator called Joe and asked, "How many stars have you in your airplanes?"

He said, "Thirteen." The Thunderbirds put together a photo album, which I still have, of the "Thunderbird ORI."

We went through the show. Young Joe rolled my socks down about ten times. It was a hell of demonstration. Most of the time, we were leaning on six g's. In the back seat, it feels more like twenty. They had no maneuver or routine that I considered hazardous. None of us five passengers had a single criticism. The symposium started that afternoon and was highly successful.

When I returned from Nellis, I wrote a one-page memo to Momyer describing the actual Thunderbird maneuvers (rolls, whifferdills and so forth), their approximate airspeeds, altitudes, and g-forces. I stated that I had checked out the show. It was one-hundred percent safe and in the hands of real professionals and I recommended letting them proceed. I clipped the album to it, to show him that we had really done our job, and put it on his desk.

He exploded! He became so mad reading it that he hollered at me to come into his office. He ran up and down the floor, pounded the desk, and kept asking, "What if you had had an accident? How would I have explained it?"

I replied, "Spike, that's exactly why we did it—to prevent something like that from happening. They know what they're doing!"

He finally simmered down and threw the report on the table with an order to "Get out of here!"

The commander of TAC acted as the chairman of the Tri-Commanders Conference, which was attended by USAFE and PACAF commanders and DOs or directors for requirements. TAC is the spokesman for the tactical forces' requirements, both on rotation and on training. The conferences were fairly useful. Some good ideas came up for revisions to the training program, reduction in TDY and deployments versus PCSs. Especially important was agreement on the next F-X or next fighter.

When I was DO at TAC, John Burns, who was my director of requirements, and I had drawn up the Specific Operational Requirement (SOR) for the F-X in 1964. It was the first fighter that was designed for the TAC mission, based on specs drawn up by TAC pilots, and was not a politically-designed aircraft. We set things down that we wanted, even though we thought they might really be unachievable by industry. They would have to go to work. The competition began in 1965.

McDonnell Douglas won the contract in 1969. Their proposed design was clearly a superior article. One reasonable competitor was Boeing, but the source selection board deemed them less responsive. Had another manufacturer proposed a really red-hot, shiny candidate, there might have been more politicization of the acquisition.

The airplane, which became the F-15 and first flew in 1972, met or exceeded every requirement we listed. It is an extraordinary machine, with all the right ordnance. It is also very survivable. An Israeli pilot managed to fly an F-15 home after he lost everything outboard of six feet of a wing! Moreover, the F-15 production program came in on time and within budget.

By contrast, all the other airplanes of that period, such as the A-7, F-16, F-111, and A-10, were political rewards and fell far short of meeting our needs. In the case of the F-16, the Air Force has spent enough money to practically replace it. This is not generally known. The accident rate for the F-16 was ten times that for the F-15! I think it still is, but this is not advertised.

The technical success of the F-15 belongs to Bob "Earthquake" Titus and John Burns; I personally thought that we were setting our sights too high and that we would just discourage the competition in technological innovation.

The greatest disappointment is that the Air Force only bought 750 of them instead of 15,000. They were highly successful in DESERT STORM in January and February 1991.

♠ ♥ ♦ ♣

Momyer hated contractors. In fact, the only people he would talk with, occasionally, were from McDonnell Douglas. He respected their product and had confidence in them. He hated all the others so much they never were admitted to his office. He thought they were crooks with their hands in the Air Force's pocket. He frequently said to me that too many contractors were retired generals and let me know that he never wanted to hear of me doing something like that. He was never going to be guilty of that. This aversion stemmed from his experience as director of operational requirements in the Pentagon, or possibly earlier, when he had the same job at TAC HQ.

Consequently, when contractors wanted to talk to some senior officer, I was designated.

CHAPTER 17

A BIG RAISE

Tokyo, Japan: COMUS Forces, Japan

In February 1970, I became Commander, U.S. Forces, Japan, a joint service position, and I was dual-hatted as Commander of Fifth Air Force. I replaced Tom McGehee. Ryan, the Chief of Staff, made the decision without consulting Momyer. The first knowledge either of us had was when Bob Dixon, the Director of Personnel (DP), was telling me on the telephone at the same time Ryan was telling Momyer on the telephone. I didn't object but I wasn't given a voice.

After Momyer hung up the phone, he was very upset. He objected violently to my transfer and thought I had engineered it. I told him I hadn't known a thing about it. The DP had just told me. I said, "I'm not particularly anxious to go over there. I'll go where I'm told to go, but I had nothing to do with this." I finally convinced him. Momyer was ready to mount his horse and race to Washington to tell Ryan he couldn't do this. Jay Robbins replaced me, which placated him somewhat. Jay had Twelfth Air Force at the time and was a very competent and experienced fighter pilot.

The Air Force commanders in Japan preceding and including Tom McGehee were heavily involved in the social whirl.

Before I left for Japan, I went to see Ryan. The compelling reason for my assignment was the reversion of Okinawa. Ryan wasn't satisfied

A Big Raise

that the Air Force was being treated right.

Whatever convinced Ryan that I had the diplomatic skills to do this better than anyone else? I'll never know. It wasn't my bag, but I did a pretty good job, I think, from both the American and Japanese standpoint.

The Japanese regarded the senior military officer in Japan as the modern day Douglas MacArthur. He had been like a god to them, so his successors were accorded the same respect and admiration. I could have been Mayor of Tokyo if I had snapped my fingers.

It bothered everyone in the American Embassy in Tokyo that I, as Commander U.S. Forces, Japan, and the senior military officer in Japan, held the position second to the ambassador's. This was established in the peace treaty after Japan surrendered in 1945. Japan is the only country in the world where a U.S. military commander is in the foreign service hierarchy. Every other place, the deputy chief of mission holds that position.

The U.S. was successful in every aspect of the negotiations on the reversion of Okinawa. I never heard any complaint from the State Department, the Joint Chiefs or any service chiefs.

Perhaps the best illustration of the care that was taken concerned the traffic. Under U.S. jurisdiction, vehicles drive on the right. Japan has vehicular traffic on the left, so the traffic had to be reversed on Okinawa. The population of Okinawa is terribly dense. They prepared everything and from one night to the next morning, while they stopped all but emergency traffic, the road signs went up, the traffic lights were changed, and the switch was completed.

A lot of important people from the American and Japanese governments, including the Defense Minister, Nakasone-san, who later became the prime minister, attended the reversion ceremony and banquet. By directive of Ambassador Meyer, all military officers, including Lieutenant General Lampert, High Commissioner of the Ryukyus, wore civilian clothes. I wore my formal white uniform because I wanted it understood that the military had a role in the events.

Nixon appointed a businessman, the past president of Ingersoll-Rand, to replace Ambassador Meyer. He was smart, in addition to being a heavy contributor to the Republican party. He did a spectacular job. I worked splendidly with him. We played a lot of tennis together. He realized and appreciated the military's role in Japan and the Far East.

♠ ♥ ♦ ♣

A Big Raise

Status Of Forces Agreements (SOFA) were in place and functioning in Japan and Korea. As a joint forces commander, I had a Navy rear admiral as force commander at Yokosuka; an Army major general as force commander at Camp Zama. The Marines have the only combat forces in Japan, except for the U.S. Air Force fighter wings at Yokota and Misawa. There was not much room for things to do or opportunity for conflict.

♠ ♥ ♦ ♣

As Commander, U.S. Forces, I reported to Admiral Jack McCain, CINCPAC. He was one of the finest people I've ever had the good fortune to work for. We played tennis when he and his wife came out, which was about every three months. His wife Roberta had an identical twin, Rowena. Rowena was the widow of a Navy captain. She was a member of the family. It was as if Jack had two wives; we'd be sitting there having a cocktail before going out to dinner and Roberta would turn to Rowena and say, "It's your turn to watch after Jack tonight, Rowena." Old Jack would just sit there puffing his cigar.

Jack loved to play tennis. He was good, but he was ten years older than me and he preferred to play doubles, because he could have a good partner. The first time he came out, he brought a Navy lieutenant commander, who was no slouch. I had discovered a good player, but he was no champion. We beat their socks off. Jack hated to lose.

The next trip, he brought a new aide. This one was a tall, rangy, young Army major who was a cannonball player. I sensed that the ante was going up. I dug up the Far East Air Force's champion, Major Frank Blazek. He was an ordinary-looking person and his appearance gave no clue about his talent. His father had emigrated from Czechoslovakia after the war. The father had been a European champion tennis player and instructor, which explained why his son was so good. Again, we beat Jack's socks off. He was really mad.

The third time he came out, he had an Air Force captain who was the Air Force singles champ. I'd seen his name in the *Air Force Times* and I guess he'd been assigned to PACAF. By golly, old Frank and I beat them, barely. With that, old Jack gave up. He didn't try another partner. He asked, "What do you all do out here? Anything besides play tennis?"

♠ ♥ ♦ ♣

A Big Raise

I ordered a study on the Kanto Plains Consolidation. The study consisted of a property inventory and a population inventory that took six months. This was the first analysis, since the beginning of our occupation, of the properties that the U.S. military owned and ran. The report became the blueprint for the structure of Fifth Air Force, particularly in Japan. The civilians continued to implement the recommendations of that study after I left.

I discovered all kinds of cats and dogs! We had little outposts of seven, eight or ten people, living in nice, neat quarters, with no mission or function. There were bomb dumps with no bombs in them, but they had a caretaker force living comfortably there on a three-year tour.

There was a timetable. For example, we had a number of housing areas, all half-full. The rationale for their having been maintained so long was that the U.S. might have to return if Korea erupted again. I didn't buy that. I planned to consolidate them into two fairly large facilities.

Almost every recommendation called for consolidation or closing. This broke a lot of rice bowls and made a lot of people angry. The report went all the way to Washington. Then I had to try it on the Japanese. I assumed that they would embrace this approach because it would lead to returning facilities to them. I was right for the wrong reasons; this was so disruptive and traumatic that they couldn't swallow it.

In the end, the plan was accepted with a few minor modifications. The installation where I was quartered was among the facilities to be closed. They duplicated the set of quarters at Yakota, literally. The Japanese copied it room by room, dimension by dimension. The results of the Kanto Plains Consolidation were extraordinary savings to the U.S. government in money and personnel. It was probably my greatest single accomplishment in Japan.

As Commander, U.S. Forces, Japan, I had jurisdiction over all the military forces in Japan and, after the reversion, in Okinawa. When the reversion occurred, General Lampert left. I had no authority in Korea.

As Commander of Fifth Air Force, however, I commanded all Air Force units in Japan, Okinawa, and Korea and, in addition, was partially responsible for the air defense of Taiwan. This was a shared chore with the BG down there. He had the units and bases; operational

A Big Raise

control reverted to me in the event of hostilities.

There wasn't much combat operational activity. Fifth Air Force had an F-4 wing at Yokota and a stand-by contingent on Misawa; Kadena and Naha on Okinawa; and a division, under a BG, with bases at Taegu, Kwanju and Osan in Korea. The Marines had a wing at Iwakuni.

Thirteenth Air Force was independent. Eighth Air Force was on Guam. The B-52s used in Southeast Asia belonged to an independent SAC command that had nothing to do with PACAF.

♠ ♥ ♦ ♣

Nakasone was the Defense Minister. He later became the Minister of International Trade and Industry, and eventually, prime minister. He was a power in the Liberal Democratic Party. He was unusually favorable to the military, for a Japanese. In October 1970, he instigated the publication by the Japan Defense Agency of its first white paper on defense. Part I was on the meaning of defense in modern society, military situation in the Far East in the future and the existing state of self-defense in Japan. He autographed a copy for me, but it's in Nihongo and I cannot read it now.

This was quite significant to the Japanese. The Japanese people and their government looked on their military establishment almost with contempt. They were second-class citizens. Their officers came from the population and attended the academy, but their military establishment was small and poorly equipped. The air arm and the navy arm were fairly modern, but the army was terribly out of date. They had no big exercises. They maintained a very low profile. On their equivalent of an armed forces day, there was a parade through downtown Tokyo of everything they had and a flyover, about which the newspapers reported very little.

There was a Security Consultative Committee, composed of the Ambassador, Admiral McCain, the Minister of Foreign Affairs, Nakasone, and me. This body ratified local agreements between the U.S. and the Japanese governments and then furthered the ratification of the papers submitted to them. There were a few policy papers, with little substance. It was a holdover from the days after the 1952 Treaty. However, in the minds of the Japanese and the U.S., it had established itself as being a fairly solid group and was a good forum for discussions and played a fairly prominent role during the Okinawa reversion negotiations.

A Big Raise

The best description of the Japanese that I have found is in the book, *The Enigma of Japanese Business.* Any Westerner who tells you he understands Japanese and is fluent in the language is deluding himself as well as attempting to delude you. A Westerner could study the culture and the language for a lifetime and never be fluent. The meaning of words varies with the way the words are used and the circumstances. There are forty-seven ways to say the pronoun "I." One uses totally different words, for example, to refer to a friend in one-on-one conversation, with a business associate, a subordinate, or a superior.

The Japanese attitude toward their military reflects their having been burned so badly by the defeat in World War II and by having been so thoroughly misled by their military leaders. They have never recovered and do not trust any military establishment. They would prefer to have no uniformed person in Japan. I don't know how they have succeeded in erasing all patriotic feeling, but such feelings are nonexistent.

Their attitude toward Americans and other foreigners, *gaijin,* who dictated all aspects of their country, military force structure, economy, and international relations after the war, is that any Western goods or services are the way to go. We taught them the labor movement and the emancipation of women. Golf is a classic example. I learned to play golf there.

Within a couple of months after I arrived in Japan, I had completed a lot of the protocol visits and welcoming parties. I received an invitation, through Nakasone-san's aide to my aide, to play golf. I sent word back politely that I didn't play golf. I would be happy to join the minister in a tennis match. The word came back, "The Defense Minister does not play tennis. He has scheduled a tee-time." I believe it was for the fifth of April, which was a Sunday about a month away.

In Japan, if someone didn't use the tee time, he paid anyway. By our standards, golf is horribly expensive. Greens fees were about $200 or $300 then, in 1970. After I was out of the Air Force and working in Japan for McDonnell Douglas five years later, I frequently invited three Japanese guests for a game. That foursome cost $1,000 for the day.

I had never held a golf club. I had nothing but contempt for golfers. I thought it was for people who were feeble, incapacitated or old.

About a week before the match, my aide reminded me of my invitation. I decided to go to Kanto Mura, a housing area where we had a practice range. It was about twenty minutes from our quarters and my office at Fuchu Air Station. I wore a pair of sneakers, since I had no golf shoes.

A Big Raise

John, the fellow who ran the driving range, was a Japanese who was very fluent in English. He was a pretty good golfer himself. His father had been president of the Bank of Tokyo in San Francisco when World War II broke out. The father, John and his younger brother were interned in a camp during the war.

I asked John to give me some left-handed golf clubs so I could hit some balls. John had never seen me before and did as I asked. I do most things right-handed, but some things I do better left-handed, like batting.

I took a couple of swings. I stepped up and hit the first ball. Then, I took a stronger whack at the next ball and missed entirely. I was holding the club like a baseball bat. I swung four or five more times. I could see I wasn't doing it right.

I said, "John, give me a couple of tips on this. This is a little different. I don't really know anything about this."

He showed me the stance, the grip and a few fundamentals. I thought, I have to really make some progress in the next week!

I bought a set of clubs and a pair of shoes and practiced every night. I had blisters on my hands from trying to learn how to hit that dumb ball.

The fatal day came; we played and it was a disaster. I had a score of 148, which was really not accurate. I picked up many times, for instance, after the fifth try to hit out of a sand trap. Old Nakasone-san thought this was the funniest thing he had ever seen. Here was an American who couldn't play golf! It was horribly embarrassing for me.

I went to Tom, John's brother, and said, "I want a golf instructor, right now."

They recommended that I be taught by Asami-san, the pro at the Yomiuri Country Club, a very fancy place. Asami-san had the reputation of being the best in the area. I had six day-long lessons, spread over six weeks. There was a playing lesson, followed by the practice range and the putting green. I needed an interpreter for the lessons, since I had no competence in the language and Asami-san spoke no English.

The first lesson, I marched out there with my left-handed clubs. Asami-san indicated, "Hold it." Through the interpreter, he said, "Tell the general I will not teach him to play golf left-handed. Golf is a right-handed game." So he went into the pro shop and brought back a set of right-handed clubs for me.

After I had swung the club a couple of times, he said, "Stop. The general plays tennis, doesn't he?" He saw that I had a lot of wrist action.

A Big Raise

"Oh, yes."

"Tell the general I will not teach him to play golf if he continues to play tennis."

"Tell Asami-san I will play no more tennis." I continued to play tennis, but didn't tell him so.

At the end of the six weeks, Asami-san told me he could teach me no more.

I invited Nakasone to a rematch. He accepted. He loved to play on the Air Force golf courses because we had carts. Japanese courses had only caddies. He beat me, but this time I was within calling distance.

Three months after I picked up my first club, I again invited Nakasone-san to play. This time, I beat him by two strokes. I had a ninety-eight and he had one-hundred. It was the first time I broke one-hundred and I was never close to him after that. He was a pretty good golfer, but by practicing constantly, I had an eleven handicap when I left Japan after three years.

I played a hell of a lot of golf. I had a practice net behind the quarters, a little four-hole pitch and putt course, with fifty-, sixty-, seventy-, and eighty-yard holes in front of our quarters. I spent hours out there. I even had lights installed so I could play at night.

Nakasone and I became very good friends. After we returned to the U.S. in 1977, Nakasone came to Washington two or three times, for very brief visits lasting only two or three days. He would send word through his establishment that he was coming and that he wanted to be sure that we could see each other. There wasn't time to play golf, but we always managed thirty or forty minutes over coffee. The people who surround a person like that were frantic. They couldn't understand how a person like me could just walk in and shake hands with their vaunted leader. Who the hell is this Graham guy?

♠ ♥ ♦ ♣

The chief of staff of the Japanese Air Self Defense Force (their Air Force), Ogawa-san, and Ishikawa-san, who followed him, were among the few Japanese with whom I became close. They wanted to know my experiences in Southeast Asia, and asked about tactics, for example.

Ishikawa was in the Japanese Army Air Force in World War II. Most Japanese ex-military admit only to having fought in Manchuria, very like the Germans, who for many years admitted only to having fought the Russians on the Eastern front. Old Ishikawa was one of the few who leveled with me. It came about after a golf game. He was a pretty good golfer for a Japanese. He was larger and stronger than average.

The game of golf, like everything else in Japan, is one long ritual. The game starts early in the morning. Everyone arrives at eight o'clock and has something to eat, usually coffee and toast. Then everyone goes to putt a little. Prime tee-time is nine or nine-thirty. At the end of nine holes, everyone takes a break and eats lunch. Forty minutes later, the starter calls your number and you report to the tenth tee for eighteen more holes. A game is thus twenty-seven holes. The game usually ends around four-thirty or five o'clock. Everyone then goes to the Japanese hot bath. After changing into a suit and necktie, there are drinks and a snack or light meal while there is a business discussion for an hour or so. By then, it's around seven-thirty and everyone goes home. The closest golf course to downtown Tokyo is over an hour and a half away. Many courses require an overnight trip.

After a golf game on the Air Force course, Ishikawa and I were having a drink. Most of the time, the Japanese will drink a beer. They have very good beer. I ordered a scotch and soda. Ishikawa ordered a bourbon and soda.

"General Ishikawa," I said, "you're the first Japanese I've ever known who drank bourbon whiskey. Where in the world did you develop a taste for bourbon?"

"Well," he said, "during the war, I went to Manila." The Japanese had taken over Clark Field, where he was a buck pilot. They found a warehouse of bourbon whiskey. He said, "It tasted better than sake."

So I knew the secret. Every time I went to see him, I took a bottle of Jack Daniels, which costs at least $100 in Japan today. The Japanese make as good a bourbon and scotch as can be bought. I actually prefer Suntori bourbon to most other brands. They also make some of the best wines. They also make the best golf clubs. But because they aren't Titleist or some other Western brand, the Japanese will not buy them. The Japanese would prefer to pay $2,000 for Western clubs when they could buy better Mizuno or Daiwa clubs for $500.

♠ ♥ ♦ ♣

One example of how regimented the Japanese are occurred in 1972. The Japanese Golf Association (JGA) decided to change the

A Big Raise

official golf ball from the English to the U.S. ball. The English ball is slightly smaller in diameter than the official U.S. ball. The day after the decision was announced, there wasn't an English golf ball to be found in any golf pro shop in Japan.

Golf courses in Japan were the only item that used the American/British measurement system (i.e., yards instead of meters). The JGA decided to convert golf courses to the metric system. Overnight, yardage markers disappeared from every golf course in Japan, scorecards were reprinted, and I learned to look for hyaku goju (150) meter markers.

♠ ♥ ♦ ♣

In September 1972, Lieutenant General George Simler was killed in an airplane accident. He had taken off in a T-38, did a roll on takeoff, and augered in. That triggered a big shuffle of all the three-stars.

At the time, Bill Pitts had been commander of Sixth Allied Tactical Air Force at Izmir, Turkey, for three months. Bill was assigned to replace Archie Old as commander of Fifteenth Air Force, at March AFB. Someone had to go to Turkey. I was nearing the completion of my three-year tour in January, but I was not eager to leave abruptly. I was ordered to go to Turkey immediately.

I protested to Dixon, the Director of Personnel: "Bob, you don't understand. First, I work for an admiral in CINCPAC and a general in PACAF. This environment requires farewell calls on everyone from Okinawa to Taiwan to Korea. Certain social functions have to be discharged." I explained it would be a minimum of thirty days.

CHAPTER 18

KNOW WHEN TO FOLD THEM
IZMIR, TURKEY: 6TH ALLIED TACTICAL AIR FORCE

It took me four or five weeks to disengage from Japan and proceed to Turkey. I went through Washington, DC, on the way because Ryan wanted to see me briefly.

Ryan told me, "We have a terrible situation in Turkey. There has been a high turnover in commanders."

Bert Harrison, an ex-SAC officer, was in the job only briefly. Joe Moore retired after only three months because his wife's twin sister had died from a heart condition and Virl feared that she had symptoms. Joe wanted her to have medical attention at Walter Reed Hospital. Dick Ellis had come in briefly but was needed to replace the commander of U.S. NATO South. Pitts had been pulled out after three months.

Ryan said, "The Turks are up in arms. They are bitter because they think Turkey is a place to dump people." He emphasized how the Air Force was in serious jeopardy with the Turks and I should know what I was walking into.

I replied, "Chief, this is one job I didn't ask for. I know what it is. I spent some time over there refereeing between the Greeks and the Turks in 1963. If I had my choice of where to give the world an enema, I would have no difficulty making up my mind. I don't think I'll be that enchanted with the assignment and, to my knowledge, from my previous experience, there isn't anything significant we can do as far as increasing NATO's capability or anything like that. That place is the pits and I think I deserve something better. If that's where you want me to go, I'll go. But I must tell you that I don't think I'll stay there for the full tour." I had a year and a half before mandatory retirement.

He said, "You must take a hard look at this. It's critical to the Air Force."

I arrived in Izmir, Turkey, in November 1972.

There were two important things that really characterized the environment over there. One, the Turks are Moslems. Their religion dominates everything, as is true in most Islamic countries. Second, there is insurmountable hostility between Turks and Greeks. Somebody will have to referee between those two countries for the next thousand years.

As an example of the impact of religion, I had a Turkish Deputy who was Major General Sabri Tavazar. He was a fine chap. I could never depend on him to do something when I wanted because he had to go to the mosque five times a day to pray. Some people spread a rug where they are, but the truly devout believers go to the mosque. It seemed to me he was always walking in or out.

As an example of the Turkish-Greek hostility, General Tavazar would enter, salute, inquire if he could close the door. He had some accent normally, but a pronounced accent when he was excited. He would tell me, "General, I regret I must report to you some actions that are being taken by the Greek members of your staff that are not in consonance with NATO and Turkish policies."

I would say, "Sabri, please give me some details."

He would rattle off some inconsequential slight. I'd assure him that I would look into it. He'd disappear.

Five minutes later, the secretary would inform me that my Deputy Chief of Staff for Operations, Greek Brigadier General Iraklis Naoum, would like to see me. Same scenario, implicating the Turks. There was never any substance but their differences are so deep they can never be eradicated.

Relationships in the office and at social affairs were always correct and proper. No one ever raised a voice, but there was a constant undercurrent of animosity and hostility just barely below the surface. I was considered the arbitrator and never was accused of favoring one side over the other.

Know When to Fold Them

The Turkish military were in the middle ages. Their equipment was outmoded, their tactics were pre-World War II, and they were top-heavy with rank which had a somewhat exalted opinion of the position that it occupied. They were dominated by the Army and there were some areas, including Izmir, that were still under military law while we were there. The commander of our district was an iron-fisted Navy admiral, Sonmetz; there was no governor or body of a democratic nature.

Turkey was absolutely paranoid about Russia and communism. They are sturdy fighters. Their soldiers are as courageous as any you might ever encounter. They have a regular force and conscripts. The regular, permanent military establishment includes the air arm. The bulk of the Army consists of conscripts who serve eighteen months. There are no exemptions. Their training is poor. Pay for "Askhars," as they were called, was about $8 per month. They were expected to send some home to their parents.

Turkey has one of the lowest per capita incomes of the civilized nations—about $400 per year. They have no heavy industry to speak of. Exports consist mainly of agricultural commodities. They have no oil. The masses are uneducated. They are supposed to have compulsory education through high school, but this is not enforced. Our golf caddies were twelve and thirteen years old, and they were there every day.

My staff was composed of approximately equal numbers of American, Turkish and Greek, with a smattering of English and Italians. It's a miracle that NATO accomplishes anything. For example, all the particular national holidays are observed by the entire HQ. Thus, we took off Italian and British holidays, as well as all the rest. I have a very low opinion of NATO and its capabilities.

The bulk of the Turkish Air Force fighter force was F-84Fs, the world's worst airplane. They had two squadrons of F-100s. They were getting some F-104s. Things looked brighter, but it was still second-line equipment and, by the time they were equipped, it would be third-line.

They had the typical Islamic view of fate, exemplified by their accident reports. If a pilot had an emergency and didn't handle it properly, say he was going to go in on a dive bomb run, he went in. The Koreans had the same attitude. One doesn't go back and around, one goes in with the plane. Loss of face when one returned was deemed worse than dying.

They copied the U.S. style of accident report. It started with the name of the pilot, the date of the accident, the time, the aircraft model and number, and paragraphs 1, 2, and 3. In the narrative, which is the important part, the U.S. writers go to great lengths to report as much as they can. This is a flash report that goes to everyone in the world with that type of airplane. Typically, it would read, "The pilot encountered mild turbulence. On checking his hydraulic gauges, he noticed fluctuation in the utility pressure. . ." and go on and on. Finally, "He ejected."

The Turks typically wrote, "Pilot encountered control problems and the aircraft became uncontrollable. He went in at a 45 degree dive... Inshallah." The final word Inshallah means "the will of Allah," or "it was fated."

The roads were two-lane blacktop and atrocious. It wasn't worth driving after dark because, half the time, they don't use lights and they drive as fast as the vehicle will go. They had huge buses, on which people would hang outside. Across the front of most of the buses and cargo trucks, in big letters, were the letters, "Mashallah," inviting Allah's protection. In other words, "Whatever happens, it's not my fault. Allah protects me."

I made no serious attempt to learn their language, which I usually would, because I really didn't think I would stay that long. Refereeing between the Greeks and Turks is a tiresome way to live. Like the Israelis and Arabs, they have been at each other's throats since before recorded history. It's never going to change. One might be up one generation or century. The other one will resurface for their turn, and so on. No matter how one tries to rationalize it, divide things up, referee, it can only be temporary at best.

I left Turkey in 1973 after six months and have not been back since.

NATO communications, command and control then were so primitive as to be almost unworkable. I couldn't visualize how the system could function in the event of hostilities. We had an underground command post in a cave not far from town. The command post was manned twenty-four hours a day primarily by Americans, Greeks and Turks, with liaison officers from Britain and Italy. We maintained a great charade about how it would function during peace and crisis. Dry runs and command post exercises were a fiasco, however. We just flat couldn't communicate satisfactorily.

General Goodpaster was SACEUR at the time. I was called up

Know When to Fold Them

there about once a month for conferences and NATO meetings during the six months I was there. Something was always going on, usually of dubious value. The communications problem persisted throughout, except between the Brits and U.S., but even that was not great. NATO HQ consisted of a large community of people taking in each other's laundry. It was an elephant tied down and unable to move. The only consolation was that the Warsaw Pact couldn't have been any better.

Turkey was divided into three regions, Western, Central, and Eastern, for air defense purposes. The HQ for each region, respectively, was at Iskeshir, Ankara, and Dyarbakir. I went around to look at them and meet their commanders, who were all three-stars. The air training establishment was relatively close to Izmir and I went there several times. The person in charge was very competent. I did the same in Greece.

I concluded that this situation was the biggest waste of time that I could ever be involved in. Transportation was equivalent to that of the turn of the century in the U.S. Our living conditions were poor. Coming from a very sophisticated environment like the Far East to the primitive conditions of the Middle East was a traumatic event.

My wife Vivian, three bird dogs and three aides were with me. We lived in an apartment in Izmir. We had a gorgeous view of the world's most polluted bay. Some people sold fish from the bay at little shops and stands, but I never ate any.

I was driven around in a station wagon with six armed Ashkars in lockstep. If we stopped, they deployed. An assassination attempt had been made on the Army General Mildren, my counterpart, before I arrived. A machine gun position had been erected on top of a building looking down into his garden. It was ready to go when the Turkish police uncovered it. After that, security was beefed up. There was an armed guard outside our apartment door twenty-four hours a day, even if he was asleep half the time. Sometimes I had to step over him to get in or out.

Both the fishing and hunting were good. I went fishing further out in the Mediterranean. Mainly, I hunted doves and wild boars.

They have a variety of dove larger than our mourning dove but not as big as a pigeon. They were delicious. Bird hunting was like a shooting gallery. The Turks harvested their grain, then processed it and bagged it in a large low building. A lot of mixed grain and chaff spilled out one end into conical piles. The doves would flock in there like a baited field. The Turks didn't care about shooting them. There was no license, no season and no bag limit. I located five of these buildings right off the bat.

The first time I went to shoot doves, I had Queenie, my Labrador, in the back of the car. The doves were so numerous they were knocking my hat off. I had hardly picked up my shotgun and stepped out of the car before ten little kids, aged from eight to twelve, appeared from nowhere. I walked about one-hundred yards from the car, while the security force deployed around me. While I set up, Queenie sat down, as she was trained to do. I dropped a bird about twenty-five to thirty yards away. She ran out and brought it in. The little kids had edged out. I asked the aide to tell the kids to stay out of the way. I didn't want to fire too close to them. He hollered at them, but they ignored him.

I shot another one, which Queenie retrieved. Queenie regarded picking up birds as her special duty. She made it clear to anyone who was along. Then I dropped one about forty yards out. A little kid ran after it. Queenie and the kid reached the bird at the same time. Queenie weighed ninety-five pounds. She hit that little kid sideways like a tackle on a block, knocked him about fifteen feet, rolled him over a couple of times, grabbed the bird and came back. The kids formed up about one-hundred yards out and never came close after that.

I had a Turkish aide, Major Demiröz, who was a heck of a swell person and who later became the air attaché from Turkey in Washington and retired in Izmir as a colonel. I still correspond with him. He writes with flowing, flowery phrases. We became godparents to his little girl. This seemed unusual, to have Christian godparents to a Moslem child.

Rifles were prohibited in Turkey. I smuggled in three, just because I knew I could get away with it. No one said anything. I'd been told about the boar hunting but I'd not done it when I was there previously.

Bornova Hunt Club was in the little town where our HQ was located, about fifteen km out of Izmir. I was the only American in the club. I tracked it down through one of my Turkish drivers, Aziz, who belonged to it. Aziz was a devout Moslem and quite a character. The club's main occupation was killing boars because they tore up the farmers' fields.

I had shot boar at night in Iran with a shotgun and a slug, from a Jeep. We didn't leave the Jeep. The animals were so big that a wounded one, if it became mad, would charge you and you'd better have a refuge. They can run very fast for a short distance.

Usually, some farmer would report that depredations had occurred the night before. About fifteen to twenty hunters would be called up.

They would form a line of beaters and bang along, the way we drive deer in this country. The four or five who were going to shoot were along the side and far end. They usually killed one. Some of the boars were quite big, weighing up to 180 to 200 pounds. They were very dangerous, with curls of four to five inches.

The first time I went with them, I had the post of honor because I had my 30.06. I was given a seat up on a little elevated area, from where I could pick the boars off at 200 yards or so, long before they came close enough for anyone else to shoot. They all had shotguns, which were legal, and shot rifled slugs and buckshot, but they were very short range. I think I shot four in a row the first time I went. I was picking them off like a shooting gallery. They thought that was great. They shot one other. The hunt took three or four hours.

I wanted one to butcher for the meat. We drove the wagon up to the closest one, which weighed about 150 pounds. I had left my knife and gun in the car, so I turned to the nearest person and asked to borrow his hunting knife. I don't think he knew what I intended to do. They were just standing around talking.

As Moslems, they never touched the boars because of their religious position on pigs. I knew this, but dumb me, I didn't think about it. I started to butcher this hog. It took me an hour to field dress it. Dressed out, the boar probably weighed 110 pounds, a pretty good-sized chunk of meat. I couldn't lift it by myself, so I asked for help. No one would come near that hog. I finally maneuvered that sucker into the back of the wagon. There was no water available, so I wiped the man's knife on some grass and sand and with an old rag I carried and handed it back to him. He wouldn't take it. He went over and kicked out a trench in the ground and motioned for me to put the knife in there, after which he covered it up. I had to buy him a new knife.

When I returned home, I had help from my three aides, Sergeants Henry Hodge, Richard Riddle, and David Parker. We cut up and quartered the hog on the sidewalk in front of the apartment house. I threw away the parts I didn't want and kept the two hams, one shoulder and some of the ribs. I cleaned these all up in the kitchen. Richard took it up to the club and told them it was beef. It was cut up and hard to recognize. They kept it in the freezer for us and we would periodically take out a package to eat.

Henry Hodge and I met when I was at Turner AFB, in Albany, Georgia. We became good friends and have hunted together ever since. Henry retired as a senior master sergeant.

The senior Turkish officers in all three services were from fairly well-to-do families, well-educated, articulate, spoke good English and understood it well. All had visited the U.S. at least once and most, more than once. As is frequently the case, half a percent of the population is wealthy and owns and runs everything; the other 99.5 percent are dirt poor.

Admiral Sonmetz, Military District Commander, was a very talented individual. He learned that I liked to hunt. He had responsibility for, among other things, an island with the harbor defenses. This island was about seven miles offshore and could be seen from our apartment. It was off limits because of the radar installation and naval gun batteries. It was teeming with wild boar. There were no farmers there, so no one did anything about it.

People who own sheep and goats drive them into the city in bands of eight to ten to twenty to sell. If a Moslem wishes to sacrifice a lamb or goat, he pays for the animal and performs the ritual. At some point, he takes the creature over to a curb to slit its throat. There, the blood runs down into the gutter. The animal is then donated to the hospital, to use as food.

On holy days, this was a common sight. It was a little upsetting to Vivian, at first.

Old Sonmetz had someone deliver a one-hundred pound carcass to us. We returned one evening to find it lying on a bloody mat in front of our apartment door. The soldier was sitting there by it. At first I couldn't figure out what it was. I thought it might be a small deer. It never occurred to me that it might be a boar, until I looked at the hooves and knew it was no deer.

Who in the hell would do that, I asked myself. It was Sonmetz's idea of a gift. I was an infidel, so pork was OK. We did the same job on that that we had done on the one I shot. Good meat!

There were reported to be some good streams for fresh water fishing. One day, I went looking for a good trout stream I'd been told about, but my driver and I never found it.

♠ ♥ ♦ ♣

Operationally, I did very little in Turkey. I acted more like an inspector general of the Turkish Air Force. I looked over their shoulder during training and exercises, tried to assess their capability and advise them on how to improve. If we had had a shooting war, I would have

Know When to Fold Them

been in charge of the air effort in the southern NATO region. I had no airplane of my own that I could take out and fly.

There was a U.S. "Rotational" squadron at the Adana base, near Incirlik. The base was American, but the base commander was a Turk. This was the base from which we staged for the effort in 1958, during the Lebanon crisis. I visited Adana occasionally, mainly because they had the best golf course of the three, total, in Turkey.

There was a golf course at Bornova, close to the HQ, that had been built in 1928 by a British firm which grew tobacco or coffee. They had many employees and, typical of the British, they soon built a club. The course originally had eighteen holes, sand greens and sand tees. Over time, it functioned fairly satisfactorily. One had to be cautious where one stepped in the clubhouse; there were holes in the floor.

When we were there, the golf course had only thirteen holes. Turkey has the most casual land and property laws of any country I know. Squatters are as common as flies. No one does anything if someone builds a ramshackle one-room rough house on someone else's property and lives there. Some entrepreneur put in an olive orchard, which wiped out two or three holes. The number one hole was transformed into a camel corral and barn. So, we teed off from the number two hole, over a pile of camel dung about thirty feet high. If you hit a low screaming shot off the tee, you didn't retrieve your ball. A couple of times, I hit a camel that wandered in the way. We heard a dull thud and it made the camel blink.

The last commercial enterprise there was a series of five high-rise, government-built housing for the poor, which took out another hole or two. Between the thirteen identifiable tees and greens, there were rocks, brush and trees. I went through a set of golf clubs in six months playing there. One time I teed off with a three-iron and the head of the club went further than the ball.

The second time we played the course, our caddy was Halil. He was fourteen, observant, sharp as a tack and spoke very good English. He was aggressive enough to knock other boys out of the way if he wanted the job. Caddy spots went to the toughest and meanest.

We took a shine to him. I asked my aide Major Demiröz to check into him, to see if there was something we could do to help him. Obviously, he wasn't in school because he was always at the club. He had a brother, about two years younger, who was also quite unusual, but not so talented as Halil. My aide learned that the boys' father worked in Germany as an expatriate. Their mother was deceased and

Know When to Fold Them

they lived with their grandmother. They had no grandfather.

I asked, "What do you recommend I do?"

"He has to go to school. There is nothing you can do to improve his lot unless he attends school."

I asked, "Would you talk to him and see if we can work something out?"

In sum, I arranged for him to enter the Turkish Air Force school system. At fourteen, he was eligible. It was an eight-year program and required intensive effort on his part. The first step was to leave Izmir to attend a preparatory school somewhere for a couple of years. Then, he would enter the Turkish Air Force Academy and, upon graduation, receive his commission. He would have it made, because the military runs Turkey. Grandmother agreed and Halil gave it a lot of thought. I even took him to see the academy and he became quite enthusiastic. We thought everything was peachy-keen. I set up a checking account for the major to draw on for his expenses. They weren't enormous, maybe $800 per year at most.

In the meantime, I had served notice that I intended to retire. Vivian and I prepared to leave. We went to play golf about two weeks before we were to leave. No Halil. His younger brother said he wasn't there and wouldn't say any more. We went out again, about two days later. Still no sign of Halil. The last time we went out, we caught sight of Halil, but he dodged us and disappeared. I asked Major Demiröz what was happening.

He checked and said, "Old Halil has aborted. He doesn't want to leave Grandma."

By then, it was too late to explore other ways to help him. We left a few days later.

♠ ♥ ♦ ♣

Vivian and I enjoyed the sightseeing and the uniqueness of Turkey. There are a lot of ruins and the country is a well-kept secret. There are places there that very few Americans have been.

We went to one site, Goreme (accent on the first syllable), in the Central Region, about twenty miles from the Iskeshir air base and Regional TAF HQ. We flew in an airplane sent down for me from Wiesbaden, from where I was supported. The Turkish Air Force officer supplied a car and arranged for us to spend the night in a little hotel in the town. Goreme was a completely self-sufficient habitation 1,500 feet underground. It was a redoubt created by the Christians during the crusades and discovered in the 1920s by a German archaeologist. It was fantastic! They had explored it. In the late 1920s, the French came in and continued. Finally, the British took up the excavation. Americans didn't take part until after World War II. Their contingent was permanent. They managed the museums on a sustained basis, photographing and restoring.

Goreme is dug into tuff, a volcanic formation that carves easily. The pulverized and refined form is used in Dutch cleanser. There are some large rooms with murals still in colors as vivid as when they were painted by the early Christians. About 1,500 people lived there. They had their own wells for water, a ventilation system, a sewage system, and food storage area. There were two entrances, the size of double doors, across each of which massive stones could be rolled to conceal the aperture. I doubt they could be moved without a forklift and a ten-ton crane.

Other than the museum contingent, we were virtually the first Americans there. They couldn't believe we'd found the place. We wandered around there for two days. There were some dim electric lights so you could find your way around. They'd provide a guide if you wanted to really probe around.

There are Roman ruins in fantastic states of preservation. The lettering is still legible.

After four or five months in Turkey, I put in my papers. I wrote a very brief letter to Ryan and said, "I am taking advantage of [whatever] paragraph in the regulation and herewith tender my resignation effective July 1, 1973." I gave him about forty-five days' notice. For retirement purposes, I had thirty-four years. Of course, the retirement request had to be approved. By then, I faced mandatory retirement in eighteen months. I did not relish the thought of eighteen more months there.

My retirement provoked a strong reaction, not from Ryan at the time, but from Dixon, the deputy for personnel, who may actually have reflected Ryan's sentiments.

Everyone had an annual physical around the date of one's birthday. Mine was in February. I went to Wiesbaden and as a result, I was grounded because of my hearing, my vision, and my back. I wasn't actively flying because I had no airplane, but I wasn't prevented from

Know When to Fold Them

it. This did not play a prominent part in my decision to retire.

This was after the Lavelle case. Practically until the day before he retired, he had been on flying status. Jack Lavelle was retired for one-hundred percent physical disability, which meant that he received retirement pay one-hundred percent income tax free. As a result of negative political coverage, the pendulum swung. Succeeding officers could not receive a disability retirement even if they were carried in on a stretcher.

After I was grounded, I put in my retirement papers. I had to take a separate retirement physical at Wiesbaden, which was shortly after the annual one. If I was deemed to be physically disabled from flying, then there was no way that I could be retired without some degree of disability. This was a logical deduction.

The surgeon general in Washington was acquainted with this box they had created for themselves. I was restored to flying status overnight and retired on flying status.

♠ ♥ ♦ ♣

Don Smith, Commander of Alaskan Air Command, replaced me when I left Turkey. He and his wife Patty and their entourage flew from Alaska to Turkey in a KC-135A, which I used for the backhaul to return to South Carolina.

I insisted that we have a two-week overlap so I could introduce him to the senior people. I took him to Greece, for example. His aide was a major whom I knew and with whom I had fished a lot in Alaska. One time, we were talking about Don and a physical. The aide said, "You know, General Smith is temporarily suspended from flying status."

I said, "Oh, is that right?"

He said, "Yes. He's been to the flight surgeon. He has these horrible, crashing headaches. They can't find anything. They give him the usual aspirin treatment and tell him to come back if he doesn't feel better."

Outwardly, there was no manifestation. Don was his cheery self. Three months later, he died suddenly of a brain tumor that was never detected.

Chapter 19

THE DEALING'S DONE
Tokyo, Japan: McDonnell Douglas

Momyer retired me at Shaw AFB in June 1973. He gave me another 4,000 words about hoping I wouldn't work for a contractor like so many other senior officers. I hadn't talked to anyone about working because I didn't intend to go to work. I was tired.

Vivian and I had previously bought some property in Sumter, South Carolina, and we were working with a building contractor on plans for a house. I started receiving phone calls from people, including Dave Lewis from General Dynamics, Bob Little from McDonnell Douglas, Johnny Allison from Northrop, and Paul Thayer of LTV, inviting me to come to work for them. I was not very interested. I told them all that I wanted to relax, hunt, fish and play golf for six months to a year. I didn't need to go to work.

We were staying with some friends, Bob and Eileen Levy, about twenty miles from where we were building on our lot. From our lot, the closest telephone was at a country store a mile and a half up the road. The only way I could be contacted by phone was to call that store. Levy gave everyone the store's number because he thought maybe it was important. The old man who ran the store would come down to tell me, "There's a fellow from Chicago [or wherever] on the telephone and he wants to talk to you, General."

The Dealing's Done

Old "Mr. Mac," Chairman of McDonnell Douglas Corporation (MDC), called. The first time, I told him no. The second time, he said, "Gordy, we need some help. We're in trouble. Could you come out here for a couple of days and give us some assistance on the Far East?"

I went back and reported this to Vivian. She warned me, "Don't you dare go back there. That old man will talk you into something you don't want to do!" She knew him well.

The house was stalled for a few days, so I flew to St. Louis. Vivian was right. MDC was attempting to sell the Japanese government the F-15 under license, Japan Air Lines the DC-10, and several other lesser programs. MDC had no qualified and experienced representative, let alone a real office, in the Far East. Old Mr. Mac wanted me to go over there. In addition, he wanted me to go to Iran and talk to the Shah and General Khatami, the Chief of the Iranian Air Force, about F-15s versus F-14s. They had already announced they were buying F-14s from Grumman.

I said, "Japan is too big a commitment. I won't go to Japan, but I will go to Iran for you." I needed to buy a suit and a few shirts. I had no suitable civilian business clothes.

I called Vivian and told her, "I'm going over to Iran for a week or so."

She reminded me, "I knew that would happen! I knew they would talk you into something!"

I said, "No, it's just a one-shot deal with no follow-on commitment."

I was over there about a month, but I succeeded in persuading them to buy 50 F-15s. Grumman was alerted and became very excited. They paid off the DO, who was also related to the Shah, so they canceled the F-15s after I left and bought all F-14s.

I came back with $3,000 worth of bills that I had paid out of pocket. I didn't carry that much cash and a lot of my checks were floating around. I told them I needed money. They sent a personnel weenie over to gather up the vouchers and lists. I received some money. I wrote everything up in a report, gave it to Bob Little and left for South Carolina. I never saw Old Mr. Mac. He was tied up or something.

I had barely walked in the door before the phone started to ring. Old Mr. Mac was terribly upset: "Gordy, you were supposed to go on to Japan!"

"Mr. Mac," I said, "There must be a terrible misunderstanding. I never intended to go to Japan."

The Dealing's Done

"Don't you remember? I wanted to talk to you about the Far East."

I said, "Yes, but you said to go to Iran, and I agreed to go there only. Don't you remember that?" Of course he did.

Two more calls and he had talked me into coming back out to St. Louis. And I did commit. I said, "I'll go for two years. If I can't do the job in two years, forget it. I'll put the house construction on hold and leave in a month."

"I can't wait a month!" he said.

I went back and told Vivian. I packed a bag and left her to clean up affairs. She joined me a week later.

That two years turned into almost five years because of a lot of things, including the Lockheed scandal that almost brought down the Japanese government.

A few months after I moved to Japan, I came back to Langley AFB. Momyer was still at TAC. I went by to learn something about F-15 tests or something. I didn't look him up but I ran into him. He didn't know that I was working for McDonnell Douglas, but it came out. He complained, "You told me you wouldn't do that. That's the dumbest thing you ever did!"

Retirement was a real change of pace. Imagine the difference: I had been the senior military person in Japan. I wasn't permitted to lift a finger. We had so many aides and maids that I was always stumbling over somebody.

I returned to Japan as a civilian, a retired officer. No one met us at the airport. We had to find our own baggage at the terminal.

As a military officer, I couldn't learn the language. There was always an interpreter interrupting me to make sure I understood. Now, as civilians, the first thing Vivian and I had to do was go to school just to live.

We leased a house, paid for by McDonnell Douglas, in Setagaya-ku, ten km from the heart of Tokyo. It was semi-Western, a beautiful house and garden. The rent was $4,000 a month, which struck me as high. Now, it would probably cost ten times that much.

The house was owned by the largest processed meat and cheese manufacturer in Japan. The real estate agent had described my position to him. He thought I was involved in McDonald's hamburgers. Soon after

The Dealing's Done

we moved in, a van drove up and a man climbed out with a box so big he could hardly carry it. It had every kind of sausage and hamburgers you could imagine. This was his present to his new tenant, as a colleague in the hamburger business!

Before we had any competency in the language, I said to Vivian, "If someone comes to the door and rings the bell, and if he is wearing a uniform of some sort, it will be OK to let him in." We had just moved in and the Japanese had all kinds of rules. "If you have any questions, call me at the office." We had a massive iron gate that closed off the driveway. We had to push a button like a garage-door opener to open the gate and drive into the yard.

The first day, Vivian called me. There was a man in a grey uniform with Japanese writing on his shirt and he had a clipboard. He wanted to go through the house. I told her, "He's probably an inspector or something." She left the phone off the hook and kept coming back.

"He must be the fire inspector." The Japanese are absolutely paranoid about fire because of the earthquake and fire they had in the twenties.

I said, "That's fine. Just get a copy of everything. You'll probably have to sign something."

That was what transpired. He bowed and left, finally, she said.

I brought the slip to the office to have it translated. We had bought $80 worth of fire extinguishers.

We went through a number of experiences like this before we took a cram course to survive. I went to the Executive Language School two hours a day, from eight to ten o'clock every morning. Vivian had a tutor who came to the house three afternoons a week. Unscrew the cap and pour it in. Within three months, we could make our way around. We had mastered the polite phrases, could ask about the train schedule, order off a menu, and, while not fluent, we could cope. After the initial surge to learn the basics, we bought a car and learned to drive on the wrong side of the road. I did something very intelligent: first I rented a car for thirty days. I thought I could get along but I was a little nervous about Vivian. My apprehension proved correct; she took care of both sides of that car before we turned it in. Most important, she learned that if she didn't assert herself on those narrow roads, the others would just crowd her over into the guardrail. After we bought a car, we had no incidents.

At the end of a little over four years, when we left, we were able to go anywhere. I could never read a newspaper because they are written in three languages—Kanji, Katakana, Hirogana, and sometimes, Romagi. I learned Kana, which was invented in 1926. It is pretty universal. You can carry on a conversation on all Westernized things. By contrast, one cannot describe modern or Western things in Kanji.

It was also fun because, among other things, I was doing business with all the people I had known before, when I wore a different hat. I had retained all the respect and attention that I had had in the military.

♠ ♥ ♦ ♣

By law, a regular officer is prevented for three years from doing business domestically with any contractor for his former service. That meant I could only work on Army or Navy contracts. In my case, the situation was very simple. I left the country. I was doing business out of the U.S., with non-U.S. companies. I spent a couple of days discussing my duties as "Corporate Vice President, Far East" and "President, McDonnell Douglas Japan" with the Air Force General Counsel before I went to work for McDonnell Douglas. In order to sign any contracts in Japan, I had to have a corporate body that was incorporated in Japan, itself. Thus, I signed the lease on the house as "President, MDC Japan."

When I returned to the U.S., I had passed the three-year limit. Nevertheless, I went back to the general counsel and gave him a copy of my job description as "Corporate Vice President, Washington." I insisted on a written opinion that in performing these duties, I was in compliance with U.S. laws and regulations.

♠ ♥ ♦ ♣

McDonnell and Douglas had merged in 1967. When I arrived in 1973, Douglas had an office in Tokyo with one man, Phil Bogart, and one woman, a secretary.

McDonnell Douglas had a representative, Zaiser, with a secretary, in Nagoya. He was the point man to look over the shoulder of the Japanese on the F-4 licensed production at the Mitsubishi factory. He had no function in a supervisory way, but someone had to report back to St. Louis.

My job, among other things, was to establish a bona fide office, hire a staff, go forth and become known as the McDonnell Douglas honcho. The biggest aerospace outfit in the world needed an office.

The Dealing's Done

Japan Air Lines (JAL) had Boeing products. My second chore was to penetrate the market and sell some DC-10s to JAL, which I did. By the time I left, they had bought over fifty, in increments of ten or fifteen at a time.

JAL was forty percent owned by the Japanese government. The same was true of All Nippon Airlines (ANA). JAL owned sixty percent of TOA Domestic, plus twenty-five percent was owned outright by the government.

ANA, the second largest airline, was a Lockheed customer. They were a closed outfit, so I never got my foot in the door. They were always nice and polite. We played golf.

TOA Domestic, the third airline, was a commuter type. They had YS-11s, the old Japanese-made Fokker, a two engine, turbo-prop which carried about thirty people. I sold them DC-9s. They were up in the double digits when I left. Now they're a big airline, with DC-10s.

♠ ♥ ♦ ♣

As a foreigner, one can not conduct business in Japan without a trading company. We had Mitsui, a large old trading company, for our commercial aircraft. Mitsubishi produced our F-4, but was not our trading company for the F-4. Mitsubishi was our trading company for missiles. Nisho-Iwai was the trading company for the F-4 and later, the F-15.

I also set up a representative for McDonnell Douglas Information Systems Company, which was very successful. He started scooping up contracts with book values that threatened to exceed those for the airplane business. But this was a temporary thing. By the time I left Tokyo, he had picked the market clean and the Japanese had learned how to do it. There is no representative there now from the company.

♠ ♥ ♦ ♣

After we had been there for about eighteen months, I was close to consummating the deal with Japan Air Lines. TOA Domestic was already on the line for DC-9s. Then the Lockheed scandal erupted. Lockheed had bribed the Prime Minister with $2 million to throw his weight to buy L-1011s for All Nippon Airways. Attempts had been made in this direction toward McDonnell Douglas. I didn't know this until I went over there and discovered this. The path was extremely dicey.

The Dealing's Done

This scandal was particularly juicy to the press; it involved high government officials and a three-star former commander of U.S. Forces in Japan (myself) was a prominent executive of one of the companies that was targeted for the investigation. This unending issue caused my original two-year assignment to extend to four years, by which time everything sorted itself out. Tanaka, the Prime Minister, was forced out in disgrace. Trials were still going on until very recently. I don't think they've cleaned up the mess yet. Japanese jurisprudence works very slowly in cases like this. They hope that they will go away. By contrast, crimes of passion are swiftly adjudicated.

Bribery is a way of life in the Middle East and the Far East. They do not consider it corruption; it is simply the way they do business. But one doesn't have to pay bribes if one's product is good. If a customer understands that, then the seller company is off limits; they don't try. If, however, a seller indicates that he is amenable to doing business that way, then they are comfortable doing it and that is the way it will happen. Both sides expect to perform accordingly.

When the scandal erupted, every American businessman, particularly in the aerospace companies, became a pariah. We were *persona non grata* everywhere. The Japanese government officials would not talk to me. The Japanese media are the grossest of their breed in the world. Scandal and sensationalism are the life blood for four or five of them. Our trading companies tried to shield us from pressures but they were not very successful. It became so bad that we obtained unlisted telephone numbers. My office was broken into twice by newsmen.

Things finally simmered down. The last year we were there was relatively uneventful and painless.

In the meantime, I turned my attention elsewhere. I sold DC-9s and -10s to Korean Airlines, DC-9s to Garuda (Indonesia), DC-10s to Singapore Airlines, DC-10s to Philippine Airlines, DC-10s to New Zealand Airlines, and four DC-10s to Malaysian Air System in Kuala Lumpur.

This last had an interesting aspect. I went down there several times. I was not marketing; I was selling, hard. There is quite a distinction. Boeing and Airbus were competing. Lockheed never entered the picture; they had no market penetration down in that part of the world. The prime minister had to sign the contract. It was a large amount, over $100 million. I got him up to the table a couple of times, but he backed off. I went back again. Finally, I told him, "If you want

The Dealing's Done

this price, you have to sign the contract. We're about to announce a steep price increase."

A big ceremony was arranged, with photographers and local TV coverage. He was so nervous he could hardly sign the contract. Afterwards, we held a cocktail party. He told me in confidence, "That is the largest single expenditure this government has ever undertaken. I want you to understand that accounts for my difficulty in signing the contract."

I never made the grade in Australia. They were too Boeing-oriented. They were nice. I enjoyed visiting them, playing golf and seeing old RAAF friends. I just couldn't peddle them anything.

My Boeing counterpart was a retired Air Force colonel who had been in SAC. I knew him well, from the Air Force. We used to play golf together all the time. We'd tell each other outright lies about things and laugh with each other because we knew we were lying. He left before we did. I didn't know his successor well, but I got along fine with him.

General Dynamics had nothing when I arrived. They came over like babes in the woods, trying to market the F-16 over the F-15. They set up an office and put an absolute rum-dum in charge. I felt sorry for the man; he didn't know anything; he was inexperienced, had never been out of the U.S. I think they eventually sold some airplanes to Japan, but I'm not sure.

Grumman was very actively selling the F-14. They didn't make the sale, but they were vigorous, persistent and professional.

Northrop finally came around, after I left, with a demo of the F-20. In fact, one of their three crashed in Korea. But Northrop never had a presence in Japan.

My greatest achievement over there was to sign the Japanese up for licensed production of the F-15, the follow-on from the F-4. They wanted 133 airplanes. Later, after I left, they added another ten or twelve to the contract. This was delayed because of the Lockheed scandal. All business with the government came to a halt for over a year and a half.

Offshore sales by American aircraft companies is the most lucrative business they can have. The Japanese knew this. On a government contract, like the sale of F-15s to the U.S. Air Force, the maximum profit McDonnell Douglas can achieve is four percent of the sale. On a contract of that magnitude, that is a lot of money. The profit on the contract with the Japanese was thirty percent. The Japanese

The Dealing's Done

knew it. The contract was as good or better than they could have done anywhere else. They accepted that they had to pay the price because they didn't have the technology to produce it. They effectively bought a lot of technology.

In fact, the issue of technology transfer was the only sticky point in that whole contract negotiation. There is an element in OSD in the Pentagon and another in the State Department that worries about what might happen in ten years if another country obtains our technology. The basic doctrine pursued by the U.S. government is to maintain a ten-year gap. This is not written into any rules; it is just policy. We are allowed to sell certain items, such as electronics or engine technology, only if we already have a ten-year lead. This is highly subjective; who is to say that it is ten years? How does one know that the other country won't make a breakthrough and do it in five?

The real advantage of the U.S. today is our methods of manufacturing and production, not the technology itself, except in the area of electronic countermeasures. Some of the black boxes would be a surprise.

I never went to China but I was instrumental in negotiating a contract with them. Their aircraft industry was owned and run by the government and very primitive, like that of the Japanese. This contract was a breakthrough. The reason I didn't go was that all the donkey-work was done by Douglas representatives themselves, out of Long Beach.

I didn't really want to be involved, beyond knowing everything that was going on. I didn't want to go over there and haggle. It appeared to me to be too much effort for the result. Step one of a twenty-year program was to license them to manufacture the landing gear fairing doors on a DC-9. A fairing door is a piece of metal of about forty square feet in size. It requires almost no technology or skill, but that was the first step. The final step was licensed production of the DC-9. This program has reached the point that MDC has given the Chinese two knocked-down kits of DC-9s that they will fabricate.

I went to Korea often. When I took the job, I was told that MACAIR had made a very vigorous effort to sell the Korean Air Force F-4s. They failed. It was a closed subject, they didn't want to discuss it. The U.S. government was opposed to it. They had F-5s and F-86s, both way behind a modern Air Force. I sold a squadron of F-4s over there within eighteen months after I arrived. That was a direct purchase in foreign military sales and was a bunch of dough. Later, they bought more and

The Dealing's Done

more. When I left, they had close to one-hundred F-4s, which is still their main airplane.

The Korean government was totally military. This is less true today. The chief of their Air Force was General Kim, one of three in a row with the same name. I had known this one during the Korean War, when he was a captain. He came back to the U.S. for training, returned to Korea and flew a P-51 with the embryonic Korean Air Force. He worked his way up to chief of the Air Force. He was a very dedicated, patriotic person, as was everyone I met at the senior level there, and had a great sense of humor. After retiring from the Air Force, he became the defense minister and was very close to President Park.

Vivian and I went over to Korea often. We had friends there and it was enjoyable. Besides, I like kimchi, which most people don't. By contrast, I never learned to like the decayed fish sauce used by the Viet Namese. It was vile. I couldn't stand the smell. The Viet Namese maids in the compound at Tan Son Nhut swallowed a gallon at every meal and I made sure to stay upwind of them.

♠ ♥ ♦ ♣

The corporate vice president of the MDC Washington office was John Allen. John had worked for Douglas for years and, following the merger with McDonnell in 1967, was the senior person and took over the show in Washington. John was a tremendous golfer. He had to retire rather abruptly and Old Mr. Mac couldn't find anyone to take his job.

I had done everything I set out to do in Japan: sold the F-15 to the Japanese; the DC-10 to Japan Air Lines, Korean Air Lines, Philippine Air Lines, New Zealand, Singapore, and everywhere else except Cathay Pacific and Australia; the DC-9 all over the Far East. The Harpoon missile went like hotcakes. I sold F-4s in Korea. I told Old Mr. Mac about six months before Allen's retirement that everything was peachy-keen, that I had run out of interesting things to do and was ready to leave.

I found a replacement, Jack Crossthwaite. Jack is about ten years younger than I am, ex-Navy, had worked five years for Republic as a test pilot before he came to MDC.

I hated Washington, but I agreed to take Allen's job for one year. Despite the job description, the job was really as chief lobbyist for the company. I worked on Navy and Army programs, as well as a lot of

The Dealing's Done

Air Force programs. All of these are really conduits to provide a manufacturer with the thinking, goals and requirements of the particular establishment buying the product. Secondly, I was there to influence the decision makers, be they military, House or Senate committee members, State Department or Commerce Department officials. It was very interesting work. I didn't like it but I didn't dislike it. I wouldn't have looked for a job doing this and, if it hadn't been for the circumstances, I would not have stayed there so long. When I started in that job, there were about fifty people working for me. When I left five years later, there were 150.

Old Mr. Mac died and his nephew Sandy McDonnell took the job as chairman. There was a huge change. I felt that I was obligated to hang on to provide some continuity. I moved all the offices out of Washington and consolidated them on two floors of leased space in Crystal City. MDC was like the Middle Ages when I took over. As one illustration, the gals had to go to the ladies room to fill plastic jugs with water to make coffee. The Crystal City office was beautifully set up.

One of my real achievements was to install a computer information system in Washington, tied to our mainframe in St. Louis, a substation at MACAIR and another substation at Long Beach. Six months were required to develop the software. We trained about three or four gals to call up, display, print and/or transmit everything that had transpired the last time Sandy McDonnell came to Washington. Sandy would receive a printout to read before he left for the next trip. For example, there would be an item "Go see Senator or Congressman so-and-so." Afterwards, Sandy would dictate the results of the discussion and the computer file would be updated.

MDC had over 2,200 vendors and subcontractors, which were in the computer along with their officers and telephone numbers, their location, their representative and senators, and everything we needed to know. When we needed support from a particular congressman, we'd punch in his name and get a printout that told us, for example, that a company that manufactured struts for the DC-9 was in that congressman's district. We'd call them and say, "Call your congressman. We have a contract that needs some help."

After five years, in January 1983, I had a little chat with Sandy. I summed up my accomplishments, that I had finished the office move, brought up the operational computer system net, and that our programs were in good shape, including the competition to build the FA-18 for the Navy. I had participated in the sale of the FA-18 to Canada, Israel, and Australia, and there were no outstanding issues or problems. I had trained a bunch of good people and I felt I could walk away in good conscience. I told him I wasn't happy there, which he knew. I told him I would leave on July 1. It went right over his head.

Over the next six months, he would come to town, we would fill his appointments, and I would remind him, "Don't forget, Sandy, I'm leaving on the first of July." It never sank in.

The day I left, he was in Washington and I was in the car with him. I said, "Sandy, I may not see you for a good while. I'm leaving."

He asked, "Where are you going?"

I said, "Sandy, you don't listen. I am leaving McDonnell Douglas as of tomorrow."

Jack Crossthwaite came back from Japan and took over the Washington office when I left.

♠ ♥ ♦ ♣

Vivian and I moved to White Stone, in the Northern Neck of Virginia, in 1983. We lived in the old fisherman's cottage on the property until our new house was built. Then we sold our house in Arlington and finished transferring our furniture and other household goods.

We have a birddog named Patsy, a large garden, sixty fruit trees, including apricots, plums, pears, apples, and nashis (a Japanese hybrid between an apple and pear), and crab traps at the end of the dock on a creek off the Rappahannock River. I have volunteered in a number of areas, including the emergency rescue squad and, most recently, as the President of the Animal Welfare League of the Northern Neck and as the court-appointed humane investigator for the four counties in the Northern Neck. I spend a lot of time reading and I go hunting whenever I have an opportunity. We play golf two or three times a week, are active in our church and keep up with our five children and ten grandchildren.

Epilogue

KNOW WHEN TO WALK AWAY
White Stone, VA

For most of my Air Force career I was very deeply involved in four major issues that were, and still are, controversial.

One issue was the gunsights and cameras in fighters. When I joined the Air Corps and first started flying P-36s and P-35s, we were flying with the same "bead-and-ring" gunsight that was used in World War I. It didn't improve much in World War II with the new reticle-sight. Toward the end of the war, the Navy's K-14 gyro-computing sight was a real breakthrough. It was still in use when we went into Korea.

After Korea, nothing happened until about 1955, when the Air Force acquired a radar-computing gunsight. The F-100 had one. For the times, it was OK. Development lagged far behind that for bombsights, by contrast. This radar-computing sight was still being used on the F-105, the most modern airplane in the early 1960s, but radar-ranging had been added. But this was a sorry piece of equipment for air-to-air gun work.

A second controversy was the "gun versus missile." I have always believed that we should build a plane with a gun and a capability for a full range of missiles (heat-seekers, radar-seekers, etc.). This controversy raged into the early part of the Viet Nam War.

In 1940 and 1941, we had .30 caliber guns from World War I. There were two on the cowl of the P-36; they fired though the propeller. In the P-40, there were four .50 caliber machine guns mounted in the wings. The P-51D had six of them and the P-47 had eight. During the Korean War, the Air Force used the same installation on F-86Es. Those .50 caliber guns were used for the F-84 series. The F-100s had the 20 mm M-39 cannon, which had a low rate of fire.

The next advance was the 20 mm Vulcan (Gatling) cannon. I fired that on a test bench in 1959. The "Vulcan cannon" gun was first installed operationally in the F-105 in 1962 and later in the F-4. It slammed those 20 mm shells out there at a rate of either 3,000 or 6,000 rounds per minute, but the airplane only carried 1,000 rounds. A minimum burst was fifty rounds; there was no interrupter switch that could be set for, say, eighty rounds. By the time you had sucked in your breath, the gun was dry. It is still in the force today. It is ancient technology.

The first Sidewinder was fired in anger in 1958, in the Taiwan crisis. The pilot had only to visually acquire the enemy, point and pickle when he heard the buzz in his headset. There was no need for a sighting solution or program. The heat-seeking Sidewinder would home on the enemy's hot exhaust. It is a very effective weapon, but it reflects poorly on our application of technology if there has been no significant improvement after forty years.

In the 1960s we acquired the Sparrow with the F-4 from the Navy. The Sparrow has a radar-guided homing system, a good acquisition and lock-on range, but is expensive. We had poor results with it in Viet Nam for several reasons—quality control, poor maintenance, firing out of parameters, poor aircrew knowledge, lack of practice. The Sparrow is still one of our major air-to-air weapons in the fighter force, through the F-15s and F-16s, even though it is not a very good weapon.

"Earthquake" Titus was the only Air Force pilot to shoot down a MiG with each of the three systems.

One dream solution to the gun was to build a caseless-round. This avoided the ammo brass-casing weight problem and the foreign-object problem, which resulted from spewing spent cases out of the side of the airplane, where it could be sucked into the next pilot's intake. I saw millions of dollars spent over the years by GE, Westinghouse and

Ford. These three contractors invariably won the contracts for this caseless round. They would show up at Eglin with a test article which rarely functioned properly. There seems to be no physical way to fit the propellant with the bullet without a case.

♠ ♥ ♦ ♣

A third controversy, which may never be settled, was the "one versus two engines." I was in favor of one engine for years, until I flew the F-4, with the J-79. Before the J-79 era, engines were too big, heavy and unmaneuverable for the air-to-air role.

The accident rate of a single-engine airplane was statistically higher but not twice as high as the rate for two-engine airplane. The statistical comparison of engine-related accidents, only, between the F-15 and F-16 was especially convincing. Given my experience with P-51s, I had been on the other side of the fence for the longest time! I had had greater range, was less vulnerable, and almost always came home on one engine—but a big airplane with one engine made a good target.

The issue arises more now because the cheap-Charlies in the Pentagon are less concerned about operational success and more convinced that one engine and one pilot have to be cheaper. If one wishes to preserve the force structure, the name of the game is "Buy the cheapest airplane." The best illustration is the following that developed during the MacNamara era from his Whiz Kids. They were advocates of a 10,000 pound airplane, with no armor plate. "Why would you want armor plate?" Fortunately, they didn't prevail, but they certainly caused a lot of wasted effort and setbacks.

♠ ♥ ♦ ♣

A fourth enduring issue, which is analogous to the last, was "two pilots versus one." With technological assistance, one pilot can do it all. With too much technology, two pilots are needed. These two situations continue to alternate.

Now, in my personal judgment, one pilot can handle it in a fighter. This isn't to say that two can't do it better, particularly some phases, such as long-range strike missions, all-weather, night, as for the F-15E. On the other hand, for a pure air-to-air mission, as for the F-16, a second pilot is a liability. First, he makes the airplane heavier, which means the airplane needs more gas. The second set of eyeballs doesn't help that much.

A little known fact is that only once during and since Viet Nam has the Air Force ever fought in a "guns-free" mode, meaning technically that we could fire without visually acquiring the air target. This one occasion lasted about seven minutes on one mission, during which Robin Olds and his pilots shot down seven MiGs. Otherwise, the eighteen-mile range of the Sparrow and equivalent or better range afforded by radar target acquisition were useless: maximum visual identification range is three miles and the rules of engagement prevented any pilot—Air Force or Navy—from toggling off without visual identification.

A second (better) reason was the mixture of airplanes in the force: Army, Navy, Air Force, Marine and Viet Namese Air Force (VNAF). One had to have a system or procedure for identifying a friend or foe with confidence before turning a missile loose. No one was willing to rely exclusively on the available "Identification: Friend or Foe" (IFF) equipment. The USAF has had an IFF system since Korea that is state-of-the-art. The issue has always been, how can one be completely sure that the enemy hasn't figured a way to fake one out?

Appendix A
DESCRIPTIONS OF AIRCRAFT

TRAINERS

PT-13 Primary Trainer, two-place biplane (one for a student and one for an instructor); 225 horsepower (hp) radial engine; fixed landing gear and tail wheel; manufactured by Stearman.

BT-9 Basic Trainer, two-place; all metal, low-winged monoplane; 450 hp engine; manufactured by North American Aviation.

BT-13 Basic Trainer, two-place; all metal, low-winged monoplane; 450 hp radial, air-cooled engine; manufactured by Vultee Aviation.

BT-14 Basic Trainer, two-place; 450 hp radial, air-cooled engine; manufactured by North American Aviation.

BC-1A Basic Combat, a larger version of the AT-6; two-place; 650 hp radial engine; manufactured by North American Aviation.

AT-6 Advanced Trainer, two-place; one .50 caliber gun in each wing; all metal, low-winged monoplane with retractable landing gear; manufactured by North American Aviation.

T-33 First jet trainer; two-place, single engine; derived from the P-80 aircraft design; manufactured by Lockheed Aircraft Corp.

FIGHTERS

PB-2 Pursuit, biplace (two people), powered by a Curtiss-Conqueror in-line liquid-cooled engine; had a turbosupercharger; was never used in combat.

P-35 Pursuit, single-place; gross weight 5600 lb. with a 950 hp radial engine; maximum airspeed of 281 mph; delivered in 1937; manufactured by Seversky Aircraft Co.

P-36 "Curtiss Hawk" - Pursuit, single-place; gross weight 6010 lb. with a 1050 hp radial engine, 3-blade propeller; maximum airspeed of 300 mph; two .30 caliber machine guns cowl-mounted; delivered in 1938; manufactured by Curtiss Wright Aircraft Co.

Appendix A

P-38   "Lightning" - Pursuit, single-place; gross weight 14,500-17,000 lb. with two in-line liquid-cooled engines, 1150 to 1475 hp; maximum airspeed of 390 to 410 mph; four .50 caliber machine guns; delivered in 1941; manufactured by Lockheed Aircraft Corp.

P-39   "Air Cobra" - Pursuit, single-place; gross weight 6,204-8,500 lb., with a in-line liquid-cooled engine, 3-bladed propeller, 1150 to 1325 hp; 37 mm cannon firing through nose and two .50 caliber guns in the wings; maximum airspeed of 370 to 385 mph; first delivered in 1940; manufactured by Bell Aircraft Corp.

P-40   "Kitty Hawk," "War Hawk," - Pursuit, single-place; gross weight 7215-10,000 lb., maximum airspeed of 350 to 370 mph; four .50 caliber wing-mounted machine guns; delivered in 1939; manufactured by Curtiss Wright Aviation Corp.

P-47   "Thunderbolt," "Jug" - Pursuit, single-place; gross weight 13,356-14,925 lb., four-bladed propeller, 2000-2100 hp radial engine, maximum airspeed of 429 to 450 mph; eight .50 caliber wing-mounted machine guns; delivered in 1942; manufactured by Republic Aviation Co.

P-51   "Mustang" - Pursuit, single-place; gross weight 8800-11,800 lb., with a Rolls Royce Merlin liquid-cooled engine 1150-1380 hp; maximum airspeed of 382 to 439 mph; six .50 caliber wing-mounted machine guns; delivered in 1942; manufactured by North American Aviation.

P-80   "Shooting Star" - Pursuit, single-place; gross weight 11,700 lb. with 4000 lb. of thrust; maximum airspeed of 560 mph; delivered in 1945; manufactured by Lockheed; first operational jet but never saw combat in World War II.

F-84   "B;" "E;" "G" were straight-wing; "F" was the first swept-wing fighter.

"Thunderjet" - Models "B," "E," and "G" - Single-place jet; straight-wing; gross weight 22,000 lb. with 5000 lb. of thrust; maximum airspeed of 600 mph.; delivered in 1949; manufactured by Republic Aviation.

"Thunderstreak" - Model "F" - Single-place jet; swept-wing; gross weight 25,000 lb. with 7200 lb. of thrust; maximum airspeed of 650 mph; delivered in 1954; manufactured by Republic Aviation. Also known as "the Lead Sled."

Appendix A

F-86	"Sabre" - Models "D," "E," "F" - Single-place jet; all swept-wing; gross weight 16,000 lb. with 5200 lb. of thrust; maximum airspeed of 650 mph.; delivered in 1948; manufactured by North American Aviation.
F-94	"Starfire" - Two-place jet; straight-wing; gross weight 16,500-20,000 lb. with 8750 lb. of thrust; maximum airspeed of 600 mph.; delivered in 1950; manufactured by Lockheed Aircraft Corp.; fired air defense missiles.
F-100	"Super Sabre"- Series of Models "A," "C," and "D" - Single-place jets; "F" - Two-place jet; gross weight 27,000 lb. with 1,600 lb. of thrust with an afterburner; maximum airspeed of 750 mph.; delivered in 1954; manufactured by North American Aviation; first USAF jet aircraft that would go supersonic in level flight.
F-101	"Voodoo" - Model "A" - Single- and Model "B" - Two-place jet; "C" and RF-101; gross weight 40,000 lb. with twin jet 30,000 lb. of thrust; maximum airspeed of 1200 mph.; delivered in 1955; manufactured by McDonnell Aircraft.
F-102	"Delta Dagger" - Single-place jet; delta-wing; gross weight 27,000 lb. with 16,000 lb. of thrust; maximum airspeed of 825 mph.; delivered in 1954; manufactured by Convair for air defense.
F-104	"Starfighter" - Single-place jet; straight-wing; gross weight 19,200 lb. with 15,800 lb. of thrust from a General Electric J-79 engine; maximum airspeed of 1,400+ mph.; delivered in 1954; manufactured by Lockheed Aircraft Corp.
F-105	"Thunderchief" - Models "B," "D," and "F" - Single-place jet; gross weight 48,400 lb. with 26,500 lb. of thrust from a single Pratt & Whitney J-75 engine; maximum airspeed of 1,420 mph.; delivered in 1956; manufactured by Republic Aviation.
F-106	"Delta Dart" - Single- or two-place jet; gross weight 35,000 lb. with 24,500 lb. of thrust; maximum airspeed of 1380 mph.; delivered in 1956; manufactured by Convair for air defense.
F-4	" Phantom II" - Model "C," derived from the Navy version "H," was originally the F-110 for the Air Force, until Secretary of Defense MacNamara changed the designation; twin jet,

Appendix A

F-4 (cont.) two-place, 34,000 lb. thrust, no gun, two Sidewinders and four Sparrow missiles.

"Phantom II" - Model "E" - Two-place jet, first with an internal gun; gross weight of 42,000 lb. with 34,000 lb. thrust from two J-79 jet engines; maximum airspeed of Mach 2+; delivered in 1963; manufactured by McDonnell Douglas.

F-111 "Aardvark" - Two-place jet; unique USAF variable-geometry-wing fighter airplane; gross weight of 70,000 lb. with twin jet 40,000 lb. thrust; maximum airspeed of Mach 2.5; delivered in 1964; manufactured by General Dynamics Corp.

F-5 or (N-156) Single-place jet; gross weight of 13,300 lb. with 7700 lb. thrust from two engines; maximum airspeed of Mach 1.4; delivered in 1963; manufactured by Northrop Aircraft Corp.

F-117 Unique USAF stealth jet, of which there is only one squadron in inventory; manufactured by Lockheed Aircraft Corp.

F-15 "Eagle" - Two-place, swept-wing jet; gross weight of 40,000 lb. with 40,000 lb. thrust from two Pratt & Whitney F-100 PW engines; maximum airspeed of Mach 2+; delivered in 1972; manufactured by McDonnell Douglas.

F-16 "Falcon" - Single-place, swept-wing jet; gross weight of 35,000 lb. with 20,000 lb. thrust from one Pratt & Whitney engine; maximum airspeed of Mach 2+; delivered in 1973; manufactured by General Dynamics Corp.

RECONNAISSANCE

The following were recconnaissance versions of the fighters, very similar but with cameras and sensors in place of any armament:

RF-51

RF-4

RF-5

U-2 High-altitude reconnaissance aircraft manufactured by Lockheed Aircraft Corp.

Appendix A

ATTACK AIRCRAFT

A-1E Derived from Navy AD-6; four-bladed propeller; conventional air-cooled radial engine; flown in Korea and after by USAF in Viet Nam.

A-3J USN twin-jet, high performance two-place attack airplane for the Navy which became the RA-5; never used as an attack aircraft; manufactured by North American Aviation.

A-4D USN single-jet, single-place, manufactured by McDonnell Douglas.

AD-6 See A1E.

A-7 USN and USAF sub-sonic single-place jet, purchased by the Navy originally, but the USAF added it to its inventory; manufactured by Ling/Temco/Vought.

A-10 USAF sub-sonic, twin jet straight-wing; manufactured by Republic Aviation for ground support.

A-26 Twin-engine conventional two-place aircraft used in World War II; later redesignated the B-26 in Korea and Viet Nam.

HEAVY BOMBERS

B-17 "Flying Fortress"- four radial engines; flown in World War II; manufactured by Boeing.

B-24 "Liberator" - World War II vintage; four radial engines; manufactured by Consolidated.

B-29 Four engine; manufactured by Boeing.

B-36 "Peacemaker" - Six-engine, propeller-driven, and four jets; largest bomber ever built in the inventory; manufactured by Consolidated.

B-47 Four-engine swept-wing jet; first of the jet bombers; manufactured by Boeing.

Appendix A

B-52   Jet bomber, manufactured by Boeing.

B-66   Twin jet engines manufactured by Northrup Aviation.

B-70   "Valkyrie" -twin engine; never went into production-only three were ever manufactured; Mach 3+; manufactured by North American Aviation.

MEDIUM BOMBERS

B-25   "Mitchell" - twin radial-engine; manufactured by North American Aviation. Used to bomb Japan in 1942 by Jimmy Doolittle.

B-26   "Marauder" - twin-engine conventional aircraft; manufactured by Martin during World War II.

LIGHT BOMBERS

B-57   "Canberra" - Twin-engine, two-place jet; used in Viet Nam; manufactured by Canberra, a British company.

CARGO AND TRANSPORT

CV-2   "Caribou" - Conventional twin-engine procured by the Army, but later taken over by the USAF; manufactured in Canada.

C-5   Four-engine jet; largest cargo aircraft; manufactured by Lockheed Aircraft Corp.

C-45   Small, 10-passenger twin reciprocating-engine conventional aircraft; manufactured by Beech Aircraft Co.

C-47   "Gooney Bird" - Twin radial-engine; manufactured by Douglas Aircraft Corp.

C-123   Twin radial-engine; manufactured by Fairchild.

C-124   Four radial-engine, heavy transport; manufactured by McDonnell Douglas.

Appendix A

C-130   "Hercules"- Four-engine, prop-jet; manufactured by Lockheed Aircraft Corp.

C-141   Four-engine, swept-wing jet, heavy lift; manufactured by Lockheed Aircraft Corp.

MISCELLANEOUS

KB-29   Tanker versions of B-29s that used four reciprocating engines; manufactured by Boeing.

KB-50   A KB-29 with two jet engines added, as well as other modifications; manufactured by Boeing.

KC-135   Four-engine, swept-wing jet/tanker; manufactured by Boeing.

EB-66   "Barracuda" - Electronic warfare version of the B-66 Bomber; twin-engine jet used for communications intercept and radar detection; manufactured by Northrup Aviation.

GERMAN AIRCRAFT

Messerschmitt-109
   Single-engine, liquid-cooled fighter, single-place.

Focke Wulfe-190
   Single radial-engine; single-place.

Messerschmitt-262
   First twin-engine, straight-wing, single-place jet with an airspeed over 500 mph. to fly in combat on either side in World War II.

Junker-88
   Twin-engine light bomber and long-range fighter.

Glossary
PILOTSPEAK

AAA Anti-aircraft artillery.
Acquisition range Range (miles) at which a radar acquires a target.
Afterburner Raw fuel is injected into the exhaust section, aft of the turbine, to create a controlled explosion for extra power; "stroking the 'burner" means to light the afterburner for full power.
Air Corps Combat arm of the air force in the Army at the beginning of World War II. The "U.S. Army Air Forces (USAAF)" was created on June 20, 1941, to incorporate all the air assets, but the Air Corps actually continued until 1942. People continued to refer to the "Air Corps" through the end of the war and considered the substitution of the USAAF as just something done in Washington. The U.S. Air Force was created as a separate military department in September 1947.
Ammo Ammunition.
Article 104 Company punishment; may be administered by an individual's commanding officer in lieu of a court martial.
ARVN Army of the Republic of Viet Nam.
Auger in Airplane crash either by spiralling in (hence the name of the carpenter's tool, "auger") or from an uncontrollable tailspin; generally, any crash.
Bail out Escape from an aircraft using a parachute.
Bandit Enemy aircraft.
Barrier Restriction at the end of a runway to stop an airplane that is going too fast and may go into the overrun.
Belly in A controlled crash landing of the aircraft, with the landing gear up.
Bingo Almost complete expenditure of ammo or fuel, with minimal reserve for emergency; preestablished point for breaking off work.
Bogey Unidentified aircraft.
Bounce Initiation of an attack on enemy aircraft; controlling the bounce gave one an advantage.
Box of bombers Bomber formation, usually comprising one squadron.
Brace An exaggerated posture of attention.
Buncher beacon A low-frequency, non-directional beacon used by the bombers as a rendezvous point.
CINC Commander in Chief.
DI Deputy for Intelligence.
DO Deputy for Operations.
Doppler Doppler systems are radar navigation systems used in virtually all airplanes today.
Exposure suit Survival suit, much like a wet suit today.

Glossary

FAC Forward Air Controller.
Frag Fragmentation bomb, usually mounted on an aircraft in clusters of three. Also a contraction of "fragmentary" for a portion of the order for a mission.
Flak car Anti-aircraft artillery mounted on a railroad car.
Flak shack Rest and recreation facility operated by the Red Cross.
Flameout (landing) Landing after engine has lost all power.
Form 1 The aircraft flying and maintenance record.
G Unit of gravity.
IG Inspector General.
Inertial Inertial systems are navigation systems commonly used in many types of airplanes today.
IO Intelligence Officer.
Jinking Rapid changes in direction and altitude to avoid anti-aircraft fire.
JP-4 Jet aircraft fuel, a less volatile fuel than high-octane gasoline.
Jug P-47 airplane.
LABS Low Altitude Bombing System.
Lock-on range Range at which a radar locks onto a target.
Mae West Slang, referring to a popular World War II female entertainer, given to a pilot's personal flotation device; the device could be inflated after a pilot bailed out of an airplane, but prior to or after a pilot hit the water; designed to keep even an unconscious pilot afloat.
MAC Military Airlift Command.
MACV Military Assistance Command, Viet Nam.
Manifold pressure Gauge that measures the pressure of the mixture in the engine going into the cylinder; measure of power, such that maximum pressure means full power.
MDC McDonnell Corporation or, after the merger, McDonnell Douglas Corporation.
Napalm Incendiary compound mixed in a container like a drop tank, referred to as a "can," jellied gasoline.
Non-rated An individual who lacks a flying rating of "pilot," "bombardier," "navigator," etc.
Open post An official pass to leave the post, for "liberty" or recreational purposes in the nearby town.
ORI Operational Readiness Inspection.
PACAF Pacific Air Force.
Peel off Maneuver to execute a rapid diving turn away from the original flight path.
Perch A position maintained by a flying instructor prior to peeling off and making a pass at a target; four student pilots in echelon formation are stacked up to the rear of the leader/instructor to observe the tactics being demonstrated; the flying instructor regains the perch to observe the performance of the students, who return to their respective position in echelon behind the instructor after a pass.

Glossary

POL Petroleum, Oil, Lubricants.

Pursuit Until the Korean War, "Pursuit" was used to designate "Fighter" pilots and airplanes.

PX Post Exchange, for general merchandise items other than those issued by the government for use by military service members.

Rat racing Series of maneuvers by one airplane chasing another through formations, loops, dives, etc., simulating combat.

Rated Having a rating as a "pilot," "bombardier," or "navigator" that qualified one for extra pay.

Sabre-Dance A situation that occurs when an airplane (originally the F-100 Super Sabre) in afterburner, very close to the gound, does not have enough forward speed to maintain lift and control and crashes; today, with ejection possible at 0 altitude/0 airpseed, a pilot can eject.

SAC Strategic Air Command.

SAM Surface-Air Missile.

Sink the stick Pull the stick back to execute a climbing maneuver or conclude the landing glide with the nose of the airplane up.

Sparrow An advanced, air-air missile developed by the Navy which was radar-guided.

Spin in Airplane crash due to pilot inability to pull out of a spin.

Spit Spitfire, a British fighter airplane.

Split-S Aircraft maneuver of a half-roll into the inverted position and a pull of the stick to dive vertically.

Stick Control column for the airplane; pushing forward resulted in "nosing over" and descending; pulling back meant "back stick" or climbing; pushing left or right resulted in banking in that respective direction; "pickling" resulted from punching the red button on the top with the thumb to release external stores (bombs, tanks, rockets, missiles) from the pylons.

TAC Tactical Air Command.

Tracers Rounds with a magnesium core, which give a visible bright white trajectory when they are fired.

Turbocharger Engine that uses compressed air to increase power; used in some automobiles today.

USAFE U.S. Armed Forces, Europe.

VIP Very Important Person.

VNAF Viet Namese Air Force.

Washout To be eliminated from the flying program.

Wingman Second aircraft and pilot in a two-ship element; responsible for protecting his leader (and vice versa) in combat.

INDEX

Numerals

12th Tactical Fighter Wing, 222
182nd Base Unit Reserve Training, 79
18th Airborne Corps, 129
19th Bomb Wing, 88
2240 Quartermaster Truck Company, 70
307th Squadron, 118, 119
308th Squadron, 119
31st Tactical Fighter Wing, 62, 101, 102, 103, 107, 109, 114, 117, 118, 119, 120, 122, 146, 192, 193, 194, 195
339th Fighter Group, 53
354th Fighter Group, 31, 32, 187, 188, 191
355th Fighter Group, 31, 65, 191, 237
361st Fighter Group, 55, 56, 60, 63, 80
366th Squadron, 242
374th Squadron, 55
405th Fighter Wing, 240
4080th Strategic Reconnaissance Wing, 103
40th Air Division, 101
41-F, flying school class, 19
41-G, flying school class, 23, 24
479th Fighter Group, 102
48th Fighter Bomber Wing, 119
4th Tactical Fighter Wing, 151, 152, 153, 155, 158, 166, 167, 249
506th Fighter Wing, 109
508th Fighter Wing, 101, 102, 103
522nd Fighter Wing, 165
555th Squadron, 242
56th Air Commando Wing, 102, 245
78th Fighter Group, 56, 59
8th Tactical Fighter Wing, 242, 246, 249
91st Bomb Group, 33
92nd Fighter Group, 95
99th Pursuit Squadron, 27

A

Adams, Paul, General, USA, 176, 177, 178
Adana, 279
Aderholt, Harry C. "Heinie", Brigadier General, USAF, 202, 245
Aeronca C-3. *See* Aircraft
Agan, "Sailor", 241
Air Force Institute of Technology (AFIT), 83
Air Force Thunderbirds, 237, 252, 256, 257, 258
Air Training Command, 87
Air Transport Command, 45, 46
Air University, 13, 83
Aircraft
  A-1, 104, 132, 137, 228, 259
  A-26, 86, 245
  A-4D, 132
  A-7, 137, 139, 140, 259
  A-7D, 139
  A-9, 137
  A3J-1, 132, 137
  AC-119, 241
  AC-130, 241
  AC-47, 241
  AD-6, 132, 137
  Aeronca C-3, 8
  AT-6, 19, 20, 21, 23, 25
  B-17, 33, 38, 39, 40, 41, 42, 43, 49, 50, 94
  B-24, 37, 39, 40
  B-25, 92, 95
  B-26, Marauder, 58
  B-36, 81
  B-47, 113, 115
  B-52, 162, 222, 231, 232, 234
  B-70, 51, 126
  BC-1A, 19, 20, 21
  BT-13A, Vultee Vibrators, 26
  BT-14, 16
  BT-9, 16
  C-123, 157, 232
  C-124, 171, 176
  C-130, 157, 167, 170, 171, 173, 175, 176, 177, 179, 216, 222, 232, 235, 241, 244, 245, 246
  C-130E, 171, 175
  C-133, 171

Index

Aircraft *continued*
    C-141, 136, 216
    C-45, 79, 117
    C-47, Gooney Bird, 67, 95, 139, 241, 242
    C-5, 136
    CV-2, Caribou, 232
    DC-10, 121, 284, 288, 289, 292
    EB-66, Barracuda, 242
    F-100, 114, 118, 120, 121, 130, 136, 162, 164, 169, 179, 230, 231, 235, 243
    F-100D, 118, 180, 192, 193, 195, 198
    F-100F, 129, 136, 170, 180, 194
    F-101, 132
    F-104, 51, 132, 148, 161
    F-104G, 121
    F-105, 104, 120, 129, 130, 131, 132, 134, 135, 136, 138, 148, 224, 236, 237, 242, 243, 248, 249, 295, 296
    F-105B, 130, 131
    F-105D, Thunderchief "Thud", 197, 237, 249
    F-110, 196
    F-111, 259
    F-117, 140
    F-14, 141, 284, 290
    F-15, 139, 259, 284, 285, 288, 290, 292, 296, 297
    F-15E, 297
    F-16, 259, 290, 296, 297
    F-20, 290
    F-4, 121, 135, 136, 138, 229, 242, 243, 257, 287, 288, 290, 296, 297
    F-4C, 196, 203, 208, 209, 210
    F-4E, 138, 140
    F-4H, 132, 134, 137
    F-5, 137
    F-84, 104, 114, 115, 296
    F-84B, 104
    F-84F, 101, 102, 103, 104, 105, 106, 108, 110, 113, 114, 115, 117, 118, 120, 128, 273
    F-84G, 102, 103, 104, 120
    F-86, 102, 118, 180, 291
    F-86E, 296
    F-94, 95
    FA-18, 293

Fairchild 24, 9
FC-47, 241
Fleet, 9
Focke-Wulfe-190, 43, 57
Folland Gnat, 169
Hawker-Hunter, 169
Jug, 43
KB-29, 107, 110, 111, 112, 128
KB-50, 128, 193
KC-135, 128, 152, 162, 208
KC-135A, 172
KC-97, 128
Luscombe, 8
Messerschmitt (Me-109), 35, 41, 43, 50, 52, 53
Messerschmitt (Me-262), 34, 41, 42, 43
MiG-21, 169, 173, 203
P-35, 20, 295
P-36, 20, 21, 23, 295, 296
P-38, 29, 39, 43
P-40, 296
P-40N, 29
P-47, 29, 55, 296
P-47N, 55
P-51, 1, 2, 29, 31, 36, 37, 39, 40, 41, 43, 45, 52, 66, 79, 92, 93, 119, 137, 187, 217, 292, 297
P-51D, 189, 296
P-80, 87, 137
PB-2, 20
Piper Cub, 9
PT-13, 14
RF-101, 161, 164
RF-4, 136, 204, 226, 229, 256
RF-4C, 202
Spitfire, 43, 52, 60, 107
Stealth fighter, 140
T-33, 95, 96, 112, 115, 132, 136, 142, 147, 155
Taylorcraft, 8
Thunderbolt, 104
Travelair 2000, 9
U-2, 161
V-1 (Buzz Bomb), 35
Vultee Vibrators, BT-13A, 26
Alabama
    Brookley Air Force Base, 159, 160
    Craig Field, 17, 19

Index

Alabama *continued*
  Maxwell Air Force Base, 27
  Tuskegee Army Air Field, 27
Alaska
  Eielson Air Force Base, 109, 110, 111, 112
  Elmendorf Air Force Base, 109, 111, 112
Alexander, David "Dave", Colonel, USAF, 152
Allen, Brooke, Brigadier General, 89, 90, 94
Allen, John, 292
Ambala, India, 168, 170, 171, 172, 173
Amen, Henry J., First Lieutenant, 16, 18
American Oil (Amoco), 75
Andrews Air Force Base, Maryland, 87, 92, 93, 143, 144, 216
Angels, Bulldogs, and Dragons, 31
ARAMCO, 76
Arizona, 16
  Luke Air Force Base, 102, 127
  Williams Air Force Base, 79, 87
Augsburg, Germany, 65

B

Backus, Ed, Colonel, 79, 95
Barker, Air Vice Marshal, 169, 173, 174
Barksdale Air Force Base, Louisiana, 107, 117
Bataan Death March, 7
Bavaria, Germany, 56
Berlin, Germany, 34, 43, 67, 128
Bergstrom Air Force Base, Texas, 117
Bernadotte, Count, 49
Bien Hoa, Viet Nam, 222
Blair, Charles "Charlie", Brigadier General, USAF, 119, 145, 240
Blazek, Frank, Colonel, USAF, 263
Blood, Gordon "Gordy", Major General, USAF, 257
Bolling Air Force Base, Maryland, 87, 92
Bowles, U.S. Ambassador to India, 168, 174
Box, Clyde, Major General, USAF, 176

Bremerhaven, Germany, 38
Brett, Devol "Rock", Brigadier General, USAF, 176
British Columbia, 6, 110
Brookley Air Force Base, Alabama, 159, 160
Brooks Air Force Base, Texas, 77, 79, 80, 81, 95
Brooks, Eloise LeFevre Graham, 75
Broughton, Jacksel "Jack", Colonel, USAF, 237, 238, 239, 240, 252
Brown, Henry "Baby", 32
Bruce, Walt, Colonel, USAF, 108, 109, 121, 194
Brunel, Dorothy, 192
Burdette, Edward "Ed", Brigadier General, USAF, 146
Burns, John J. "J.J.", Lieutenant General, USAF, 105, 162, 249, 258, 259
Buzz Bomb. *See* Aircraft, V-1

C

Cabell, Pearre "Pree", General, USAF, 95
California
  Edwards Air Force Base, 132, 133, 134
  El Segundo, 6
  Fort MacArthur, 10, 79
  George Air Force Base, 118, 122, 147
  Hemet, 11, 13, 15, 16, 17, 18
  Long Beach, 9, 291, 293
  March Air Force Base, 76, 87, 270
  Redlands, 15
  Redlands University, 15
  Taft, 2, 6, 7, 8, 66, 186, 187
  Taft College, 7
Cannon Air Force Base, New Mexico, 165, 168
CAPTIVAIR, 87
Caracas, Venezuela, 75
Carswell Air Force Base, Texas, 81, 115, 116, 117. *See also* Fort Worth, Texas
Cassidy, Emmet, Major General, USAF, 160

Index

Catton, Jack J., Brigadier General, USAF, 162, 163
Caviness, Roy, Colonel, USAF, 55
celestial navigation, 106, 120
Central Intelligence Agency, 95, 127, 229
Chang, Lieutenant General, 206
Chapman, Wilson, Colonel, USAF, 83
Chidlaw, Ben, General, USAF, 88, 89
Childs, Maurice E. "Deke", Colonel, USAF, 129
Clark Air Force Base, Philippines, 148, 240, 243
Cluster Bomb Units, 236
Cochran Field, Macon, Georgia, 26, 27
Coiner, Richard, Major General, USAF, 152, 160
Colorado
  Denver, 6
  Ouray, 5, 186
  Peterson Air Force Base, 107, 108
Combat Air Patrol (CAP), 2
Combat, He Wrote, 33
Compton, Willie B., Major, USAF, 10, 79, 80
Conner, Richard E. "Crash", Lieutenant Colonel, USAF, 27, 28, 59, 60
Corona Avenue, Redlands, California, 15
Corps of Engineers, 76, 77, 221, 222, 252
Corregidor, 7
Corum, Del, Lieutenant, 114
Cox, Rod, Major, USAF, 53
Craig Field, Selma, Alabama, 17, 19
Creech, Wilbur "Bill", General, USAF, 172, 252, 253
Crossthwaite, Jack, 292, 294
Crum, Bill, Major General, USAF, 126
Cuba, 127, 161
Cuban Missile Crisis, 161, 198
Curtiss-Conqueror, in-line engine, 20
Cyprus, Greece, 179

D

Dale Mabry Replacement Training Unit, 29
Davis, Benjamin "Ben", Lieutenant General, USAF, 27, 95
Defense Petroleum Agency, 125
Demiröz, Yasar, Colonel, Turkish AF, 276, 279, 280
Denver, Colorado, 6
Depression era, 6
DESERT STORM, 62, 259
Devasher, Group Captain, 170
Dickey, Leonard, Lieutenant, 83
Dien Bien Phu, Viet Nam, 230
Directorate of Intelligence, HQ USAF
  Air Targets Division, 89, 91, 92
  Petoleum Section, 91
Disosway, Gabriel P. "Gabe", General, USAF, 136, 138, 139, 140, 148, 217, 233, 255
Dixon, Robert "Bob", General, USAF, 252
Dollar Steamship Line, 9
Dominican Republic Air Force, 217
Dominican Republic Crisis, 216
Don Muang, Thailand, 222
Doolittle, Jimmy, General, 85, 86, 87, 88, 89, 90, 92
Doppler, 118, 120, 121
Doppler-inertial navigators, 121
Druen, Walter D., Jr. "Dan", Major General, USAF, 122
Duffy, James E., Jr. "Jim", 191
Dunham, William D. "Dinghy", Brigadier General, USAF, 147
Dunning, John "Big John", Brigadier General, USAF, 147
Duran, Master Sergeant, 193
Duxford, England, 56, 59, 60

E

Eagle Squadron, 61, 153
Eaker, Ira C., Major General, 45, 46, 47
Edwards Air Force Base, California, 132, 133, 134
Eglin Air Force Base, Florida, 21, 29, 127, 130, 131, 158, 162, 241, 247. *See also* Fort Walton Beach Army Air Field
Eielson Air Force Base, Alaska, 109, 110, 111, 112
Eighth Air Force, 32, 38, 45, 60, 68, 85, 265

Index

Eighth Fighter Command, 42
Eighth Tactical Fighter Wing, 242, 246, 249
El Segundo, California, 6
Elmendorf Air Force Base, Alaska, 109, 111, 112
England
   Duxford, 56, 59, 60
   Little Walden, 55, 58, 60
   Steeple Morden, 31, 46, 65, 187, 189, 191, 192
   Sturgate, 109
Enthoven, Alain, 139
Estes, Howell, General, 206
Eubank, John, Major General, USAF, 161
Everest, Frank, General, USAF, 216

F

Far East Air Force, Japan 62, 87, 95, 263
Fifth Air Force, Japan 62, 95, 99, 169, 209, 213, 261, 264, 265
First Tactical Air Force, 213
Fletcher, Jack, Lieutenant, USAAF, 48, 191
Florida
   Eglin Air Force Base, 21, 23, 29, 127, 130, 131, 158, 162, 241, 247
   Fort Walton Beach Army Air Field, 21, 23, 25
   Homestead Air Force Base, 162, 163, 164, 198
   McCoy Air Force Base, 114, 162
   McDill Air Force Base, 162, 216, 256
   Naples, 29, 31
   Pensacola, 8, 9
   Tallahassee, 29
Fontenot, Dr., Captain, USAAF, 47
Ford, Lieutenant, 13
Fort Bragg, North Carolina, 155, 157, 197, 198
Fort MacArthur, San Pedro, California, 10, 79
Fort Walton Beach Army Air Field, Florida, 21, 23, 25. *See also* Eglin Air Force Base
Fort Worth Army Air Field, Texas, 79, 80, 81
Fortier, Norman J. "Bud", Lieutenant Colonel, USAF, 46, 47, 191, 201, 202, 204, 205
Fourth Tactical Fighter Wing, 96, 151, 152, 153, 155, 158, 166, 167, 249
Fowler, Jack, Brigadier General, USAF, 94, 95
Franklin, R.C., Colonel, USAF, 218
French Foreign Legion Air Force, 59, 60, 61, 62
Fritzlar, Germany, 57, 58
Fuchu Air Station, Tokyo, Japan, 209, 212

G

g-suit, 48, 113
Galland, Adolph, 42, 43
Garland, William M., Brigadier General, USAF, 94
Gates, Bob, Colonel, USAF, 130
General Robert F. Worley Hall, 252
George Air Force Base, California, 118, 122, 147
   William Tell Meet, 122
Georgia
   Cochran Field, 26, 27
   Turner Air Force Base, 101, 104, 108, 117, 120, 123, 130, 161, 215
Germany
   Augsburg, 65
   Bavaria, 56
   Berlin, 34, 43, 67, 128
   Bremerhaven, 38
   Fritzlar, 57, 58
   Templehof, 67, 68
Glantz, Mike, 39, 42, 45
Godfrey, Arthur, 201
Going Downtown, 240
Goodpaster, Andrew, General, USA, 274
Göring, Hermann, 67
Gould, Bob, Colonel, USAF, 96
Graham, Alexander, 5
Graham, Billy, 205
Graham, Jacquie, 7

313

Index

Graham, June Claire "Jay", 6, 7, 186,
Graham, Marshall Roberts "Bob", Colonel, USAF, 83, 96, 107
Graham, Mary Bruce, 5
Graham Report, 218
Graham, Vivian, 207, 212, 275, 278, 280, 283, 284, 285, 286, 292, 294
Greece, 157, 166, 179, 275, 282
  Cyprus, 179
Grey, Sarah, 187
Grieger, William "Bill", Colonel, USAF, 174
Grubbs, "Rosie", Brigadier General, USAF, 16
Guam, 88, 89, 101, 105, 234, 265
Guarino, "Larry", Colonel, USAF, 146

H

Hagemann, Joseph A. "Tony", Colonel, USAF, 165, 166
Haiphong Harbor, Viet Nam, 237, 238, 239
Haiphong, Viet Nam, 237, 240
Halliday, Gilbert, 8
Halliday, Walter, 8
Hanoi, Viet Nam, 237, 240
Hardman, Charles "Chuck", Colonel, USAF, 83
Harkins, Paul D., General, USA, 147
Harmon Trophy, 51
Harris, Hunter, General, USAF, 229
Harrison, Bertram "Bert", Lieutenant General, USAF, 113, 271
Harry Sham's Flying Service, 9
Hauver, Charles D., "Chuck", 80
Hawaii
  Hickam Air Force Base, 223, 238
  Pearl Harbor, 24, 26, 94
Hayao Kinugasa, General, Chairman, Joint Staff, 212, 213
Heard, 26
Heaton, 191
Hemet, California, 11, 13, 15, 16, 17, 18. *See also* California
Herbes, Ed, Colonel, USAF, 25, 29, 87
Hester, John, Major General, USAF, 157
Hickam Air Force Base, Hawaii, 223, 238

Higgins, Walter, 8
Hipps, William G. "Bill", Brigadier General, USAF, 160
Hitler, Adolph, 42
Ho Chi Minh Trail, 229, 230, 241, 245, 247
Hodge, Henry, Senior Master Sergeant, USAF, 277
Hoisington, Perry, Colonel, USAF, 13, 14, 15
Homan, Harold A. "Bud", First Lieutenant, USAF, 194
Homestead Air Force Base, Florida, 162, 163, 164, 198
Honolulu Oil Corporation, 9, 73, 76
Hopkins, Zeke, 132, 133
Hopwood, Lloyd P., Major General, USAF, 13
Horton, Charles "Chuck", Colonel, USAF, 105, 107, 194
Hudson, Charlie, 33
Hunziger, Dick, Colonel, USAF, 109
Hurd, Peter, 115

I

IBM, 68
Idaho
  Coeur d' Alene, 6
India, 166, 167, 169, 171, 173, 175
  Ambala, 168, 170, 171, 172, 173, 199
  Gauhati, 175
  Ladakh, 166
Indian Air Force, 169, 172, 199
Iran, 157, 158, 166, 176, 177, 179
Iranian Air Force, 179, 200
Ishikawa-san, 268
Iskeshir Air Base, 275, 280
Italy
  Naples, 45, 46, 47
Itazuki, Japan, 95
Izmir, Turkey, 179, 213, 214, 270, 271, 272, 273, 275, 276, 280

J

J-79, engine, 297

Index

Jabara, James "Jabbie", Colonel, USAF, 32, 191
Japan
   Fuchu Air Station, Tokyo, 209, 212
   Okinawa, 101, 218, 261, 262, 264, 265, 270
   Tokyo, 95, 97, 209, 212, 261, 262, 265, 267, 269, 283, 285, 287, 288
   Tokyo Bay, 96
   Yokota Air Force Base, 210
Johnson, Art, Major, USAF, 194
Johnson, Gerald W. "Jerry", Lieutenant General, USAF, 96, 101, 102, 103
Johnson, President, 127, 235
Jones, David "Dave", General, USAF, 126, 127

K

K-14 gyro-computing gunsight, 37, 38, 295
Kanto Plains Consolidation, 264
Kasler, James H. "Jim", Colonel, USAF, 153
Kennedy, Jackie, 175
Kennedy, John F., 155, 163, 164, 166, 174
Khatami, General, Chief of Staff, Imperial Iranian, 178, 200, 284
Kiel, Emil, Brigadier General, 65
Kimpo, Korea, 96
Kinnard, Claiborne H., Jr. "Clay", Colonel, USAF, 40
Korat, Thailand, 218, 222
Korea, 95, 96, 103, 127, 206, 295
   Kimpo, 96
Korean War, 81, 137, 292, 296
Krone, Bob, 107
Kruzel, Joseph J. "Joe", Major General, USAF, 168
Kuntz, Captain, USN, 221
Ky, General, Commander Viet Namese Air Force, 201

L

Lampert, Jim, General, USA, 262, 264
Landers, John D. "Jack", Colonel, USAF, 55

Langley Air Force Base, Virginia, 137, 148, 164, 215, 252, 255, 285
Laos, 218, 227, 228, 241, 245, 247, 248. *See also* Ho Chi Minh Trail
Las Vegas, Nevada. *See* Nellis Air Force Base
Laughlin Air Force Base, Laredo, Texas, 103
Lavelle, "Jack", General, USAF, 282
Laven, George, Colonel, USAF, 132, 133, 134, 135, 137, 196
Lebanon crisis, 179, 279
Leffingwell, Vernon "Monk", Lieutenant Colonel, US, 89
LeMay, Curtis, General, USAF, 101, 105, 107, 113, 117, 126, 127, 128, 130, 135, 136, 146, 215
Letterman General Hospital, 7
Libya, 141
Lincoln Grammar School, 187
Little, Robert C. "Bob", 256, 283, 284
Little Walden, England, 55, 58, 60
Long Beach, California, 9, 291, 293
Louisiana
   Barksdale Air Force Base, 107, 117
Luftwaffe, 40, 41, 42, 67
Luke Air Force Base, Arizona, 102, 127

M

Mackenzie, Innes, 9
MacNamara, Robert N., Secretary of Defense, 137, 138, 139, 140, 156, 163, 196, 218, 219, 223, 235, 246, 247, 248
Macon, Georgia. *See* Cochran Field
March Air Force Base, California, 13, 87, 270
March Field, California, 13, 76
Marshall, Bert W., Jr., Lieutenant Colonel, USAF, 31, 40
Martin, Glen, Lieutenant General, 218
Maryland
   Andrews Air Force Base, 87, 143, 144, 216
   Bolling Air Force Base, 87, 92
Maxwell Air Force Base, Alabama, 27
Maxwell Instructor School, 27

Index

McBride, Willie P., Major General, USAF, 257
McCain, John S. "Jack", Admiral, USN, 167
McClure, William C. "Mac", Lieutenant Colonel, USAF, 115, 116
McConnell, John P., General, USAF, Chief of Staff, 218
McCoy Air Force Base, Orlando, Florida, 114, 162
McDill Air Force Base, Florida, 162, 216, 256
McDonnell Aircraft Corporation, 196
McDonnell Douglas Corporation (MDC), 138, 284, 287, 291, 292, 293
McDonnell, J.S. "Old Mr. Mac", 284, 292, 293
McDonnell, Sandy, 196, 293, 294
McGehee, "Tom", Lieutenant General, USAF, 261
McNair, Govenor of South Carolina, 207
McNaughton, Major General, USAF, 99
McNickle, Marvin "Marv", Lieutenant General, USAF, 251
McQuillen, John D., Captain, USAF, 164
Meacham Field, Texas 116
Mellen, Joe, Lieutenant, 191
Mendenhall, Lee, Captain, 46, 47, 188
Messerschmitt. *See* Aircraft
Michigan
  Selfridge Air Force Base, 142
Middle East Air Force, 45
Mildren, General, USA, 275
Military Airlift Command (MAC), 155
Missiles. *See* Sidewinder missile; Sparrow missile
Mobil Oil, 75
Momyer, William "Spike", General, USAF, 132, 146, 204, 205, 207, 221, 226, 228, 229, 230, 231, 232, 234, 238, 239, 240, 245, 249, 251, 252, 255, 256, 258, 259, 261, 283, 285
Montana, 6

Montgomery, "Monty", Colonel, USAF, 102
Moore, Ernest "Mickey", Brigadier General, USAF, 95
Moore, Joseph Jr. "Joe", Major General, USAF, 257, 258
Moore, Joseph Sr. "Joe", Lieutenant General, USAF, 132, 219, 228, 271
Moore, William G., Jr. "Bill", General, USAF, 176, 177
Morris, Abe, 60
Muldoon, Bernard "Bernie", Colonel, USAF, 238
Murray, John J. "J.J.", 188, 189
Myers, Gilbert "Gil", Major General, USAF, 219

N

Naderi, Colonel, 200
Nakasone, Defense Minister of Japan, 211, 262, 265, 266, 267, 268
Nakhon Phanom Air Base, Thailand, 202, 222, 245, 247
Naoum, Iraklis, Brigadier General, Hellenic AF, 272
Naples, Florida, 29, 31
Naples, Italy, 45, 46, 47
National Automobile Theft Recovery Association, 18
National Military Home for Veterans, 5
Nazzaro, Joseph J. "Joe", General, USAF, 162
Neal, Bascomb, Major, USAF, 125, 145
Nevada
  Nellis Air Force Base, 102, 121, 127, 129, 138, 141, 161, 194, 195, 255, 256, 257, 258
New Mexico
  Cannon Air Force Base, 165, 168
  Roswell, 115
Nha Trang, Viet Nam, 222
Nickerson, Captain, USN, 8
Nielsen, 20
Nineteenth Air Force, 151, 152, 166, 181
Ninth Air Force, 32, 118, 152, 160, 231, 251

Index

Norley, Louis "Red Dog", Colonel, USAF, 61
North Carolina
   Fort Bragg, 155, 157, 197, 198
   Pope Air Force Base, 155
   Seymour Johnson Air Force Base, 151, 152, 154, 155, 156, 158, 159, 166, 172, 197, 251
North Viet Nam. *See* Viet Nam
Northrop N-156. *See* Aircraft, F-5
Nuremburg Trials, 67

O

Offutt Air Force Base, Omaha, 105, 115
Ogawa-san, 268
Okinawa, Japan, 56, 101, 218, 261, 262, 264, 265, 270
Oklahoma
   Tinker Air Force Base, 109
Olds, Robin, Brigadier General, USAF, 87, 242, 246, 298
Olds, Thayer, Brigadier General, USAF, 101, 103
O'Malley, Jerry, General, USAF, 253
Orlando, Florida. *See* McCoy Air Force Base
Ouray, Colorado, 5, 186
Outlaw, Eddie, Vice Admiral, USN, 135

P

Pak, President, 211
Palestine, 60
Pan Am, 75
   navigation school, 119, 120
Parker, David, Master Sergeant, USAF, 277
Parrish, Noel, Brigadier General, USAF, 28, 29
Partridge, Lieutenant General, USAF, 99
Pearl Harbor, Hawaii, 24, 26, 94
Pensacola, Florida, 8, 9
Pershing, General, 17
Peterson Air Force Base, Colorado, 107, 108
Pettee, Dr., 91
Phan Rang, Viet Nam, 222

Philippines
   Clark Air Force Base, 148, 240, 243
Pierce, Arthur "Art", Brigadier General, USAF, 239
Pinto, Air Vice Marshal Indian AF, 169, 170, 173, 174
Pitts, William "Bill", Lieutenant General, USAF, 270
Pleiku, Viet Nam, 222
Pope Air Force Base, North Carolina, 155
Potter, Captain, 67, 68
Preston, Maurice "Mo", General, USAF, 122, 123, 125, 126, 134, 142, 144, 145, 166
Price, David, Major General, USAF, 85, 92
Priest, Royce W. "Deacon", 40
Pritchard, Gilbert L. "Gil", Brigadier General, USAF, 219
Pueblo crisis, 251
Pugh, Paul, Vice Admiral, USN, 135
Purcell, Robert "Bob", Colonel, USAF, 146
pursuit, 19
Pursuit-Biplace, 20
Putnam, Benny, General, 147

R

Rad, Naimi, Brigadier General, 200
Ramey Air Force Base, Puerto Rico, 113
Ramey, Roger, Brigadier General, USAF, 81,
Randolph Field, San Antonio, Texas, 16, 17, 19
Ray, Wilbur "Will", Lieutenant Colonel, USAF, 115
Rechlin Larz, 39
Redlands, California, 15
Redlands University, California, 15
Reichstag, 67
Republic Aviation, 104
Research and Development, 23, 24, 39
Riddle, Richard, Senior Master Sergeant, USAF, 277
Ritchie, William D., "Bill", Colonel, USAF, 128

Robbins, Jay, Lieutenant General, USAF, 261
Roswell, New Mexico, 115
Rousher, Woodrow "Woodie", Lieutenant Colonel, USAF, 230
Royal Air Force (RAF), 2, 26, 36, 38, 59, 65, 107
Royal Canadian Air Force, 61
Rubel, A.C., 84
Russ, Robert "Bob", General, USAF, 253
Russian Air Force, 53
Russian Army, 53
Ryan, John D. "Jack", General, USAF, 115, 117, 234, 239, 248, 249
Ryan School of Aeronautics, Hemet, California, 11
Ryan School of Aeronautics, San Diego, California, 13

S

Saigon, South Vietnam. See Viet Nam
Salt Lake City, Utah, 6, 134
Santry, John, Colonel, USAF, 62
Saudi Arabia, 76, 166, 180
Schilling, David C. "Dave", Colonel, USAF, 101, 102, 119, 128
Schinz, Al, Major General, USAF, 257
Scott, Robert "Bob", Colonel, USAF, 130, 132, 237
Seattle, Washington, 6, 106, 148
Second Air Division, 219, 221, 228
Second Air Force, 101
Selfridge Air Force Base, Michigan, 142
Selma, Alabama. See Craig Field
Seoul, South Korea, 211
Seventh Air Force, 200, 201, 204, 205, 206, 221, 222, 227, 228, 232, 233, 234
Sewart Air Force Base, Tennessee, 176
Seymour Johnson Air Force Base, North Carolina, 148, 149, 151, 152, 154, 155, 156, 158, 159, 166, 172, 197, 251
Shaw Air Force Base, South Carolina, 152, 231, 251
Shell Oil Company, 84, 85, 86, 88, 92

Shell Union, 84, 85
Sidewinder missile, 236, 242, 296
Silva, Stan, 191
Simler, George, Major General, USAF, 218, 219, 257, 270
Simon, Meyer "Mike", Sergeant, 188
Singh, Arjan, General, Chief of Indian AF, 169
Sixth Allied Tactical Air Force, 179, 213, 214, 270
Smith, Don, Lieutenant General, USAF, 282
Smith, Stanton T., Colonel, USAF, 119
Socony Oil Company of Venezuela, 62
Socony-Vacuum Oil Company, 75
Sonmetz, Admiral, Turkish Navy, 273, 278
South Carolina
   Sumter, 207
South Korea
   Seoul, 211
South Viet Nam. See Viet Nam
Southeast Training Command, 29
Sparrow missile, 138, 296, 298
Speck, Elldred, Captain, 188
Spencer, Robert "Bob", Brigadier General, USAF, 142, 143
Spitfire. See Aircraft
St. Louis, Missouri, 196
Stalcup, Oran, Lieutenant, USAF, 2, 51
Standard of California, 75
Standard of Indiana, 75
Standard of Ohio, 75
Standard of Texas, 75
Stanton, "Long John", Lieutenant, USAF, 191
Starbird, Lieutenant General, 247
Stark, Herb, 73, 74
Status Of Forces Agreement, 98, 263
Stealth fighter. See Aircraft: F-117
Steeple Morden, England, 31, 46, 65, 187, 189, 191, 192
Steeple Morden Strafers, 34
Steeves, Jerry, Colonel, USAF, 103, 112
Storm Troopers (SS), 57
Strand, Raymond, 8
Strategic Air Command
   airplanes in, 114, 115, 128, 234

Index

Strategic Air Command *continued*
  author's supervision of division of, 126
  bases in, 81
  commander's conference of, 115
  conversion to Tactical Air Command from, 117, 118
  directives, rules, and policies of, 106, 113, 114, 215
  Director of Logistics of, 125
  imitation by Tactical Air Command of, 215
  independent command of, 265
  officers and ex-officers of, 107, 115, 161, 271, 290
  preparing target list with aid of, 92
  profile missions of, 105
  responsibilities on base of, 81
  Turner Air Force Base in, 101
  war plans and targeting material of, 89, 94
Strother, Dean C. "Doc", General, USAF, 129
Sturgate, England, 109
Suez crisis, 110
Sumter, South Carolina, 207
surface-air missile, 161, 163, 170, 235, 236
Sweeney, Walter C., Jr., General, USAF, 127, 147, 148, 153, 154, 155, 156, 157, 160, 161, 162, 164, 167, 172, 173, 180, 183, 215, 216, 217, 255

T

Tactical Air Command
  airplanes converted from Strategic Air Command to, 114
  airplanes of, 128, 129, 130
  author's involvement with, 126, 148, 151, 183, 218, 252
  Blue Chip One exercise, 155
  check flights from HQ of, 161
  communications to, 171
  decentralization of functions of, 255
  deployment of forces of, 129
  Director of Materiel for, 160
  duty of commander as chairman of conference of, 258

Tactical Air Command *continued*
  General Momyer of, 259, 285
  HQ of, 137, 255
  inside knowledge of Viet Nam operations, 128
  interest of President Kennedy in Air Force, 155
  manning from units of, 166
  modifications of 105s by, 159
  organizations in, 166
  presence in Viet Nam of, 222, 229, 232
  under direction of General Sweeney, 152, 162, 216
Taft, California, 2, 6, 66, 186, 187
Taft College, California, 7
Taiwan crisis, 296
Takhli, Thailand, 222, 237
Tallahassee, Florida, 29
Tan Son Nhut Air Base, South Viet Nam, 200, 201, 202, 204, 205, 206, 221, 224
Target Research Branch, 91, 92
Tavazar, Sabri, Major General, Turkish AF, 272
Taylor, Zack, 257
Taylorcraft. *See* Aircraft
Templehof, Germany, 67, 68
Tennesse
  Sewart Air Force Base, 176
Tenth Air Force, 77, 79, 95
Texas
  Bergstrom Air Force Base, 117
  Brooks Air Force Base, 77, 79, 80, 95
  Carswell Air Force Base, 81, 115, 116, 117
  Fort Worth Army Air Field, 79, 80, 81, 115, 116, 140
  Laughlin Air Force Base, 103
  Meacham Field, 116
  Randolph Field, 16, 17, 18, 19
  San Antonio. *See* Randolph Field
Thailand, 202, 218, 222, 227, 234, 242, 245, 247
  airfields built in
    Korat, 222
    Nakhon Phanom, 222

Index

Thailand
  airfields built in *continued*
    Takhli, 222
    U-Tapao, 222
    Ubon, 222
  airfields expanded in
    Don Muang, 222
    Udorn, 227
The First and the Last, 42
The Hollow Threat, 81
Thirteenth Air Force, 265
Thomas, Art, Colonel, USAF, 122, 123
Thomas, Marie, 187
Thompson, Brigadier General, USAF, 205
Throckmorton, Major General, USA, 199
Thud Ridge, 240
Thunderbirds. *See* Air Force Thunderbirds
Thunderbolt. *See* Aircraft
Tilley, Reade, Colonel, USAF, 107
Tinker Air Force Base, Oklahoma, 109
Titus, Robert "Earthquake", Brigadier General, USAF, 248, 256, 259
Todd, Ray, Colonel, USAF, 191
Tokyo Bay, Japan, 96
Tokyo, Japan, 95, 97, 209, 212, 261, 262, 265, 267, 269, 283, 285, 287, 288
Tonkin Gulf incident, 217
Toshihaya Baba, Lcdr Aide to General Kinugasa, 213
Travelair 2000. *See* Aircraft
Treaty of Peace and Mutual Cooperation, 98
Triantafellu, Rockly, Brigadier General, USAF, 161, 170, 218
Truesdale, Carl, Major General, USAF, 147
Turkey
  Izmir, 179, 213, 214, 270, 271, 272, 273, 275, 276, 280
Turkish Air Force, 273, 278, 280
Turner Air Force Base, Albany, Georgia, 101, 104, 108, 117, 120, 123, 130, 161, 192, 193, 194, 195, 215, 277
Turner, Slim, Major General, USAF, 79
Tuskegee Army Air Field, Alabama, 27
Tuskegee County, Alabama, 27
Tuskegee Institute, Alabama, 27
Tuskegee Negro Veterans Home, 27
Tuy Hoa, Viet Nam, 222
Twelfth Air Force, 147, 242, 255, 261

U

U-Tapao, Thailand, 222
U.S. Coast and Geodetic Survey, 8
Ubon, Thailand, 222
Udorn, Thailand, 227, 237
Union Oil Company, 83, 84
United States Armed Forces, Europe (USAFE), 119, 157, 181, 258
University of California, Berkeley, 9
University of Pittsburgh, 83
Utah
  Salt Lake City, 6, 134

V

Vahdati, Iran, 200
Venezuela, 73, 75, 76
Victory in Europe (VE Day), 44, 53, 55, 56
Victory in Japan (VJ Day), 62
Viet Cong, 205, 224, 245
Viet Nam
  airfields built in
    Bien Hoa, 222
    Cam Rahn Bay, 222
    Nha Trang, 222
    Phan Rang, 222
    Pleiku, 222
    Tuy Hoa, 222
  airfields expanded in
    Danang, 222
    Tan Son Nhut, 222
  airplanes in, 140, 146
  author parachuting and flying in, 157, 230
  briefings in, 223
  build-up of forces in, 136
  Cam Rahn Bay, 222, 227, 228, 230, 235, 242
  direction of war under President Johnson, 127
  F-5, use of in, 248

Index

Viet Nam *continued*
  gun vs. missile controversy, 296
  "guns-free" mode in, 298
  intelligence reports on, 231
  North Viet Nam, 203, 227, 228, 229, 231, 236
    Haiphong, 227, 237, 238, 240
    Haiphong Harbor, 237, 239
    Hanoi, 237, 240
  POWs, 153
  radar use in, 249
  role of surface-air missiles in, 235
  South Viet Nam, 216, 218, 227, 229, 230, 242, 245
    Danang Air Base, 205
    Tan Son Nhut Air Base, 200, 201, 202, 204, 205, 206, 221, 222, 224
  strikes, sorties, and targets in, 227, 232, 235, 241, 246
  Tactical Air Control Center, 224
  U.S. commitment in, 219
  Westmoreland's management of war in, 231, 233, 235
Viet Namese Air Force, 224, 234
Virginia
  Langley Air Force Base, 137, 148, 164, 215, 252, 255, 285
  White Stone, 294, 295
Vogt, John W., Jr., General, USAF, 239, 249
Vultee Vibrators. *See* Aircraft

W

Warner, James R., 5
West, Jerry, Major, USAF, 204
West Side Cemetery, Taft, California, 6
Westmoreland, William C. "Westy", General, USAF, 147, 221, 224, 229, 231, 233, 234
Westover, Charles B., Lieutenant General, USAF, 216
Wheeler, Clermont E. "Pudge", Colonel, USAF, 102
Wheeless, Hewitt T. "Shorty", Lieutenant General, USAF, 81
White, Alvin S. "Al", Captain, 191
White, Robert M. "Bob", Major General, USAF, 51

White Stone, Virginia, 294, 295
White, Thomas D. "Tommy", General, USAF, 191
Whitehead, Ennis "Ennis The Menace", 87
Williams Air Force Base, Arizona, 79, 87
Williamson, Brady, 188
Wilson, Bud, 14
Wilson, Cy, Colonel, USAF, 27, 101
Wilson, Enos W., 5
Wilson, Joseph "Joe", Lieutenant General, USAF, 246
Wilson, Louisa Lance, 5
Wilson, Margaret, 5
Winchester, Model 12, 20
World Wide Fighter Weapons Meet, 121
World Wide Gunnery Meet, Nellis Air Force Base, Nevada, 194, 195
Worley, Robert F. "Bob", Major General, USAF, 216, 251, 252
Wright Patterson Air Force Base, Ohio, 83, 84, 85, 89
Wrightham, Buck, Master Sergeant, USAAF, 39, 48

Y

Yalta Conference, 46
Yeager, Charles E. "Chuck", Brigadier General, USAF, 240
Yokota Air Force Base, Japan, 210

Z

Zemke, Hubert "Hub", Colonel, USAF, 102, 103, 112, 115, 117, 118
Zimmerman, Don, Brigadier General, USAF, 96
Zuckert, Secretary of the Air Force, 217